Integrated Assurance

Integrated Assurance

Risk Governance Beyond Boundaries

VICKY KUBITSCHECK

GOWER

Published by
Gower Publishing Limited
Wey Court East
Union Road
Farnham
Surrey, GU9 7PT
England

Gower Publishing Company
110 Cherry Street
Suite 3-1
Burlington, VT 05401-3818
USA

www.gowerpublishing.com

British Library Cataloguing in Publication Data
A catalogue record for this book is available from the British Library

ISBN: 9781409423591 (hbk)
ISBN: 9781409423607 (ebk – ePDF)
ISBN: 9781409474739 (ebk – ePUB)

Library of Congress Cataloging-in-Publication Data
Kubitscheck, Vicky.
  Integrated assurance : risk governance beyond boundaries / by Vicky Kubitscheck.
    pages cm
  Includes bibliographical references and index.
  ISBN 978-1-4094-2359-1 (hardback) -- ISBN 978-1-4094-2360-7 (ebook) -- ISBN (invalid) 978-1-4094-7473-9 (epub) 1. Risk management. 2. Corporate governance. I. Title.
  HD61.K83 2015
  658.15′5--dc23

2014021935

Printed in the United Kingdom by Henry Ling Limited, at the Dorset Press, Dorchester, DT1 1HD

Contents

PART IV   CASE STUDIES

List of Figures

List of Tables

Acknowledgements

This book is richer for the contribution of my colleagues. Despite busy lives, back to back meetings and demanding board agendas, they have made time to share their views, knowledge and experiences with me. I am forever grateful for their support and insights. For gaps and omissions in my interpretation of their wisdom, I apologise. There are too many to list here, but I would like to mention a few by name.

To Lord Smith of Kelvin, a renowned proponent of corporate governance and a firm champion of risk assurance, I would like to make particular mention for his support not only for this book but for my other pursuits in governance over the years. His ability to impart wisdom and guidance with humour and humility remains exemplary and inspirational in my daily role.

To Glen Moreno, I would like to say special thanks not only for his contribution to this book but also for his support, and for widening my horizons, in my career in governance.

I would like to make special mention of Andrew Alsop, Peter Bowen, Tanya Castell, Andrew Katz, Davida Marston, Kathryn Morgan, Charlie Puddicombe, Paul Smith, Patricia Templeton, Louis Wong, and members of the Insurance Internal Audit Group who worked on the Good Practice Development Group's integrated assurance work stream, for their valuable input.

To Stephen Mann and Police Mutual, UK's largest affinity friendly society who gave me the opportunity to develop my concepts for integrated assurance and enterprise risk management, I owe a debt of gratitude.

To all the boards and their organisations, who opened their minds and doors to me, I am thankful for their trust, experience and the opportunity to hone my perception and insights.

To Jonathan Norman and staff at Gower Publishing for the platform to talk about one of my areas of passion, and patience for this book, I am most grateful.

To my sister, Keen, for looking out for me since my young days at school and support for this book, I would like to make a special thanks.

Finally, to Manfred, whose constant encouragement and support made this book possible.

Glossary of Key Terms

Assurance

Assurance within the context of corporate governance refers to confirmation of the *integrity* and effectiveness of systems of risk management and control. Assurance is not just an activity but a transaction to inspire and maintain confidence. It involves at least two parties – the assurance *stakeholder* who requires or seeks assurance and the assurance provider. The terms *assurance* and *risk assurance* are used synonymously. Assurance is discussed particularly in Chapter 6 on *Rethinking Assurance*. See also *confidence in assurance*.

Assurance Food Chain

The assurance food chain refers to the connectivity between those who require or seek assurance and those who provide assurance in respect of a risk, control process or any other related matters. Assurance stakeholders generally refer to those who require or seek assurance to be able to discharge their responsibilities, which may include providing assurance to those higher in the food chain. From an internal perspective, the board resides at the highest level of the food chain, seeking assurance necessary for the proper discharge of its corporate governance accountabilities to the organisation's external stakeholders. The assurance food chain is discussed in Chapter 6.

Assurance Map

The assurance map or integrated assurance map is the output of the *assurance mapping* process.

Assurance Mapping

The assurance mapping process is a methodical approach for identifying and assessing the nature, validity, and interconnectivity of the sources of assurance across all lines of defence in the organisation. The focus and purpose of the assurance mapping process varies depending on the level at which integrated assurance is applied – from planning assurance, enhancing assurance and harnessing collective risk and control intelligence. Assurance mapping helps an organisation gain better insights into the way assurance is organised across the organisation as well as the effectiveness of its systems of control and risk management. Assurance mapping is discussed in Chapter 11.

Confidence in Assurance

This refers to the level of confidence an organisation has in the overall effectiveness of its systems of risk management in respect of the organisation's principal risks and business activities. The overall level of confidence depends on two factors: firstly, a judgement of the quality of the controls and mitigations (and therefore residual risk) as reported by the risk assurance activities, that is, the *result of assurance*, and secondly, trust in the reliability of the assurance activity itself, that is, the *quality of assurance*. Confidence in risk assurance is covered particularly in Chapter 14.

Control or Internal Control

A control or internal control refers to an action, activity or process such as a verification check, validation and authorisation put in place by the organisation for managing a particular risk. The purpose of a control is two fold: firstly, to help ensure that a process operates as required, and secondly, to help reduce the likelihood and/or impact of a risk. In this context, a control is a form of risk mitigation and is designed to help the organisation manage risks in line with its risk tolerance. A system of control is a collective term to refer to a set of actions or processes that, together, help to manage a risk to a target level of exposure. See also *optimal control*.

Core Business Process

A core business process is a fundamental or essential activity for operating the business. It is usually determined by the business model and its operating environment.

Integrated (Risk) Assurance

Integrated assurance refers to a structured approach for gaining a holistic picture of the principal risks and the level of residual exposure an organisation is required to manage. It involves aligning and optimising the organisation's assurance over the management of those risks, and the core business activities in line with the board's risk appetite, and exists to support the board's risk oversight and risk taking. It promotes shared risk intelligence and accountability with a common goal to strengthen the organisation's risk management and oversight. The terms *integrated assurance* and *integrated risk assurance* are used synonymously. The integrated assurance framework is discussed particularly in Chapter 10.

Optimal Control

An optimal *control* is one that manages risk to a target level of acceptable risk or exposure at an appropriate cost.

Optimal Risk Decision

An optimal risk decision is one that balances the level of risk taking within the organisation's *risk appetite* against the expected reward or return.

Principal Risk

A principal risk refers to an existing, evolving or emerging risk that could threaten the successful delivery of the organisation's business objectives, strategy or the viability of its business model. It includes the risk of missed opportunities.

Quality of Assurance

This refers to the level of trust in the reliability of the assurance activity itself. Quality is judged by the degree of relevance in respect of the risk under consideration, formality and integrity of the approach taken to provide the assurance.

Result of Assurance

This refers to the judgement of the quality of the controls and mitigations, and therefore of the resulting residual risk, as reported by the risk assurance activities.

Risk Appetite

Risk appetite refers the board's expressed tolerances and limits for taking, accepting as well as avoiding risks. These tolerances and limits are expressed in quantitative and/or qualitative terms as necessary to inform decision making within the organisation. In this regard, the board's risk appetite statement is expected to cover strategic, financial, reputation and operational risks; it is integral to the organisation's risk management framework.

Risk Assurance

See assurance.

Risk Based Decision Making

A risk based decision making process balances the level of acceptable risk-taking with the expected benefit, reward or return.

Three Lines of Defence Model

The three lines of defence model is an approach for distinguishing the different layers of risk mitigation activity or control in respect of a particular risk or business process. The first line of defence refers to front line management and those who are direct owners of or are accountable for the risk or business process. The second and third lines of defence refer to activities by resources which are not owners of the risk under consideration with activities from the third line of defence being regarded as independent. The three lines of defence model is discussed in Chapter 8.

Foreword

Sleep walking into a disaster is likely to be every company board's nightmare. Whether it is a result of excessive risk taking or unintended consequences of decisions in the boardroom, risk blindness is hard to defend. Board risk blindness is unfortunately not uncommon, as we are reminded almost daily by headlines of some dysfunctional corporate behaviour or of regulators demonstrating their increased powers to impose fines on those they hold personally accountable.

The trust bestowed on company boards by stakeholders who simply want promises made to them to be delivered fairly, or for their investments to be protected, has been severely dented in the wake of the financial crisis. The confidence boards had in the internal systems of management and governance hitherto must inevitably have been shaken. If lessons are to be truly learned from events since the start of the new Millennium – of which there are plenty to choose from, such as Enron, Parmalat, BP, Olympus, News Corporation and the recent financial crisis – rebuilding the confidence of those who have entrusted us requires company boards to adopt a more conscious approach to risk governance than ever before.

To this end, this book provides a fresh perspective from the lens of the board. It invites boards and the organisations they oversee to rethink *assurance* – particularly, the way they consciously seek and gain assurance against the risks that could destabilise the organisation, or that exceed the board's risk appetite. The book is practical, providing an approach by which the process can be supported by management, and is illustrated with case studies. The approach recognises that knowing about the risks is not enough, as this can neither ensure that the residual risk remains within the board's risk appetite nor prevent *excessive* risks being taken. To facilitate sound and confident risk-informed decision making, it is logical that assurance from all lines of defence must therefore be fully aligned with the principal risks and business model of the organisation providing a full picture that is based on collective risk intelligence.

This seemingly simple concept of risk assurance is central to Vicky's definition of integrated assurance – yet, it is probably the first that has been framed from a board's perspective. It promotes accountability across functional boundaries for a more joined-up and holistic risk picture of the organisation. As our business environments continue to grow in complexity, greater risk oversight is demanded of our boards. For conscious risk-taking, our boards need the support of an assurance process that is capable of peering through the organisation without boundaries and for affirming the effective management of risks through shared intelligence. This provides the foundation for restoring and maintaining the confidence of our stakeholders.

But first, as champions of risk governance, our boards must seek this holistic and integrated level of risk assurance.

Lord Smith of Kelvin

A leading figure in business and public life, Lord Smith is a Knight of the Thistle and has served on several boards across a range of industry sectors. He currently chairs the boards of SSE plc, the UK government-backed Green Investment Bank plc, and Glasgow 2014, the Organising Committee for the Commonwealth Games. He is also a non-executive director of Standard Bank Group, Chancellor of Strathclyde University and Patron of Foundation Scotland. His past roles include chairman of Weir Group plc, governor of the BBC, a board member of the FSA and chairman of the FRC Group on Audit Committees, responsible for the Smith Report (2003) on guidance on audit committees.

Preface

As an opening remark, it is worth noting that, for most of us, *assurance* is intuitive and an integral part of the governance process. Assurance within the context of corporate governance refers to confirmation of the *integrity* and effectiveness of systems of risk management and control. Intrinsic in the assurance process is its link to risk management. Without clarity of this link, assurance has limited value. In this book, the term *assurance* is therefore synonymous with *risk assurance*.

Integrated assurance, as I found when I started research for this book, means different things to different people and organisations. As a concept, it ranges from being described as enterprise wide risk management to major project governance to the coordination of the internal audit plan. Integrated assurance, as I hope this book will help me unfold, is not a rigid process but an approach or a discipline for supporting effective risk management across functional boundaries in our organisations – large and small alike.

With lessons in corporate governance in abundance from the financial crisis of 2008, and the resulting sharper regulatory attention on boardroom performance in both the private and public sectors, it seemed timely for the book to take a fresh look at assurance and the role of integrated assurance in the new order of corporate governance. It is the aim of this book to support those in governance in the proper discharge of their duties – whether these involve seeking or providing assurance, or both – a relational process which I refer to in the book as the *assurance food chain*.

When I was approached to write this book, it was clear in my mind that there would be three main design principles. Firstly, the book should not be an academic essay but one that is based on practical lessons and experience for supporting the governance process through effective assurance both inside and outside the boardroom. Secondly, the concepts and recommendations contained in the book should be injected with current insights from those in the assurance food chain that include board members and regulators as well as assurance providers. Thirdly, while my background in financial services inevitably leads me to draw on events experienced by this sector – which appears to have had more than its fair share in recent times – I was keen that we should pick up lessons and good practices from other sectors. Assurance, after all, is the bedrock of the governance process and corporate failure is indiscriminate of sector.

With these design principles and the goals of supporting effective corporate governance and finding more value in our approach to risk assurance, I have laid out the book in four parts. Part I of the book provides the backdrop for defining integrated assurance by taking a fresh look at the role of risk assurance in corporate failures and for supporting *Corporate Governance in the New Order*. Part II moves on to explore *Risk Assurance beyond Boundaries* by defining integrated assurance and examining its key characteristics. Part III discusses the practical aspects for *Implementing Integrated Assurance* and Part IV provides a number of *Case Studies* that illustrate the different levels at which integrated assurance can be applied. At the end of each chapter is a set of key points for quick reference. A summary of each part of the book is provided below.

Part I sets out the case for integrated assurance by first considering in Chapter 1: *Corporate Governance on Trial*, the effect of sub-optimal assurance in high profile events including those associated with the financial crisis of 2008 and the flight to a new order of governance. Chapters 2–5 go on to examine the relationship between assurance and effective corporate governance with particular attention to risk oversight, excessive risk taking, openness and transparency as well as accountability. Chapter 6 concludes Part 1 of the book by re-examining the concept of assurance across the assurance food chain and the need for it to be applied more consciously because of the role it plays in effective governance and risk based decision making.

Picking up the case for a fresh approach to assurance, Part II of the book develops a definition for integrated assurance. It begins with a discussion in Chapter 7 of the challenges facing many boards in gaining a holistic picture of risks and of the effectiveness of controls and risk mitigation strategies in the organisation. As risk assurance across functional boundaries is essential for developing integrated assurance, we dedicate Chapter 8 to discussing the three lines of defence model for expressing an organisation's system of risk management and control. After considering the various ways in which the discipline of integrated assurance is being applied in current practice in Chapter 9, we conclude Part II in Chapter 10 by providing a definition for integrated assurance and describing the three main levels at which it can be applied.

Part III of the book explains the practical implementation of the different levels of integrated assurance by beginning with a description of the assurance mapping process in Chapter 11, which is common to all three levels of application. Chapters 12–14 describe each of the three levels of application in turn. Chapter 15 on *Getting Started* provides guidance for scoping and selecting the level at which integrated assurance can be implemented as determined by the needs and capability of the organisation. To help organisations be more prepared, Chapter 16 discusses the key implementation challenges experienced by others.

Part IV of the book provides nine case studies, selected to illustrate the ways in which integrated assurance as a discipline can be applied to support the governance process in different organisations with their particular areas of focus. Each organisation in the case study shares its rationale for implementing integrated assurance, the approach it has taken and the value gained from the process, examples of which include supporting an audit committee's review of the need for an internal audit function, approval of the internal audit plan, enhancing the organisation's risk governance to match growth ambitions and for promoting collective risk intelligence across the group.

My hope is that the book will inspire organisations and their boards to do two things: firstly, to look at assurance in a more conscious fashion that is intrinsically linked to the organisation's risk management and, secondly, to champion integrated assurance as a discipline for gaining holistic insights into the organisation's principal risks and for optimising its assurance. By recognising that every individual in the organisation is part of the assurance food chain, integrated assurance transcends functional boundaries to help organisations embed their strategy for risk management and systems of control. A good outcome is governance with increased confidence.

In case I am coming across as over positive, I hasten to stress that integrated assurance is an approach or discipline for supporting the governance process and not an end in itself. Risks will continue to evolve and emerge to test the resilience of our organisations. Integrated assurance is merely a tool to harness the collective capability of the organisation and optimise its capacity to accept and manage risks.

Like any tool, integrated assurance will evolve through its use. If you have experiences or comments you would like to share, please let me know at: iabook@vicky.kubitscheck.com.

Vicky Kubitscheck

PART I
INTRODUCTION – THE CASE
FOR INTEGRATED ASSURANCE:
GOVERNANCE IN THE
NEW ORDER

Chapter 1
Corporate Governance on Trial

In this opening chapter we consider, in the first two sections, the role of ineffective assurance and information – particularly over risk taking in the breakdown of corporate governance that contributed to the financial crisis of 2008 and major corporate failures. Risk taking and its assurance is further discussed in Chapters 2 and 3. In section two of this chapter, we also highlight the *different* truths which boards should be alert to when seeking assurance. We consider in the last section of the chapter the emerging trend in regulation for a more holistic and integrated values based approach to corporate governance that is multidimensional in its consideration of risks. This sets the scene for Chapters 4–6 where we spotlight those key elements of corporate governance that refer to transparency, accountability and assurance in a new order.

Corporate Governance – The Dog that didn't Bark?

Surprises in the boardroom are seldom welcomed, even when good things happen, especially when this is due to luck and associated with a near miss event. Good or bad, an outcome of an event that was within reasonable expectation is more acceptable – and manageable – than one which totally blindsided the board. We know bad things happen in life. In any complex systems which include life, and in business, things do not always go as planned. When they do go wrong, particularly in business, the people at the helm are held to account. Board members who speak regularly about wanting no surprises in the boardroom are essentially referring to the need for effective alert systems. Could they be referring to a dog in the boardroom called *corporate governance* that barks?

The call for better corporate governance has reached new heights since the global financial crisis, triggered by the credit crunch, which started to reverberate across the financial markets and world economies in 2008. It proved to be one of the biggest surprises that ever surfaced in virtually every boardroom in the corporate and non corporate world. The quality of assurance expected by key stakeholders of major organisations in the financial market system was found wanting as the crisis unfolded. One notable example was contained in the Financial Crisis Inquiry Commission report in the US which stated that *'Throughout the summer of 2007, both Federal Reserve Chairman Ben Bernanke and Treasury Secretary Henry Paulson offered public assurances that the turmoil in the subprime mortgage markets would be contained'*. It went on to say that *'Days before the collapse of Bear Stearns in March 2008, SEC Chairman Christopher Cox expressed "comfort about the capital cushions" at the big investment banks'*.[1]

Whether or not these assurances were appropriate given the mood of the economic and political climate at the time, the crisis exposed the weaknesses in the accessibility and quality of information, judgement and also the credibility of the decision makers. The same report stated that *'just before Lehman's collapse, the Federal Reserve Bank of New York was still seeking information on the exposures created by Lehman's more than 900,000 derivatives contracts'*. How does a board seek assurance of the level of risks that is being taken by the firm in such a situation? When should the alerts have started? What kind of management controls were really in place? How credible was the assurance provided by management's attestation of the internal controls for financial reporting required under the Sarbanes Oxley Act?[2]

Similar questions could be raised in the case of the bail out[3] of the US insurance giant, American International Group Inc. (AIG) in 2008. Prior to the bottom falling out of AIG, how did the board assure itself that the risks taken by management were acceptable and within their expectations? For example, when the senior executive at AIG advised the board that the credit default swaps (CDS) protection they had sold to banks would never go into default (characterising them as 'gold' and 'free money'), how was the assertion monitored, verified and reported? As CDS were unregulated, and with no mandated capital requirements or regulatory filings, was management reporting of the multimillion dollar CDS business sufficient and open? Was the board further aware that, unlike banks and hedge funds, AIG had no form of reinsuring itself against the protection it was selling to the banks and hedge funds in respect of their CDS holdings? Was the board aware that CDS sold with subprime mortgage loan exposure was amounting to $61.4bn? Did the board and management rely wholly on the AAA rating assurance of the CDS provided by the credit agencies at outset?

Many such questions were asked by the numerous post crisis inquiries and studies. I have stopped counting the number of reviews, committees and inquiries that have been initiated by each nation since the global financial crisis. The International Federation of Accountants[4] (IFAC) lists no less than 17 international organisations that have set up dedicated resources for addressing the issues relating from the global financial crisis. The list includes organisations such as the European Commission, HM Treasury in the UK, the International Monetary Fund, the Global Public Policy Committee (Standards Working Group), the Basel Committee of Banking Supervision, the Financial Stability Forum, the United Nations Development Policy and Analysis Division and the World Bank.

Without exception, the inquiries concluded dramatic breakdown of corporate governance as one of the main contributory factors of the crisis. The Financial Crisis Inquiry Commission has gone one step further than other inquiries by concluding that the turmoil was *avoidable*. It said in its report that:

> The crisis was the result of human action and inaction, not of Mother Nature or computer models gone haywire. The captains of finance and the public stewards of our financial system ignored warnings and failed to question, understand, and manage evolving risks within a system essential to the wellbeing of the American public. Theirs was a big miss, not a stumble.[5]

The report suggests that the financial crisis was predictable had the *captains* and *stewards* acted on early signs and warnings.

A similar conclusion was reached by the US Senate Permanent Sub Committee on Investigations on the US's largest corporate bankruptcy at the time, Enron. The Subcommittee stated that the failure of the board to heed warning signs and to ask an 'awful lot of questions' in the months leading to the collapse of Enron contributed to its demise. According to its report on 'The Role of the Board of Directors in Enron's Collapse', the Subcommittee stated that:

> it identified more than a dozen red flags that should have caused the Enron Board to ask hard questions, examine Enron policies, and consider changing course. Those red flags were not heeded. In too many instances, by going along with questionable practices and relying on management and auditor representations, the Enron Board failed to provide the prudent oversight and checks and balances that its fiduciary obligations required and a company like Enron needed. By failing to provide sufficient oversight and restraint to stop management excess,

> *the Enron Board contributed to the company's collapse and bears a*
> *share of the responsibility for it.*

By failing to challenge and seek appropriate assurances from management, the Subcommittee said that the Enron Board had transformed the company from a 'well-respected and award-winning company to a disgraced and bankrupt enterprise in less than 3 months'.[6]

An obvious question, articulated appropriately by Senator Joseph Lieberman[7] who chaired the Senate Government Affairs Committee at a hearing in May 2002, is 'why all that experience, and so much more, accomplished so little for shareholders of Enron'. Pulling no punches, Lieberman stated in his testimony that he thought the directors not only lacked diligence but were also greedy by profiting from their positions and 'toasted marshmallows over the flames … even as those flames shook our economy and engulfed the dreams of thousands of dedicated Enron employees who lost not only their jobs but their retirement security'. Lieberman goes on to say that 'The flagrant failure of Enron's board of directors is a warning we must heed'.

Unfortunately, warnings of such breakdowns in the boardroom are neither new nor unique to Enron. *Greed*, when mixed with *hubris and the desire for power*,[8] according to Hamilton and Micklethwait, forms one of the six common toxic cocktails for corporate failures. In their indepth analysis of eight specially chosen high profile case studies from around the globe that include Enron, WorldCom, Swissair and Marconi, Hamilton and Micklethwait identified that the other five interlinking root causes of corporate failure were: poor strategic decisions, overexpansion and ill-judged acquisitions, dominant CEOs, failure of internal controls and ineffectual or ineffective boards.

Nearly six years on, the indiscriminate impact of the 2008 financial crisis across nations, industries as well as private and public sectors is still unfolding. The UK Government's Spending Review[9] published in 2010 refers to taking *decisive action* for example with a 34 per cent cut in its administration budgets by 2014–2015 while the US Department of the Treasury[10] announces a plan to cut 10 year deficits by 2.1 trillion US dollars from the start of 2013 to manage the long term fiscal challenges exacerbated by the economic crisis. The ultimate and full impact is still being felt by each nation's citizens – that is all of us. In the UK, the pressure of the financial crisis has seen the disappearance of some household names – such as one of UK's oldest stores, Woolworths, with over 800 branches nationwide and 1960s homeware icon, Habitat, as they went under administration.

The rate of corporate mortality as a direct impact of the financial crisis is not expected to slow down. The US Federal Deposit Insurance Corporation[11] (FDIC), which is a primary regulator and often appointed as receiver for failed banks, listed in July 2013 over 450 bank failures since 2000, the majority of which occurred since 2008. The FDIC 2010 Annual Report Highlights[12] reported that some 884 banks (12 percent of all federally insured banks) with assets totalling nearly $400 billion were on their *problem list*, the highest level in 18 years.

The timescale to full recovery remains uncertain as economies in Europe, the US and in Asia continue to wrestle with the challenges. It is hardly surprising that sweeping changes to the banking and financial market systems have been proposed, and are being implemented, to prevent the recurrence of another systemic market failure. Early indications are that the face of corporate governance is set to change as regulators take a more intrusive and preemptive approach to seeking assurance from boards of their effectiveness – ensuring that corporate governance *is* a dog that barks.

Defective Information, Intelligence and the 'One Truth'

Being alert to relevant information and acting appropriately on them are the two pertinent lessons, as considered in the last section, from the global financial crisis and major corporate breakdowns. It would indeed be a waste of a crisis if we do not examine their practical implications for restoring confidence in boardroom practice. We should, however, first acknowledge that not all boards are as dysfunctional as those characterised by the high profile corporate disasters. Most boards seek to do well for the organisations they represent. While boards must take personal responsibility to equip themselves for the task they are, however, also reliant on the support, integrity and diligence of the organisation's management to provide them with appropriate and timely information.

Seeking *sufficient information* is an art which boards must hone if they want to avoid the *road to ruin* – a sentiment reflected in a study by the Cass Business School. In this investigation of 18 high profile corporate breakdowns that include AIG, Arthur Andersen, BP, Cadbury Schweppes, Coca Cola, EADS Airbus, Enron, Firestone, Maclaren, Northern Rock and Société Générale, internal communication and information flow was found to be defective. In addition to improving their approach to risk management, boards and in particular non-executive directors are advised to seek 'full information and ask challenging questions'[13] about the underlying risks.

This is put succinctly by the UK Financial Reporting Council in its recommendations for *Enhancing corporate reporting and audit* that are aimed at both financial and nonfinancial companies. The proposals stated that:

> *The financial crisis highlighted the importance of the identification, analysis and management of risk. That is not only true in financial services. Companies in all sectors still get into trouble because of failures in this respect. Our aim is to reduce the likelihood that the message will be forgotten – as it has been after past crises – by increasing transparency in the way that directors report on their activities, including their management of risk.*[14]

Directors are called to better understand those risks that should be avoided as well as those that could be prevented. The span of oversight of such risks is potentially wide and directors face an increasing challenge in not allowing risks to fall between the cracks in their oversight activities.

Sufficiency of board level information is therefore critical. At the operational level, managing risks in a business environment is an integral part of any manager's process; it involves proactive recognition of risks, assessment of their significance to determine the nature of the controls and risk mitigation actions required, monitoring and reporting on the sound management of those risks. Management assurance is presumed to be integral to the reporting process. Directors, in particular independent non-executive directors rely on managers to provide such information accurately, sufficiently and on a timely basis to enable them to form sound judgement on risks.

Fundamentally, directors rely on the *integrity* of management. What is sufficient or timely can depend on the judgment of those providing the information. To help directors direct and seek the *right* kind of information, it is useful for them to be alert to, and be able to distinguish between, three potential forms of *accuracies* and *truths* – expected, alleged and actual – when assessing the assurance they receive from management in respect of a system or process.

- *The expected system or process*

    - This refers to what the directors, or senior management, have specified in terms of expected outcomes, performance or requirements of a system of processes and internal control to be in operation; this may include tolerances and limits for risk taking.

- *The alleged system or process*

  - This refers to what management believes, or thinks, to be happening based on expectations rather than through verified means.

- *The actual system*

  - This refers to the true state and actual functioning of the system or process that has been confirmed by tests or validation.

A board that receives assurance over a system or process that is not based on tests or validation cannot be certain that the system being described reflects the actual system. Such form of assurance is passive assurance. Assurance that cannot be supported by some form of positive confirmation is *empty* and increases the risk of unpleasant surprises in the boardroom. A board that seeks more active forms of assurance is more likely to gain better insights to the actual functioning of the organisation's risk management and systems of internal control. A board that seeks more active forms of assurance would also help ensure that management maintains systems that resemble what is expected as well as what is being alleged.

To help form a rounded judgement, and informed choices, some directors speak of getting the *one truth*. They are not necessarily referring to dishonest reporting or deliberate lies but the apparent inconsistencies in the information they get which together can lead to a confused picture. The unknown risk taking within some organisations as exposed by the financial crisis illustrated the quality of the assurance received at board level. For governance to work better, directors and senior management need to gain a clear and *single* view of the risks they are taking. I hasten to add that having a *single* view of risks does not mean having *one* report but a *consistent understanding* of the risks taken from as many valid perspectives as necessary to form a *rounded judgement* of the exposures in the business.

Information that is provided in an uncoordinated fashion or without adequate context of the risks can serve to mislead rather than inform the board. Management assurance that is joined up and coordinated would help provide the boards with the *one truth* it needs to make informed choices for discharging its oversight responsibilities. Boards can help steer management on this new path by seeking more active and joined up assurance of the organisation's risk management systems. Boards need to take a more conscious approach to seeking assurance and exercising oversight that is required for delivering effective corporate governance.

Modernising Corporate Governance in the New Order

In the flight to recovery and restoring confidence in the market, a raft of new governance codes and regulatory architecture reforms has been introduced, for both private and public sectors, in recent years. Implementation measures and standards are still being determined in many areas. The need to raise standards of corporate governance and ethics is the focus of current regulatory change. There is sufficient understanding by policy makers that public policy and regulatory change alone cannot prevent another crisis. The Sarbane-Oxley Act of 2002 that was rushed through congress at lightning speed within four months with the aim of preventing another Enron is a case in point. It requires fundamental behaviour change. The Walker Review warns that *'The behavioural changes that may be needed are unlikely to be fostered by regulatory fiat, which in any event risks provoking unintended consequences'*.[15]

Perhaps a more values based approach to governance is required such as that advocated by King III which defines corporate governance as 'the expression of ethical values and standards'. In particular, King III Principle 1.1 states that the 'The board should provide effective leadership based on an ethical foundation' and in Principle 1.2 that the board should 'ensure that the company is and is seen to be a responsible corporate citizen'. This means the company should 'protect, enhance and invest in the well-being of the economy, society and the natural environment' which the Code refers to as the *triple context*.

King III believes that because of the responsibilities attached to its status and because responsible corporate citizenship 'implies an ethical relationship of responsibility between the company and the society in which it operates',[16] the board is required to act in accordance with its social and moral standing in society. In this regard, King III states that the board is required to govern within such a triple context and should receive integrated reports on those areas. King III believes that a values based approach that operates in such a triple context is necessary for modernising corporate governance frameworks and to help secure trust and rebuild confidence in the market.

Customers, investors and other key stakeholders need to be assured that the boards and management can be trusted to protect their interests. This need was articulated plainly in November 2009 by Andrew Bailey of the Bank of England and current CEO of the new Prudential Regulation Authority who said that 'the answer to a depositor's question "Is my money safe?" must be yes – no hesitation or qualification can be added'.[17] As the European Union moves forward with its agenda to boost consumer protection and market confidence, it was unsurprising that this sentiment was expressed again in July 2010 by Michel Barnier, the European Commissioner responsible for internal Markets and Services when he said 'European consumers deserve better. They need reassurance that their savings, investments or insurance policies are protected no matter where in Europe they are based'.[18] The need to reassure and protect the interests of customers and other key stakeholders of an organisation applies equally to financial services and all other sectors of our economy, and to do this, organisations must first not fail.

It is significant and timely that the new Companies Act (2006)[19] for all businesses incorporated in the UK stresses that the duty of a director is to not only act in the interest of the organisation but also for its long term success. Resilience is the key principle that underpins the new prudential regulation for banks and insurance companies that is being framed under the Basel III Accord[20] and EU Solvency II[21] Directive respectively. To restore confidence in the market, the assurance sought by the board must also take a forward looking view of the adequacy of its risk governance and systems of internal control for the long term success of the organisation.

In response to rising standards of probity in the public sector the Intelligent Board (2006),[22] based on a study led by a steering group of eminent figures and board members in the UK National Health Service (NHS), poignantly called for boards to reexamine the questions they are asking in the boardroom and in doing so improve the information they are getting to enhance their decision making and strategy. The report asserts that to modernise, boards need to work differently and move away from the traditional line of enquiry and think more strategically in line with the concept of an *integrated governance* model as described in a Handbook issued by the UK Department of Health in 2006.[23]

The King III Code would agree that boards need to work differently and state that on the basis that 'good governance is essentially about effective leadership'; it believes that modernisation of boards must start at the top. Leadership says King III is 'characterised by the ethical values of responsibility, accountability, fairness and transparency and based on moral duties that find expression in the concept of Ubuntu', and which operates in an integrated manner within the triple context of economic, social and environmental performance. 'Strategy, risk, performance and sustainability have become inseparable'[24] and like the NHS integrated governance model King III advocates *integrated reporting* in its Code.

King III believes it helps to increase transparency and the legitimacy of the operations of a company thereby increasing business opportunities as well as improvements in its risk management. Trust and confidence of its external stakeholders should also be enhanced. Internally, King III believes the integrated reports would enable the company to evaluate its ethics, fundamental values and governance. King III's integrated reporting concept is also bolstered by its call for 'combined assurance' which refers to coordinated assurance between internal and external providers of assurance – which is central to this book.

The challenge for leaders in the boardroom is one of modernisation: firstly, to recognise the implications of corporate governance in a new order that is more values based and, secondly, to deliver corporate governance that is multidimensional in its context. Put together, corporate governance is required to be more joined up in its consideration and oversight across matters affecting the entire enterprise – strategy, economic, social and environment that is underpinned by sound principles of risk management.

Our discussions above show an emerging trend for a more integrated enterprise wide approach to corporate governance, reflected in the approaches of public policies, legislation and regulation introduced since the start of the new Millennium. The emerging modern approach is one that is not 'fostered by regulatory fiat'[25] but one which needs to strike the right balance between conformance and delivering long term strategic success for the organisation and its stakeholders through performance.

To Conclude this Chapter ...

To conclude this opening chapter, we acknowledge that it is difficult to deny that corporate governance has been ineffective when it really counted. Assurance given and received in those organisations as they collapsed can only be described as empty. The information upon which the assurances were formed could also be described as defective. The reasons for this are many, including the lack of board challenge, inadequate risk management and defective board level information. The severity and wide reaching impact of the financial crisis has made an indelible mark on the future approach of policy makers and regulators alike. Corporate governance is expected to mature and modernise by taking a more holistic and integrated values based approach to managing the affairs of the organisation with a longer term view.

With this in mind, it is our aim in this book to help boards gain the assurance they need to discharge their responsibilities with confidence, which in turn will enable them to assure those who have entrusted them.

Key Points from this Chapter

1.   A modern approach to corporate governance is values based, holistic and integrated across all aspects of the enterprise: strategy, economic, social and the environment that is underpinned by sound principles of risk management that take a longer term view.

2.   Boards should reexamine the questions they ask to gain better quality assurance that is joined up to provide *one truth* – that is, a consistent view and understanding of the risks and state of control.

3.   Failure to be alert to or to act on red flags can render corporate governance ineffective, as found in the downfall of major organisations.

4.   Assurance that is based on defective information – that is, incomplete or unvalidated – cannot inspire confidence.

5.   Assurance can be provided against three truths – expected, alleged and actual.

6.   Assurance in the boardroom cannot be taken for granted as regulation is heightened to strengthen standards of governance.

7.   A more conscious approach to corporate governance is necessary to help restore trust and confidence in the boardroom.

Endnotes

[1]   Financial Crisis Inquiry Commission (May 2009–February 2011), *The Financial Crisis Inquiry Report – Final Report of the National Commission on the Causes of the Financial and Economic Crisis in the United States*. Official Government Edition. Submitted by Pursuant to Public Law 111-21 (Washington, DC, U.S. Government Printing Office, 2011), xxi.

[2]   U.S. Government, Sarbanes-Oxley Act 2002, 'Public Law No. 107-204', formally known as the 'Public Company Accounting Reform and Investor Protection Act and Corporate and Auditing Accountability and Responsibility Act' (Washington DC, *U.S. Government Printing Office*, 2002), Sections 404 and 302.

[3]   William K. Sjostrom, Jr., '*The AIG Bailout*' (Lexington, Virginia, *Washington and Law Review*, 2009), 954–957.

[4]   International Federation of Accountants (IFAC), *The Global Financial Crisis*. Accessed 29 May 2011 http://www.ifac.org/financial-crisis/international-resources.php.

[5]   Financial Crisis Inquiry Commission (May 2009–February 2011), xvii.

[6]   Unite States Senate, Permanent Sub Committee on Investigations of the Committee of Governmental Affairs, 'The Role of the Board of Directors in Enron's Collapse', 107th Congress 2d Session (Washington, DC, *U.S. Government Printing Office*, Senate Prints 107–70, July 8, 2002) 11–16, 55.

[7]   Senator Joe Lieberman, Chairman of the Senate Government Affairs Committee, 'Statement at the hearing on 7 May 2002: The Role of the Board of Directors in Enron's Collapse'. Accessed 20 July 2013, http://hsgac-amend.senate.gov/old_site/050702lieberman.htm.

[8]   Stewart Hamilton and Alicia Micklethwait, *Greed and Corporate Failure – The lessons from recent disasters* (Hampshire, England and New York, Palgrave MacMillan, 2006), Chapters 1, 4.

[9]   H.M. Treasury, *The Spending Review 2010: Presented to Parliament by the Chancellor of the Exchequer by Command of Her Majesty* (London, HM Treasury, October 2010), 10.

[10] Timothy F. Geithner, 'A message from the Secretary of the Treasury, Department of the Treasury, Washington D.C.'. Accessed on 22 July 2013. http://www.gao.gov/special.pubs/longterm/debt/debtbasics.html#largefeddebt.

[11] Federal Deposit Insurance Corporation (FDIC), Bank List Updated 12 July 2013. Accessed 20 July 2013. http://www.fdic.gov/bank/individual/failed/banklist.html.

[12] FDIC '2010 Annual Report Highlights', Section Risk Management, updated 06 June 2011. Accessed 20 July 2013 http://www.fdic.gov/about/strategic/report/2010highlight/chpt1-02.html.

[13] Cass Business School/AIRMIC, '*Roads to ruin – A study of major risk events: their origins, impact and implications, Executive Briefing*, 2011'. Accessed 4 October 2011. http://www.airmic.com/roads-ruin-study-major-risk-events-their-origins-impacts-and-implications.

[14] Financial Reporting Council (FRC), *Effective Company Stewardship: Enhancing Corporate Reporting and Audit* (London, *FRC*, January 2011), 5.

[15] H.M. Treasury, *A Review of the Corporate Governance in UK Banks and other Financial Industry Entities – Final Recommendations* ('The Walker Review'), 26 November 2009. Website last updated 7 April 2010. http://webarchive.nationalarchives.gov.uk/+/http:/www.hm-treasury.gov.uk/walker_review_information.htm, 9.

[16] King Committee on Corporate Governance and Institute of Directors in Southern Africa (IoDSA), *King Code and Report on Governance for South Africa* ('King III') (Johannesburg, *IoDSA*, 2009), Principles 1.1 and 1.2.

[17] Andrew Bailey, Deputy Governor at the Bank of England and CEO of the new Prudential Regulation Authority, 'The UK Banking Resolution Regime', a speech delivered to the Institute of Chartered Accountants England and Wales Financial Services Faculty breakfast, London 26 November 2009. Retrieved 27 May 2011. http://www.bankofengland.co.uk/publications/Documents/speeches/2009/speech414.pdf.

[18] European Commission, Press Release IP/10/918 Brussels 12 July 2010, 'Commission proposes package to boost consumer protection and confidence in financial services'. Retrieved 27 May 2011. http://europa.eu/rapid/press-release_IP-10-918_en.htm.

[19] H.M. Government, *UK Companies Act 2006* (London, HM Stationery Office, 2006), Directors' Duties, Sections 171–177 that came into effective from 1st October 2007.

[20] Basel Committee, 'Basel III: A global regulatory framework for more resilient banks and banking systems', December 2010 (rev June 2011). Accessed 27 December 2013. http://www.bis.org/publ/bcbs189.htm, 1–2.

[21] European Commission, 'Directive 2009/138/EC of the European Parliament and of the Council of 25 November 2009 on the taking-up and pursuit of the business of Insurance and Reinsurance', commonly known as 'Solvency II'. Accessed 11 April 2011. http://eur-lex.europa.eu/LexUriServ/LexUriServ.do?uri=OJ:L:2009:335:0001:0155:EN:PDF, Article 45.

[22] Dr Foster Intelligence, a joint venture with the Department of Health 'The Intelligent Board, 2006'. Retrieved 25 December 2012. http://drfosterintelligence.co.uk/thought-leadership/intelligent-board/, 4, 7.

[23] UK Department of Health, *Integrated Governance Handbook – A handbook for executives and non-executives in healthcare organisations*, February 2006. Accessed 27 December 2009. www.dh.gov.uk/governance.

[24] King Committee on Corporate Governance and Institute of Directors in Southern Africa (IoDSA), *King Code and Report on Governance for South Africa* ('King III') (Johannesburg, *IoDSA*, 2009) Principles 1.1 and 1.2 (10, Practice Notes on Chapter 2 on improving board functioning and Practice Note Chapter 9 on integrated reporting).

[25] H.M. Treasury, 'The Walker Review', 2009.

Chapter 2

Risk Taking and Oversight

In Chapter 1 we considered the cracks in many organisations' corporate governance and risk taking strategies, exposed by the financial crisis of 2008 and high profile corporate failures. In this chapter, we consider the nature of excessive and blind risk taking, and the challenges facing organisations to gain an effective oversight of risks. In the last section of the chapter, we consider the steps for gaining appropriate (rather than perfect) risk knowledge.

Nature of Excessive and Blind Risk Taking

No legitimate organisation wants to fail. It is probably fair to say that organisations strive to strike the balance between taking sufficient risks in order to innovate and grow the organisation and avoiding risks that are excessive in relation to the capacity and capability of the organisation. This leads us to wonder how organisations fail in the midst of the assurance we assume they must be seeking, and getting, to help them maintain that balance. Putting aside greed, hubris and power, how do legitimate organisations with highly experienced boards and competent individuals allow excessive risk taking to take place to the detriment of the organisation?

Borrowing lessons from the 2008 financial crisis, we would attribute the lack of knowledge or information, particularly relating to areas of new development and change, as one of the key reasons for unintentional excessive risk taking. Acquisitions or entering new markets and launching new products without prior experience in a market are particular examples where unknown risks may be taken. The credit default or derivative swaps (CDS) which were central to the credit crunch financial market crisis were a relatively new product category that was not fully understood by analysts, let alone board members.

A case in point is American International Group (AIG). The US based National Association of Insurance Commissioners (NAIC) stated that:

> *The AIG financial holding company took on more risk than they could handle when investing in collateralized debt instruments, such as credit derivative swaps on mortgage-backed securities. It is important to note that these types of investments are financial products, not state-regulated insurance products. When the U.S. housing markets experienced a downturn, these risky investments lost lots of money for the AIG financial holding company.*[1]

AIG's demise, according to NAIC, is a direct consequence of poor judgement of risks beyond what it could handle.

In his analysis of these toxic products, 'One Way to Stop Bear Raids', George Soros concluded that AIG did not understand the nature of the product it was selling and failed 'because it sold large amounts of credit default swaps (CDS) without properly offsetting or covering their positions'. He asserted that 'AIG thought it was selling insurance on bonds, and as such, they considered CDS outrageously overpriced. In fact, it was selling bear-market warrants and it severely underestimated the risk'. Mispricing of these financial instruments and the asymmetric risk reward profile of the CDS market which effectively meant that buying a CDS contract to go short on bonds 'carries limited risk and unlimited profit potential' while 'selling CDS offers limited profits but practically unlimited risks';[2] AIG's failure to understand the lethal combination of these risks led to its demise.

Most of us would, however, argue that unknown risk taking is inherent in life and in business. Managing uncertainty and the unexpected in our organisations is, after all, what risk management is about. Managing risk involves anticipating the unknown and filling the gaps with *best available* information. Best available information should not, however, be confused with knowledge which refers to higher grade fact based information. When the imperfections in best available information are ignored, judgement on risk taking is more likely to be inhibited. The lessons from the financial crisis unfortunately exposed weaknesses in both the quality of information as well as knowledge which combined with a lack of challenge served to undermine the risk assessment and governance process in a dramatic way.

To summarise, on the premise that organisations and their boards have all intentions to exercise effective risk management and governance, excessive risk taking is more likely to arise because:

- They are unaware of the risks and exposures they are running in the first place.

- They do not have the information necessary for them to form sound judgment or to take conscious decisions either to avoid or accept risks that could be regarded to be excessive with hindsight.

- The profile of the initially accepted risks has changed and the speed at which those risks could become catastrophic is either not recognised or not monitored.

- It is too late to stem the momentum of hazard by the time the excessive risk is recognised, and/or

- At a fundamental level, the board and the organisation have not defined their tolerances and limits for taking or accepting risks and therefore what *excessive* risk taking means.

These are all aspects of the organisation's corporate governance framework that includes the systems of strategic planning, risk management, management control and assurance. Given such a broad definition of corporate governance, it is hardly surprising that virtually all analysis attributes the governance process to organisation successes as well as failures.

In its study of the financial crisis, the Walker Review concluded that major governance breakdowns (within banks) 'contributed materially to excessive risk taking and to the breadth and depth of the crisis'. The Walker Review stressed that these governance issues need to be brought closer to the centre stage to ensure that companies are better governed because while 'Better financial regulation has much to accomplish, but [it] cannot alone satisfactorily assure the performance of the major banks at the heart of the free market economy'.[3] The inference is that better risk governance is necessary if an organisation is to avoid taking a risk of total failure too far.

Putting Risk Governance at the Heart of Corporate Governance

The rush to review corporate governance codes in direct response to the financial crisis of 2008 across the globe has been unprecedented. In the UK, the Walker Review of corporate governance, particularly in UK banks, makes no less than 29 (out of a total of 39) recommendations that are specific to improving governance in financial institutions. They relate to the way boards are made up and function. They are set out under the following four headlines:

- governance of risk;

- board size, composition and qualification;

- functioning of the board and evaluation of performance; and,

- remuneration.

The Walker Review studied the lessons from UK banks, although the principles of their recommendations are applicable across other sectors. These principles[4] are reflected in the new UK Corporate Governance Code (2010) published by the Financial Reporting Council (FRC), which is the UK's independent regulator accountable to Parliament for monitoring the implementation of the Code.

The Code sets out detailed principles for sound boardroom practice in companies that cover leadership, effectiveness, accountability, remuneration and relations with shareholders in which the management of risk is an integral component. In addition to providing 'entrepreneurial leadership of the company within a framework of prudent and effective controls which enables risk to be assessed and managed,'[5] the board, according to the Code, is also 'responsible for determining the nature and extent of the significant risks it is willing to take in achieving its strategic objectives. The board should maintain sound risk management and internal control systems'.[6] By being clear about tolerances for taking and accepting risks, boards are more likely to guard against excessive risk taking in their organisations.

The Code refers to a set of guidance,[7] issued by the FRC to directors immediately after the financial crisis, on the need to carry out *rigorous* assessments of the continued viability and ongoing concern of the organisation – as part of, but not limited to, the regular preparation of financial statements. This is particularly important when organisations are operating in difficult economic conditions and/or are experiencing financial stress. Further, recognising the need for boards to take an integrated approach to assessing business viability risks and the organisation's risk management, control and reporting processes, the FRC has proposed further changes[8] to the UK Corporate Governance Code in 2014.

In South Africa, we saw the Institute of Directors replace the existing King Code and Report on Corporate Governance (commonly referred to as King II) with King III in 2009 for implementation in 2010. As covered in Chapter 1, King III advocates a holistic approach to corporate governance that stresses the importance of building sustainable businesses such that strategy, risk, performance and sustainability are regarded as inseparable. Poignantly, King III places much emphasis on the organisation being a *responsible corporate citizen*[9] that is led by effective leadership with high standards of ethics and values of responsibility, accountability, fairness and transparency. This includes the appropriate oversight of risks in the organisation.

Across the Atlantic, the principles in Walker and King III are also found in the set of principles launched by the National Association of Corporate Directors (NACD), a US based non-profit organisation created by, and for, directors. These principles are known as the *Key Agreed Principles to Strengthen Corporate Governance for U.S. Publicly Traded Companies*. The first set was published in 2008 and updated in 2011. The NACD identified four key areas of concerns to most directors which relate to risk oversight, strategy, transparency and executive compensation, and issued guidance to directors accordingly.

In its guidance, the NACD recognised a 'new need for stronger risk oversight' and advises that 'improving the oversight of risk will require directors to assign risk oversight responsibilities, establish risk identification procedures, evaluate risk models, and improve overall information flow'.[10] The NACD's recommendations relating to risk oversight is underpinned by the findings from the financial crisis, that excessive risk taking was either not detected or not identified early enough for boards to take appropriate action.

The NACD makes a raft of recommendations for increased transparency relating to board decisions. In addition to setting the tone for managing risks, the NACD indicate that effective governance requires boards to be more proactive in monitoring risks and where, or if, their tolerances have been exceeded. More open and useful communication by boards is expected to provide foundations for constructive management oversight to facilitate better decision making by shareholders as well as for supporting clearer accountability of management and the board.

Recognising that the board's core responsibility is to engage with management in the development of an effective corporate strategy, the NACD recommends that boards should also improve their ability to balance strategy and risk. This requires boards to work in greater collaboration with management and to increase timely access to strategic information to ensure that strategy is better aligned with short, medium and long term goals.

Additionally, boards should also establish executive compensation objectives and metrics that are aligned to these long term goals. In particular, executive compensation systems should reflect the company's risks, attitudes to risk, as well as the behaviours it is trying to incentivise. The NACD goes on to recommend that boards should improve their oversight of human capital development and executive compensation through performance metrics. Increased independence of compensation committees and use of independent compensation advisors, together with more proactive shareholder communication are also regarded to help improve standards of board governance.

Challenges in Risk Oversight Widen Cracks in Governance

In practice, for a board to achieve a full and complete picture of the risks across the organisation is challenging for many reasons. In its review[11] of the progress of implementing the new UK Corporate Governance Code (2010), the Financial Reporting Council indicated that there were two main challenges facing board members in their risk governance responsibilities, which are:

- The practical implications of the board's remit in respect of risk oversight and risk management.

- Clarity over the board's attitude to risk or risk appetite (which is explained in the next chapter on *Assurance against Excessive Risk*).

According to the review, many board members believe that there is greater awareness and discussion of risks although there is more skepticism over the improvements in the practice of risk management. In particular, there is a concern as to whether or not it is practical or even possible for a board to apply a single, aggregate risk appetite for the company as a whole. For non-financial services organisations such as those in energy and health industries, the challenge could be greater where the nature of significant risks could span across financial, people and environmental risks.

A member of an audit committee from an organisation at the UN did not hesitate to highlight to me that the challenge is multiplied in larger and more complex organisations where the objectives are more social than economic, such as to reduce world poverty or increase empowerment in women. Such altruistic qualities in the strategic aims of these organisations make it even more challenging for board members to define their risk appetite across the organisation, exercise risk governance and measure success in their organisation's risk management efforts.

The geographical spread of organisations, and therefore the range and number of jurisdictions and regulatory regimes (not to mention multicultural dimensions) affecting the organisation's operating environment, is another major challenge for effective board oversight. Size and complexity would undoubtedly extend the risks that the board would have to deal with and to exert appropriate oversight. Can some organisations become just too complex and large to manage or oversee such that they should be broken up?[12]

At the time of its collapse in 2008, AIG operated in over 130 countries and comprised 71 state regulated insurance entities in the United States alone. As part of its bail out agreement, AIG and its board undertook to use part of the loan to facilitate an orderly sale of certain parts of its businesses 'with the least possible disruption to the overall economy'.[13] One of the credit agreements also required AIG to work with the trustees of the AIG Credit Facility Trust to ensure appropriate corporate governance arrangements are established.

The debate as to whether or not an organisation can be too large to manage is likely to run for a while as boards take steps to strengthen their governance arrangements in line with revised governance codes and enhanced regulation. The participants in the FRC review mentioned earlier acknowledged the practical challenges by indicating that 'all that could be realistically be expected of the board was to have a clear understanding of the company's overall exposure to risk, and how this might change as a result of changes in the strategy and operating environment'.[14] This involves the board agreeing its appetite and tolerances for individual key risks as well as the types of risk which are either acceptable or unacceptable.

The Eversheds Board Report concurs with the views of board members and participants in the FRC discussions to the extent that risk is moving up the board agenda. There is overwhelming' acceptance (93 per cent in the study) of the role of directors in risk management, although the Eversheds Report thought that there was less agreement amongst those who were surveyed about what the role constituted. The majority (88 per cent) also thought that risk management is not a new thing and that its move to become part of the company DNA is the biggest development noticed by directors. This has led a Chair of an international bank to say that 'Next time there is a bank crisis, it won't be on risk, but it might be on something else which people haven't focused on'.[15] The uncertainty, however, over the remit on risk at board level means there is potential for risks falling between stools or just not being recognised.

A similar review in 2010, entitled 'A new risk equation?',[16] supports the view that risk is moving up the agenda, although organisation capability to evaluate and assess its impact is yet to be developed fully. Nearly half of the 465 senior executives interviewed thought that their review of the strategic financial and operational risks before the financial crisis of 2008 did not fully capture the impact of the downturn; furthermore, only 30 per cent indicated that risk management was effective in helping them manage the impact of the recession.

The events and aforementioned studies indicate that the practice of risk management is far more complex than realised and also less mature in development and in embedding than expected. My own discussions with board members confirm this. For example, one non-executive director of a global organisation which operates in over 160 countries observed that risk, while understood by all in an organisation to be important, is complex and riddled with terminology that can confuse and impair clear thinking, even at the highest level. He further observed that many risk logs or registers are mere lists of worries which can obscure the real messages and threats requiring management attention.

The implication is that (even) risk professionals find it difficult, partly because risk management is a broad discipline that involves a complex mix of technical and non-technical skills, experience, intuition as well as objective analysis. The views of this non-executive director have been put plainly and are shared by many non-executive and executive directors alike. Risk professionals and assurance providers should take note.

It is clear that there is more for organisations to undertake to develop and mature their risk management practices. This challenge will continue to grow as risk management evolves with the changing environments of markets, economies and businesses. Effective assurance over the sound risk management must be fundamental to a board's risk governance agenda to help ensure that risk taking is not excessive but operates within the board's appetite and tolerances. Surprises, as one non-executive director had surmised for me should ideally come in 'little blue [Tiffany] boxes'.

Being Alert to Limitations in Risk Information

Uncertainty is inherent in risk based information. By its nature, perfect knowledge in risk management is unrealistic. Managing risk involves anticipating change from expectations on evolving conditions with laser focus from different angles of the *risk lens*. The failure of AIG arising from its credit derivative swaps business activities as mentioned earlier reinforces the importance of understanding the nature of risks and its behaviour under different conditions, some of which may not be known. The AIG case also helps to remind us of the limitations of current risk modeling for decision making in managing our businesses and over reliance on rational behaviours.

Imperfect knowledge economics,[17] as defined by Frydman and Goldberg, recognise the shortcomings in current risk models with their tendency to focus on what could be measured. Imperfect knowledge economics focuses instead on change and looks for structural change and qualitative regularities, not quantitative ones. Frydman stated in an interview that 'To understand markets, one must put together statistical knowledge, with theoretical knowledge with some experience to arrive at accurate, albeit qualitative, predictions that are much more accurate than so-called 'precise' predictions generated by econometric models'.

Recognising that the process of forecasting is multi-layered, Frydman goes on to say that organisations should be alert to structural changes for continual reassessment of reliance on models. Reflecting on the over reliance placed on the ratings of credit derivative swaps that was central to the financial crisis, Frydman levied criticism on the rating agencies as well as the entire ratings system of forecasting 'that allowed the credit rating agencies to claim scientific basis for their predictions on the back of "scientific" models that in reality have no scientific basis themselves'.[18]

Open, constructive, challenge and discussion of risks, including assumptions underlying probabilistic risk models, are therefore necessary to allow innovation particularly in new markets without inappropriate risk taking. However, judging how much information is required is a challenge for many boards.[19] Management should support the board's risk oversight process by issuing appropriate *health warnings* when providing information to guard against over reliance of what could be imperfect (human) predictions, assumptions and yet to be proven theories. In a nutshell, to be risk informed, information should contain appropriate signposting of its limitations to help optimal decision making.

In support of more rigour in debate in the boardroom in the health sector, a report[20] published by the Audit Commission in 2009 observed that many boards of National Health Service (NHS) trusts and foundations trusts do not always have access to the right kind of information and appeared too trusting with little constructive challenge or debate about strategic issues. Steve Bundred, then Chief Executive of the Audit Commission, said when the report was published that:

> The NHS has, in many cases, been run on trust. But those who are charged with running our hospitals must be more challenging of the information they are given and more sceptical in their approach. Healthcare is inherently risky and complex, and assurance is not easy in the public or private sectors.[21]

The aforementioned report noted that where integrated governance and rigour in the assurance process had been applied, performance was enhanced, and boards of NHS and foundation trusts are asked to rethink their assurance frameworks.

To help boards, and senior management alike, to seek such information as is necessary to support their decisions and be assured with reasonable level of confidence of the risks being accepted, we summarise below the insights required – many of which I have collected from board members themselves:

- Know the risks facing the organisation:

    - Understand the principal areas of risks which the organisation is exposed to by virtue of its business model, including potential areas of lost opportunities;
    - Understand those principal risks that could 'break the business model';
    - Understand the rationale and robustness of the approach for identifying the current, evolving and emerging risks;
    - Understand the likelihood of the risks materialising and their potential impact, without being over focused on the net or residual risks;
    - Understand the imminence, speed or velocity at which any of these risks may materialise;
    - Understand what risks may not be recognised because of their accounting treatments such as off balance sheet items;
    - Understand the stretch of the organisation in terms of capacity and capability for managing the risks which the organisation are exposed to or plans to accept.

- Know what risks are being taken, accepted, tolerated or avoided:

  - Understand whether or not the risks being taken, accepted or being tolerated across the organisation are consistent with the board's expectations or appetite for risk;
  - Understand the nature of the stress testing carried out to assess the sensitivity of the risks;
  - Understand the rationale for the accepting risks that are higher than the board's expectations and appetite for risk;
  - Understand the implications for accepting or agreeing to tolerate the positions;
  - Understand the implications for not accepting certain risks or adjusting the board's current risk appetite and tolerances.

- Know the controls and actions required to reduce any risks outside the board's tolerances or expectations – potential *excessive risks*:

  - Understand the significance, effectiveness and reliability of the controls in place for managing the risks within the tolerances of the board;
  - Understand that there is clear ownership of the risks as well as the actions;
  - Understand the actions being taken to rebalance the risk and results to the business;
  - Understand the nature and adequacy of the assurance being received over the residual level of risk and exposure to the organisation.

- Know that optimal choices and informed decisions have been made:

  - Understand whether or not the right people and subject experts have been consulted to help identify the options available and assess the value – that is the loss as well as reward – of each option;
  - Understand whether or not the options considered have been unnecessarily restrained or have been based on shaky assumptions;
  - Understand whether or not the risks of deselecting or selecting options have been properly assessed by the right people;

- Understand whether the decisions required are time sensitive and how delays in making decisions may or may not affect the outcome.

- Know the limitations of the information for making decisions:

    - Understand the nature of the underlying assumptions, how they have been derived and their limitations such as untested parameters, robustness of the stress tests, short shelf life of advice given and how they may change the quality and outcome of the information;
    - Understand the conditions under which the information should be used to give reliable results;
    - Understand the implications of the shortcomings of the assessments and models.

Risk insights cannot just happen but are gained by open discussion and asking questions. As observed by Louis Wong, an audit committee member of an organisation at United Nations, 'discussion and challenge by board members is important to get beneath the skin of risk and assurance reports to clarify what the risks actually are and what has actually been done to minimise those risks as some of those reports tend to look good on paper'.[22] Open discussion is also conducive for board members to share their knowledge and experience which is critical for better informing the risk evaluation process. A summary of the headline questions which the board and the organisation should ask about its risk, to support more conscious risk taking, is provided in Table 2.1.

Table 2.1   What the Board Should Know About its Risks

The big threats	What are the principal risks of the organisation – as a whole and within its entities – that could undermine the viability of the business model or strategy?
Changeability	Are the risks stable or sensitive to change at high velocity, and for what duration?
Capacity for risk	Does the organisation have the capacity and capability for managing the risk?
Acceptability	Are the risks being accepted, tolerated or avoided in line with the board's expectations?
Mitigation	How effective are the required key controls and actions for managing and reducing those risks outside the board's tolerances or expectations? How do we know this?
Options	Are the bases for forming optimal choices and decisions sufficiently sound?
Limitations	What are the limitations of the information for making such decisions?

If a reminder is at all necessary, the rationale for seeking timely, useful and relevant *risk informed* information is to enable the board to:

- Better engage with the organisation, its executive and management teams to debate and discuss risks for more robust and optimal decision making.

- Feel more assured that the underlying risks are being managed in accordance with its expectation.

- Feel more confident that management have thought through the risks and that decisions have been made on an informed basis.

- Know the limitations of decisions so that they can be reassessed appropriately;

- Discharge its duties appropriately and responsibly.

In addition to being able to demonstrate that it has discharged its risk oversight and governance over the organisation's risk management system effectively, the board is also able to promote sustainable, long term success of the business. This level of conscious risk taking is consistent with the obligations of directors in respect of Section 172 of the UK Companies Act (2006) which requires directors to 'act in the interests of the company and promote the success of the company for the long term'.[23]

To Conclude this Chapter ...

In conclusion, sharpening the organisation's risk governance is clearly the new focus in the boardroom. A clear line of sight of risks across the organisation is ideal but not always feasible especially in complex and large structures. Knowing the limitations of risk information is essential for forming sound judgement on the risks which the organisation is able to take, accept or avoid. Risk insights are best sought through open discussions allowing collective knowledge in the boardroom to be gathered for better decision making. Conscious risk taking is one step towards guarding against excessive risk taking. Seeking appropriate assurance of the organisation's risk taking capability and capacity for risks is another important step towards effective risk governance. This, we will consider further in the next chapter on assurance against excessive risk taking.

Key Points from this Chapter

1. Risk management is a complex, multilayered discipline even for experienced boards and more attention is required to develop and mature current practices.

2. Sound corporate governance means knowing the capacity an organisation has for taking and absorbing risk.

3. Excessive risk taking occurs when there is a mismatch between the risk exposure and the organisation's capacity for taking the risk; it can also occur when risk taking exceeds the board's risk appetite.

4. Being alert to imperfect knowledge is vital for informed and conscious risk taking as well as assessing the level of information required for optimal decision making.

5. Seeking appropriate information to assure the board that risks are being managed in accordance with the board's risk strategy and appetite is critical for effective risk oversight.

6. Effective risk oversight will require everyone in the organisation to work consistently, and joined up, to avoid risks falling between stools.

7. The board is expected to spend more time on risk management than ever before, to ask the right sort of questions that cover, in particular:

    - *The big threats* – those principal risks that could undermine the viability of the business model or the organisation's strategy;
    - *Changeability* – stress testing, sensitivity and velocity of the risks;
    - *Capacity for risk* – resources and capability for managing the risks;
    - *Acceptability* – risk of exceeding the board's tolerance and risk appetite;
    - *Mitigation* – strength of controls and actions for managing the risks, as well as their assurance;
    - *Options* – bases of decision making;
    - *Limitations* – of information in the decision making process.

Endnotes

1   National Association of Insurance Companies (NAIC), News Release September 2008, 'AIG: Conversation should stay focused on the facts'. Retrieved 22 October 2011. http://www.naic. org/Releases/2008_docs/AIG_facts.htm.

2   George Soros, 'One Way to Stop Bear Raids', *The Wall Street Journal*, 23 March 2009. Retrieved 22 October. 2011, http://online.wsj.com/article/SB123785310594719693.html.

3   H.M. Treasury, *A Review of the Corporate Governance in UK Banks and other Financial Industry Entities – Final Recommendations* ('The Walker Review'). Published 26 November 2009. Website last updated 7 April 2010. http://webarchive.nationalarchives.gov.uk/+/http:/www.hm-treasury. gov.uk/walker_review_information.htm, 10.

4   Financial Reporting Council (FRC), *The UK Corporate Governance Code* (London, FRC, September 2012), 10.

5   Ibid., Section A.

6   Ibid., Section C.

7   FRC, *Going Concern and Liquidity Risk: Guidance for Directors of UK Companies* (London, FRC, 2009).

8   FRC, *Risk Management, Internal Control and the Going Concern Basis of Accounting: Consultation on Draft Guidance to the Directors of companies applying the UK Corporate Governance Code and Associated Changes to the Code* (London, FRC, November 2013).

9   King Committee on Corporate Governance and Institute of Directors in Southern Africa (IoDSA), *King Code and Report on Governance for South Africa* ('King III') (Johannesburg, *IoDSA*, 2009) Principles 1.2

10 National Association of Corporate Directors (NACD), *White Papers Series I: Risk Oversight, Strategy, Transparency, Executive Compensation* (Washington, DC, *NACD*, 2009), Chapter 1.

11 Financial Reporting Council (FRC), *Boards and Risk: A summary of discussions with companies, investors and advisers* (London, FRC, September 2011), 3, 5.

12 H.M. Treasury, 'The Walker Review', 2009. 38.

[13]   Federal Reserve Board, Press Release September 16 2008 'Announcing the authorisation of the loan from the Federal Reserve Bank of New York to AIG under Section 13(3) of the Federal Reserve Act'. Retrieved 30 May 2011. http://www.federalreserve.gov/newsevents/press/other/20080916a.htm.

[14]   Financial Reporting Council (FRC), *Boards and Risk: A summary of discussions with companies, investors and advisers* (London, FRC, September 2011), 8.

[15]   Eversheds LLP, *The Eversheds Board Report: Measuring the impact of board composition on company performance* (London, *Eversheds LLP*, May 2011). The report involved a study of 241 companies headquartered in the UK, continental Europe, the USA and the Asia-Pacific region that was supplemented by 50 in-depth interviews with directors, 16, 26.

[16]   Grant Thornton, 'A new risk equation? Safeguarding the business model' (London, *Grant Thornton UK LLP*, 2010), 6.

[17]   Roman Frydman and Michael Goldberg, *Imperfect Knowledge Economics: Exchange Rates and Risk* (New Jersey, Princeton University Press, 2007).

[18]   Roman Frydman, 'Mechanics of risk', *Business & Finance*, 15 February–28 February 2008, 38–39.

[19]   Financial Reporting Council (FRC), *Boards and Risk: A summary of discussions with companies, investors and advisers* (London, FRC, September 2011), 3.

[20]   Audit Commission for Local Authorities and the National Health Service, *National Report: Taking it on trust – A review of how boards of NHS trusts and foundation trusts get their assurance* (London, *Audit Commission*, April 2009).

[21]   Steve Brundred, CEO Audit Commission, Press Release on 29 April 2009 'NHS boards should challenge more to assure themselves'. Retrieved 24 May 2011. http://archive.audit-commission.gov.uk/auditcommission/pressoffice/pressreleases/Pages/29042009takingitontrust.aspx.html.

[22]   Louis Wong, an audit committee member of an organisation at UN and a former auditor general of the Asian Development Bank, who has exposure in both the private and public sectors in a private discussion in August 2013.

[23]   H.M. Government, *UK Companies Act 2006* (London, HM Stationery Office, 2006), Section 172.

Chapter 3

Assurance against Excessive Risk Taking

In this chapter we delve deeper into one of the most significant lessons from the 2008 financial crisis and from major corporate failures – excessive risk taking and lack of risk oversight. After discussing the significance of an organisation's attitude to risks in judging the level of risks it takes and setting the board's risk appetite, the rest of the chapter considers securing appropriate risk oversight and assurance over the effectiveness of the organisations's risk mitigation strategies.

Intrinsic Link between Attitude to Risk Taking and Decision Making

No responsible board member would knowingly take risks that exceeded either their personal appetite or that of the organisation's capacity to take risk. There are of course exceptions. We have all heard or read about, and some of us may have even come across, individuals such as a dominant chief executive or marketing development director who chose to take a bet on behalf of the organisation in the belief that they can single handedly bring glory to the organisation by breaking into a new market or pushing through an acquisition. The problem with the analyses of such events is the benefit of hindsight. Also, in reality, the individuals are either unlikely to admit that excessive risks had been taken or that they misjudged the risks they were taking; they could have put forward a self convincing case for the level of risks to be taken in exchange for the likely returns to the organisation.

Risk taking, in other words, is largely based on judgement. Judgment is a complex process that is influenced by a number of factors, in particular at a personal level by the individuals involved and at a group level when personal and organisational influences are fused together to provide a combined outcome. It was no coincidence that the supervisory approach of the UK financial services regulators has changed radically since the financial crisis to one that is not only more intensive and outcomes based but which involves assessing the judgement of firms on a forward looking perspective. In his last speech as Chief Executive of the UK Financial Services Authority (FSA), Sants acknowledged that risk taking is necessary for firms to generate returns but that:

> the chances of management making the right decisions will be greatly improved if they are supported by good governance. In particular, this should ensure that judgements made do not go outside a firm's risk framework as agreed and overseen by the board.[1]

Sants alluded to two key roles of the board. Firstly, the board is required to set a framework for good risk governance. Secondly, the board is required to ensure the decision making and judgement across the organisation consistently reflects the board's attitude and tolerances to risk. This challenge is the focus of this chapter and the heart of this book.

DEFINING RISK APPETITE

The board's attitude to risk taking has acquired a common expression in the term – *risk appetite*. The term is used to refer to the board's expressed attitude to taking, accepting, tolerating and avoiding risks. In practical terms, risk appetite refers to a *spectrum of risk taking* that includes the types and their levels of risks which:

- The board is willing to take, for example, openness to explore new markets within specified limits of capital exposures or investment costs;

- The board would want to avoid altogether including *no go* areas, for example, no business activities outside the core knowledge of the organisation;

- The board would accept or tolerate only within limited exposure or tolerances; this category covers many aspects of risk taking on a day to day basis such as tolerance for processing errors or delays in services.

Collectively, these attitudes to risk provide a form of *risk compass* within the organisation to guide judgment and optimal decision making on a day to day basis at all levels of the organisation. We define *optimal* decisions as those decisions that balance the level of acceptable risk taking against expected reward or return.

When the board's risk appetite and attitude to risks are unclear, the void is likely to be filled either by the individual's own risk attitude or by second guessing the level of risk the board or senior management might take or tolerate. As a result, suboptimal decisions are made. When the organisation's reward system is inconsistent, or misaligned with the board's attitude to risk taking, the chance of excessive risk taking is likely to increase. Adair Turner, Chairman of UK Financial Services Authority identified 'absurd bonuses for excessive risk taking'[2] as a contributory factor to the financial crisis of 2008.

Any mismatch between the individual's and the board's attitude to risk usually results in surprises, which may manifest themselves in the following ways:

- Excessive risk taking occurs (as discussed in the last chapter) because the board's appetite for risk taking is over estimated.

- Missed opportunities, because the board's appetite for taking or accepting new risks is underestimated.

- Issues are not escalated or reported for attention because the board's tolerances are overestimated until the impact greatly exceeds the board's appetite for bad news.

- Excessive reporting of issues that clouds the big risks because the board's tolerances are underestimated.

- Inappropriate risk mitigating actions and excessive controls, because the board's tolerances are underestimated resulting in more checks and processes at an unnecessary cost to the organisation.

In summary, clarity and consistency in the board's risk appetite is critical for informing decision making and judging the level of exposures which are acceptable to the board. Excessive risk taking and resulting surprises in the boardroom should be exceptional; inefficient management of risks and systems of internal control at an operational level should also be minimised.

The UK Corporate Governance Code recognises the importance of the board's role in defining its attitude to risk taking by codifying in its main principle *C2: Risk Management and Internal Control* which states that 'The Board is responsible for determining the nature and extent of the significant risks it is willing to take in achieving its strategic objectives. The board should maintain sound risk management and internal control systems'.[3] While some directors think that setting risk appetite is not the board's primary role, most would agree that an appropriate statement of risk appetite is required in organisations.[4]

The intrinsic link between risk appetite and decision making implies the need to articulate the board's attitude to risk potentially for all kinds of decision making across the organisation. This clearly poses many practical challenges for organisations. To keep it at a pragmatic level, I would suggest the following main principles for determining the types of decisions which should be included in the board's risk appetite statement:

- Key decisions that relate directly to delivering the organisation's vision or strategy, such as financial strength, innovation, growth and expansion into new markets, products and territories.

- Key decisions that impact the way the organisation deal with its key stakeholders such as its customers, business partners, regulators, governments and communities, which may already be included in the codes of conduct in some organisations.

- Any overriding decisions for managing reputation risks.

In brief, risk appetite should be stated for key decision areas, that is, areas of decision making that affect the sound and successful delivery of the business at the group as well as subsidiary levels. A single or aggregate risk appetite for the whole group in respect of a decision area is feasible if the decision area it affects applies consistently across the group, for example, reputation damage to the brand.

The imprecise science of judgment and decision making means that risk appetite and tolerances cannot always be expressed in financial terms or as a single target number. Where it is not viable to set a single limit for risk taking, a board should consider setting a tolerable range or boundary for acceptable risk taking – like drawing *markers in the sand* outside of which risks may become unacceptable. By providing these boundaries, appropriate trigger points can also be determined for escalating potential risks and *red flags* for further consideration before decision if necessary. In other words, to guide decision making on a practical basis, the board's risk appetite statement would involve describing thresholds for risk taking in quantitative as well as qualitative terms.

By maintaining focus on the principal areas of decision making which the board would like to influence it should be possible to keep the risk appetite statement at a manageable level. To ensure such influence is maintained appropriately, it is crucial for the board to review its risk appetite statement at regular intervals to reflect the organisation's evolving strategy and business operating environment at group as well as subsidiary level.

Managing Risks within the Board's Appetite

The means by which an organisation manages its risk within the board's risk appetite and organisation capacity for accepting risk is referred to as its risk mitigating strategy. The risk mitigation strategy broadly consists of the organisation's policies, actions and processes to protect again excessive risks. Risk mitigation is sometimes also referred to as a *control* that is installed by management to ensure that the risk it aims to manage does not exceed the limits set by the board. A risk is therefore said to be managed or *controlled* within risk appetite if:

- The likelihood of the risk materialising is within expressed tolerances, and can refer also to the frequency of a risk materialising.

- The impact of the risk should it materialise is within tolerable limits.

The level of exposure to risk remaining, despite the organisation's risk mitigation strategy and systems of internal control, is known as the *residual risk*. Residual risks that are outside the board's tolerances or comfort zone will require further attention. A risk mitigation or control is said to be effective and optimal when the residual risk and cost of implementation is appropriately balanced. Optimal controls should mean that risks are not *over controlled* or *out of control*. Over controlled risks usually mean that more than necessary resources are being used to maintain risks below their acceptable or target level of exposure. The corollary point is that resources are, therefore, not being used efficiently and that the costs which include the cost of missed business opportunities outweigh the benefits to the organisation. A risk that is out of control, on the other hand, would mean that the organisation is most likely to be exposed to a level of risk that exceeds the board's risk appetite.

Risk mitigation strategies and controls are more likely to be designed intuitively rather than objectively when the organisation has not expressed or published its attitude to risk taking. This could lead to suboptimal decisions and ineffective design of risk mitigation and controls. The board's tolerances for risks effectively put down markers in the sand against which controls and risk mitigation can be determined objectively as far as possible and implemented effectively. Managing risks without an agreed point of reference, such as the board's risk appetite, is more likely to give rise to surprises in the boardroom and excessive risk taking.

Risk Oversight: Compliance with the Board's Risk Appetite

Having laid down markers for risk taking, the board is better placed to seek assurance from executive and senior management that key decisions are being taken accordingly and consistently. Assurance can effectively be sought at three main levels although the nature by which it is provided will vary depending on the nature of the risks and decisions considered. A brief summary of each level or type is described below.

I   COMPLIANCE WITH THE BOARD'S RISK APPETITE AT A SPECIFIC RISK OR DECISION LEVEL

This is a common level of assurance that is provided, for example, on the organisation's investment and market positions, counterparty exposures, reputation risk exposures, health and safety incidents and other operational events that may have occurred outside tolerances. The focus on specific risks and related decision making enables the board to conduct deeper discussion on trends of past as well as projected exposure levels of risks, and consider the adequacy of the organisation's risk mitigation strategies and controls. Discussion of risks at the specific level should give due regard to exposures at the *gross* as well as *net* or residual level, where net or residual exposure as described above, is taken after the effects of risk mitigation strategies and controls. Some boards, and in particular their risk and audit committees, find it useful to have a view of those risks with the largest difference between gross and residual exposures as this provides insights to the perceived robustness of management's risk mitigation and controls. Such reports enable the board to seek appropriate information including independent assurance over the robustness of management's risk mitigation and controls.

2   COMPLIANCE WITH THE BOARD'S RISK APPETITE AT THE AGGREGATE LEVEL

This involves providing an aggregate picture of the residual exposures across the areas in the board's risk appetite; deviations would be highlighted for discussion. Progressive reports tend to provide a forward looking view of risks that may exceed the board's risk appetite. The reporting at the aggregate level allows the board to determine the overall resilience of the organisation in relation to the total capacity of the organisation to absorb risks across all entities. Aggregate views of compliance with the board's risk appetite can also be used to identify any particular risks as well as areas of the business such as a remote operation that require deeper discussion.

3   ASSURANCE OVER SHIFTS IN RISK TAKING BEHAVIOURS

This type of assurance is sought when a board, or the organisation, is seeking to determine if and how any changes in the risk appetite statement may be affecting decision making in the organisation. Examples where this type of assurance may be required include a change in the organisation's strategy to avoid certain markets and reduced appetite for reputation damage arising from customer complaints. This type of assurance reporting reinforces the view that the board's risk appetite plays a significant part in influencing behaviours and decision making – and the culture of the organisation in the longer term. This type of reporting also helps the organisation to assess the degree of integration of the board's risk appetite in the risk management *DNA* of the organisation.

As mentioned earlier, the board's risk appetite and risk taking is necessarily dynamic to reflect the changing picture of the business. In this regard, the board will require appropriate support for maintaining currency of its risk appetite and tolerances. Reporting on compliance with the board's risk appetite, therefore, also needs to evolve and be sensitive to the changing focus of the board. More importantly, as discussed in Chapter 1, openness in discussion of the reports and any apparent red flags is necessary for proper insights to be gained by the board.

To Conclude this Chapter ...

In summary, to guard against excessive risk taking, an organisation must first know what its risk appetite is – that is, risks it is willing to take, accept or must avoid. As risk appetite is integral to judgement and the decision making process, it follows that clarity and consistency in articulating the board's attitude to risk taking and tolerances is critical for influencing and directing the strategy of the organisation. The board's risk appetite effectively sets the tone of behaviour in the organisation; risk mitigation strategies and systems of internal control are designed accordingly in order that the residual exposures to the organisation remain within the board's tolerances for risks.

To maintain effective risk oversight, the board seeks appropriate risk and assurance reporting at the specific and aggregate level so that it can assess that the risks are being managed in line within the board's appetite for risks. The reports themselves are limited in value, without openness in discussion to gain appropriate insights to the organisations risk taking and residual exposures.

Key Points from this Chapter

1. Risk appetite is intrinsic to decision making and judgement.

2. The board's appetite for risk taking and tolerances should cover the key decisions that it wants to influence and direct across the organisations – at the group and subsidiary level as appropriate.

3. As the level of risk to take or avoid involves judgement, it is useful for the board to provide boundaries of its tolerances for risk taking in quantitative and qualitative terms, especially when a single target number is impractical.

4. A clear understanding of the board's tolerances and appetite for risk taking is necessary to steer and influence the development of appropriate risk mitigation strategies and systems of control. The board needs support for maintaining currency of its risk appetite.

5. Excessive risk taking is more likely to occur when there is a lack of understanding of the board's acceptance of risks or where inappropriate reward systems incentivise behaviours that are inconsistent with the board's risk appetite.

6. The board should not only seek, but also discuss, assurance to confirm consistent application of the board's risk appetite across

the business at the specific and aggregate level with appropriate focus on both gross and net or residual level of exposures.

7.   Assurance should consider both those measureable and non measurable risks which the board wishes to influence, such as culture and behaviours.

Endnotes

[1]   Hector Sants, Chief Executive FSA, 'Delivering effective corporate governance: the financial regulators role'. A speech delivered on 24 April 2012 at Merchant Taylor's Hall. This was to be Sants' last speech as CEO of the FSA one year before restructure of the new regulatory system commenced in April 2013 (FSA). Accessed 26 April 2012. http://www.fsa.gov.uk/library/communication/speeches/2012/0424-hs.shtml.

[2]   Adair Turner, Chairman, FSA (2008–13), 'Successful regulatory reform'. A speech delivered on 28 September 2010 at the Eurofi Conference, Brussels. Retrieved 29 October 2011. http://www.fsa.gov.uk/pages/Library/Communication/Speeches/2010/0928_att.shtml.

[3]   Financial Reporting Council (FRC), *The UK Corporate Governance Code* (London, FRC, September 2012), Principle C.2: Risk Management and Internal Control.

[4]   Eversheds LLP, *The Eversheds Board Report: Measuring the impact of board composition on company performance* (London, Eversheds LLP, May 2011), 17. 'Setting risk appetite: Risk management per se was not considered the primary function of the board (only 6 per cent of directors believed the contrary to be the case). It was thought to be an important function but not one that was necessarily top of the list'.

Chapter 4
Openness and Transparency

We considered, in Chapters 1 and 2, the criticisms leveled at organisations following the 2008 financial crisis and major corporate failures that related to defective information. We also considered the importance of risk based information and the need for open discussion and constructive challenge for the board to gain effective risk oversight. In this chapter we further explore the important aspects of openness and transparency in information, without which reliable assurance required by the board against excessive risk taking will be greatly impaired.

Transparency beyond Regulatory Compulsion

A truism which we all would accept is that information – formal and informal – is the bloodstream of any business. It is fundamental for decision making at all levels of the organisation. It is, however, the quality and timing rather than its quantity that determines its usefulness. This is especially true if we want to make not just any decision but informed and balanced decisions for taking or accepting risks. Implicit in the decision making process – to stop or to go – is the assurance that the potential risks and rewards have been considered appropriately (as covered in the last chapter on assurance against excessive risk taking). Lessons from the 2008 financial crisis and major corporate failures indicated however the importance for such assurance to be gained more explicitly and consciously in the boardroom through discussions. Openness in discussion through constructive challenge helps to clarify understanding and adds value to imperfect information that is inherent in risk information systems.

The benefits of open discussions are also recognised by investors as reported by the Financial Reporting Council (FRC) following a discussion with board members and investors in 2011. The FRC reported that some investors:

placed more importance on the assurance they received from discussions
with boards and management than on the words in the annual report.
This was particularly the case when it came to assessing the quality of
risk management and internal control, for which their main source of
assurance was the quality of the Board.[1]

To facilitate more informed and open discussions, the board is not only
dependent on useful risk based information but on information that is relevant,
open and transparent. Providing useful information of decision grade to the
board for the purpose of effective risk oversight involves making the right
call on the level, depth and timing of information required. Too much can
be as unhelpful as too little, since the real issues and risks can be obscured;
information that seeks to assure the board can arguably have the opposite
effect if badly timed.

An organisation's risk appetite, as considered in Chapter 3, plays a key part
in influencing judgment and therefore the type, level and timing of information
provided to the board. In other words, the board can be very dependent on the
diligence and risk compass of the executive of the organisation – unless it is
active in influencing, and in seeking, the type and level of information it needs
for its oversight.

A LITTLE HELP FROM THE REGULATORS

Recognising the importance of information for board risk oversight in the
governance process, it is no coincidence that regulation at state, industry
and professional levels is vocal in this area. To ensure consistency between
organisations, as well as between global platforms, legislation and regulation
play a significant part in prescribing the type and level of information and
disclosure required by organisations. Professional institutions also play a
major role in setting supplementary standards for reporting by organisations.
Required reporting by organisations can be summarised into four main
categories:

1.   Mandatory public reporting such as the annual company filings
       and financial reporting requirements of incorporated companies
       and public listed companies, which are generally aimed at
       investors. Some examples include UK Companies Act, the UK
       Corporate Governance Code and reporting requirements for US
       listed companies under the Sarbanes Oxley Act.

2.   Mandatory private reporting to regulators, such as those required by banks and insurers of their assets, liabilities and capital positions, to enable the regulators to assess potential individual and systemic risks. Since the 2008 financial crisis, the appetite for greater quality and disclosure has increased significantly following work by the financial regulators internationally such as that led by the Enhanced Disclosure Task Force of the Financial Stability Board.[2]

3.   Mandatory event based reporting to the relevant authorities such as financial crime and money laundering.

4.   Guided internal reporting based on professional standards, industry and regulatory practices and guidance. Compliance with many of these reporting requirements is principles based which involves interpretation by the organisation for appropriate application.

Mandatory reporting has, unfortunately, not prevented corporate failures. It is also unlikely to do so in the future. As discussed in the earlier chapters, minimising the risk of corporate failures requires the directors and stewards of organisations to adopt a different approach to exercising risk oversight by influencing the right kinds of behaviours that put the long term success of the organisation at the heart of everything it does. This approach cannot happen by compulsion but only with the mutual support of regulators and organisations.

One such example is the Financial Reporting Council (FRC)'s paper entitled 'Effective Company Stewardship – Enhancing Corporate Reporting and Audit'. The paper sets out a number of proposals for enhancing public corporate reporting that include describing steps the directors take to ensure 'the reliability of the information on which the management of a company, and therefore directors' stewardship, is based; and [to ensure] transparency about the activities of the business and any associated risks'. In respect of assuring integrity and confidence in corporate reporting, the proposals call for 'a more effective and transparent assurance regime'[3] that include fuller reporting by audit committees on how they have discharged their responsibilities.

Taking the views from investors in another report, the FRC published four main suggestions which are worth noting here. They are:

- integrating commentary on risk throughout the report, rather than treating it as a standalone section;

- specifically, linking reporting on risk to discussion of strategy and the business model;

- explaining changes in the company's risk exposure over the previous 12 months, as a result of changes to the strategy or business environment, and indicating if it might change in the future; and

- disclosing how key risks were being mitigated.[4]

Guided reporting from regulators is useful to allow mature and appropriate application by organisations. It is however also open to interpretation with reference to the organisation's risk compass and the tone set by the board. In Chapter 2, we considered the significant role played by the board's attitude to risk in influencing judgment within the organisation. The resulting risk compass of the board and organisation will determine what, how much and how frequently information is appropriate for assuring the board of the affairs of the business.

Malfunctioning Risk Compass Obscures Board Oversight

As discussed in Chapter 2, if an organisation is unclear of the board's attitude to risks then individual judgement will fill the void. Where this is combined with a lack of conscious seeking of assurance, surprises in the boardroom are likely to occur. To help us illustrate such a risky combination, we consider the House of Commons select committee inquiry[5] on phone hacking that concluded in 2012.

At the inquiry, Rupert Murdoch, Chairman and Chief Executive Officer of the global media holding company News Corporation, revealed that he was wholly unaware of the improper practices or ethical issues within the organisation. Did it reflect bad judgment on the part of the executive management for not keeping the board informed or blind trust by the board for not seeking appropriate assurance over the fundamental standards of media practice within the organisation? It was both, according to the inquiry. Murdoch attempted to justify being blindsided by the issue by stating that it happened in a very small part of the group. His failure to grasp the severity of the impact of improper practices in News Corporation led the select committee to conclude that Murdoch as Chairman of News Corporation:

did not take steps to become fully informed about phone-hacking, he turned a blind eye and exhibited wilful blindness to what was going on in his companies and publications. This culture, we consider, permeated from the top throughout the organisation and speaks volumes about the lack of effective corporate governance at News Corporation and News International. We conclude, therefore, that Rupert Murdoch is not a fit person to exercise the stewardship of a major international company.

The case of News Corporation illustrates the significance of the need for appropriate oversight of *principal* risks from across the group that includes risks from remote parts of the organisation. The case also illustrated complexities as well as the significance of corporate culture and ethics in decision making or the culture of decision making. A board sets the tone for managing a risk or an issue by how it discusses and seeks information and assurance over a particular risk or issue. When the issue or risk relates to conduct and ethics, conscious and open discussion is even more important because of the complex nature of culture and ethics that is demonstrable only through behaviour.

The conduct of the board and senior management of the organisation continually sets and resets the risk compass of the organisation by which others would follow. For effective management of risks to organisations, management and boards must want to be informed – with the full picture of risks that could render their organisations unviable – so that they can direct with confidence for the long term success of the organisation.

Avoiding Blind Trust and being Blindsided

We have so far considered the importance of open discussion that is supported by diligent and transparent information for supporting effective risk oversight by the board. In this section we acknowledge the challenges faced by board members when using information and engaging in open discussions. We highlight two particular areas that could trip up even the most experienced board members, namely technical information and risks of *group think*.

TECHNICAL INFORMATION

Board information will from time to time contain highly technical information, more so when reporting on financial and taxation matters. We learnt from the 2008 financial crisis (as covered in Chapter 1) that the *clever use* of financial reporting protocol enabled items to be reported *off balance sheet*; as a result, liabilities were understated. This obscured any opportunity for scrutiny of the full picture of the affairs of the business. The small print associated with the limitations in the use of mathematical models for forecasts and projections was either over looked or omitted altogether. The key message here is the need to be alert to the difference between being technically right and being true to the big picture.

Decision making in the absence of complete or reliable information should be expected in any business environment, particularly, in a dynamic and progressive organisation. The deliberate *hiding* or *obscuring* of information for the purpose of presenting a rosier picture is highly questionable especially if this results in the board being misled with an inaccurate aggregate picture of the risk. Having blind trust or being blindsided by numbers, models and computations from a computer are unfortunately not uncommon in business, but it is risky.

As discussed in the last chapter, management and boards are required to be mutually supportive by working together to ensure that limitations in the information and underlying models used are visible. Mutual trust that such open and transparent information will be used maturely in discussion is fundamental to instill confidence on both sides. This also applies to reporting to, and discussions with, other stakeholders such as investors and regulators.

Clearly, having an appropriate mix of skills on the board to cover its oversight needs is fundamental, although reliance on one or two individuals carries risks which should be subject to regular review as part of the board's evaluation of its structure, composition and effectiveness.

GROUPTHINK

The second source of blind trust and blindside arises from what is commonly known as *groupthink*. The post analyses of corporate failures confirmed the phenomenon of *groupthink*, a theory first put forward in the early 1970s by Irving Janis, professor emeritus at the University of California, Berkeley. The theory refers to the systematic errors made by collective and concurrence seeking decision making in a group process. It causes even the shrewdest, most intelligent and experienced directors to lose individual objectivity and intuition and to be swayed by prevailing thought in the room. Janis defined groupthink as:

> *A mode of thinking that people engage in when they are deeply involved*
> *in a cohesive group, when the members' strivings for unanimity*
> *override their motivation to realistically appraise alternative courses*
> *of action.*[6]

As a result of groupthink, the old adage *when things look too good to be true,*
they usually are too good to be true did not survive when the property boom,
technology bubble or investments in subprime mortgages promised significant
returns. We also refer to the remarks of Senator Lieberman[7] at the inquiry on
Enron when he expressed surprise over how Enron could have failed with such
breadth of experience in the boardroom.

Groupthink, as Janis revealed, is not merely the preserve of directors
in the corporate boardroom. The theory was developed after his study
of five 'fiascos' resulting from miscalculations of the practical and moral
consequences of decisions made during the administration of five American
presidents – Roosevelt, Truman, Johnson, Kennedy and Nixon. While often
important decisions cannot be made by one individual alone on the premise
of the limited information processing capacity of one brain, the use of groups
in decision making also have their flaws. In other words, groupthink is a social
psychological phenomenon that arises as part of group dynamics where the
'we-feeling of solidarity', group consensus seeking behaviours and conformity
to group norms are stronger than individual thought.

Group dynamics happen. Being alert to groupthink allows us to manage
it to some extent. Effective chairing that seeks the views of others and
encourage constructive challenge by playing devil's advocate is one way to
prevent unhealthy groupthink. Janis makes a number of other suggestions for
preventing groupthink that include the leader encouraging each member of
the group to be a 'critical evaluator', use of experts from outside the group and
ensuring that sufficient time is spent on reviewing the warning signals from
rivals.

In summary, by seeking objective information and encouraging open
discussion with the aim of ensuring that the risks have been appropriately
stress tested, the board can optimise the benefits of the collective intelligence of
the group and minimise the flaws of groupthink.

To Conclude this Chapter ...

The board's strife for better quality assurance should encourage more open reporting and improved consideration of the bases for managing risks. The board's risk appetite, and their actions in seeking or ignoring information, is influential in setting the tone for reporting and discussing risks and issues. Open and transparent reporting of information and discussion is fundamental for effective risk oversight and for guarding against unintended excessive risk taking.

By being open to imperfect information and alert to limitations in the information, better decisions can be made. In other words, a holistic picture of risks and issues are necessary for effective risk oversight and balanced decision making. Openness in reporting, that is accompanied by mature discussion, helps to build trust and confidence. This also reduces the risk of the board having blind trust or being blindsided by risks and issues across the organisation.

Key Points from this Chapter

1. Open and transparent reporting that facilitates mature discussion allows for effective risk oversight and guards against excessive risk taking.

2. The board's risk appetite sets the tone or norm for information flows across the organisation as well as for the culture of decision making.

3. Being picture accurate is better than being technically right, which could actually obscure the view of risks across the business.

4. By encouraging critical evaluation and mature discussion, the chairman and leaders within the organisation can promote collective intelligence for informed rather than consensus seeking decision making.

5. Active and conscious seeking of assurance that risks are being well considered minimise the detrimental effects of groupthink.

6. Assurance without openness can destroy trust and confidence.

Endnotes

1   Financial Reporting Council (FRC), *Boards and Risk: A summary of discussions with companies, investors and advisers* (London, FRC, September 2011), 14.

2   Financial Stability Board, 'Enhancing the Risk Disclosures of Banks Report of the Enhanced Disclosure Task Force', 29 October 2012. The report makes recommendations for enhancing disclosures particularly of major banks with the aim of rebuilding investors' confidence and trust in the banking industry. Accessed 1 November 2012, http://www.financialstabilityboard.org/publications/r_121029.htm.

3   Financial Reporting Council (FRC), *Effective Company Stewardship – Enhancing Corporate Reporting and Audit* (London, FRC, January 2011), 10, Chapters 2 and 4. Since its issue in January 2011, the FRC published two further reports in September 2011 that were expected to lead to further consultation of the UK Corporate Governance Code and related guidance.

4   FRC, *Boards and Risk: A summary of discussions with companies, investors and advisers* (London, FRC, September 2011), 14.

5   House of Commons, Culture, Media and Sport Committee, 'News International and Phone-hacking, Eleventh Report of Session 2010–2012 Volume 1 (C)' (London, *The Stationery Office*, 2012), Sections 201, 226–229.

6   Janis, J. Irving, *Groupthink*, 2nd edition (Boston, MA, Wadsworth, 1982).

7   Senator Joe Lieberman, Chairman of the Senate Government Affairs Committee, 'Statement at the hearing on 7 May 2002: The Role of the Board of Directors in Enron's Collapse', accessed 20 July 2013, http://hsgac-amend.senate.gov/old_site/050702lieberman.htm.

Chapter 5

Accountability

In this chapter we consider one of the core principles that underpin effective delivery of governance. We explore the significance of personal and corporate accountability in current governance codes and regulation, as more focus is placed on gaining assurance over the organisation's ability to run successful and sustainable businesses.

Personal Accountability – Doing the Right Things versus Doing Things Right

Accountability is one of the core principles underpinning good governance. Quite simply, without accountability, getting things done will be laboured. It is required for delivering good governance and conversely, good governance demonstrates accountability. In this regard, accountability in corporate governance refers to ownership and answerability throughout the organisation. Delivering corporate governance, therefore, involves accountability at the personal and corporate level. We consider first, the features of personal accountability in governance.

Personal accountability is implicit in being a leader, a role that is assumed by those in governance. In practice, however, accountability is not as well understood as one might expect. The word conjures up a degree of ethical and emotional attachments that include responsibility, integrity, duty and *blameworthiness*. Based on his study of public accountability, Schedler indicates that the term consists of two basic elements – 'answerability', which refers to the obligation to inform about and explain what one is doing, and 'enforcement', which refers to the resulting sanctions imposed on those who violate their public duties.

In its simplest form, accountability involves a level of account giving and according to Schedler refers to a relationship between two parties A and B such that 'A is accountable to B when A is obliged to inform B about A's (past or future) actions and decisions, to justify them, and to suffer punishment in the case of eventual misconduct'.[1] The obligation on A to inform B is de facto a duty to provide assurance on the actions taken and the decisions made in order to avoid the risk of the punishment. This obligation to provide assurance arises from five main sources where accountability is:

- Bestowed on a body or individual because of their position, for example, as a public listed company that is required to operate within the prevailing listing regulations or as a registered director, who is required to carry out the duties as set out in the relevant companies acts.

- Associated with operating within a certain industry, such as public utilities, the pharmaceutical industry or financial services where the degree of formal and self regulation is high.

- Attached to a contract of engagement or employment, which sets out the expected services and roles to be performed in exchange for some form of reward.

- Associated with a professional body, where the registered individual such as a lawyer, accountant, auditor, actuary or medical practitioner is required to act within the professional codes of practice, conduct and ethics.

- Accepted implicitly based on the individual's interpretation of personal responsibility or the corporate sense of duty, which is largely influenced by the internal culture set at the top, namely the board of directors.

In practice, all five forces exist together to ensure, first and foremost, that the required actions and decisions are executed. Accountability that is imposed, for example, through regulation and formal stipulations by the organisation is more likely to result in *boiler plate* compliance behaviours. Such behaviours tend to be process led with focus on *doing things right* in line with the corporate message. Conversely, accountability that is accepted implicitly is more likely to result in a higher level and quality of commitment to doing the right things for the organisation rather than merely ticking the compliance box.

By focusing on *doing the right things* rather than merely *doing things right*, organisations are more likely to promote personal accountability and gain more

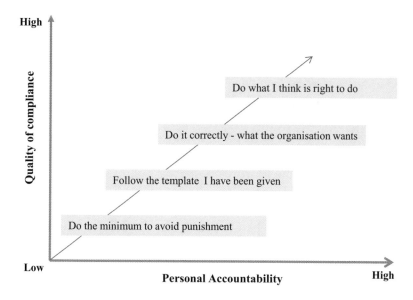

Figure 5.1   Relationship between Personal Accountability and Compliance

value from their governance and risk management processes. Individuals with a personal sense of accountability can help make poor structures and processes work; in contrast, the best designed structures and processes are unlikely to function well when there is no personal sense of accountability.

Corporate Accountability

In a well functioning organisation, each decision and its resulting actions, as well as their consequences, will have an owner. Such ownership of decisions and their related outcomes which include rewards as well as risk of loss enables an organisation to deal with issues and to make progress efficiently. Personal accountabilities come together collectively to provide corporate ownership of decisions, actions and consequences. Without corporate accountability, an organisation is likely to experience situations such as:

- business objectives and targets being delayed or not achieved at all;

- an executive team that is required to be very hands on in order to achieve progress;

- difficulty in implementing policies and standards consistently;

- recurrence of issues because problems either remain unresolved or are patched up superficially; and,

- over reliance on a core set of individuals who have emerged as reliable persons with a *can do* attitude who fix things.

It is through the assurance process that organisations understand and confirm that individuals have carried out their respective responsibilities and accountabilities. In the boardroom, having a clear sense of personal and corporate accountability helps to drive appropriate challenge and debate as directors seek to better understand the risks they are facing and the decisions they are required to make. In Chapter 2 we considered how the lack of challenge in boardrooms contribute to excessive risk taking and undermine board effectiveness.

While most boards recognise the importance of the quality of challenge, as was confirmed in the Eversheds Board Report,[2] the way in which they can hold individuals accountable without creating a blame culture is, however, not straightforward. One way to do this objectively is with the help of an appropriate assurance reporting framework that involves explaining the approaches taken when forming judgement and making decisions. This should not obstruct intuition in risk governance but provide a conscious and objective structure for decision making.

The Link between Assurance and Accountability

The provision of assurance is critical to demonstrating accountability and proper execution of responsibilities and duties. One of the most significant legislation that formally recognises the link between assurance and accountability is the Sarbanes-Oxley Act (SOX). It was issued by the US Securities and Exchange Commission (SEC) in 2002 in response to a number of high profile corporate failures of US public listed companies, notably, Enron, Worldcom and Tyco. SOX, which attracted global attention for its highly prescriptive rules placed the spotlight on corporate and management accountability and the need for formal assurance to be provided in company annual reporting. This is set out explicitly, particularly in Sections 302 and 404.

Section 302 requires the principal executive (namely, the chief executive officer or equivalent persons) and principle financial officer (that is, the finance director or equivalent individuals) to certify the integrity of the organisation's financial reports and systems of internal control. Formal statements from the chief executive and finance director are required to confirm, for example, that the organisation's reports do not 'contain any untrue statement of a material fact or omit to state a material fact'[3] that would cause the report to be misleading, that the organisation have evaluated the effectiveness of its internal controls and reported any significant deficiencies and resulting corrective actions to the organisation's auditors and audit committee.

Supporting Section 302 is the more talked about Section 404 of the Act, which prescribes the requirement for management to provide an 'internal control report'[4] in its annual report. The report involves a formal assessment of the effectiveness of the organisation's internal control structure and procedures for financial reporting. Additionally, the external auditors of the annual report are required to attest to the assessment carried out by management. This last requirement attracted significant attention and contention mainly because of the expected additional cost of compliance.

The listing standards of both the New York Stock Exchange (NYSE) and the National Association of Securities Dealers Automated Quotations (NASDAQ) stock exchanges, which were approved by the SEC in November 2003, supplemented the reforms introduced by SOX. The reforms, similar to the new regulations that followed the 2008 financial crisis, were regarded to be critical for enhancing corporate governance and restoring investor confidence. At its introduction, the explicit and highly prescriptive nature of Section 302 of SOX required all US public listed companies to review and overhaul the way the way they operated in the boardroom and throughout the organisation, regardless of geographical locations.

The level and detailed description of the nature of assurance required indicates that the SEC did not have any appetite for either the standards of governance or operations to be misinterpreted by the boards of organisations. Several years on, and after some rationalisation of the approaches within the organisations, the principles underlying Sections 302 and 404 are better understood and adopted globally on a *SOX light* basis.

SOX also recognised the significance of the cultural undercurrents within an organisation which influence accountability and behaviours. In the analyses that led to its introduction, unethical corporate behaviour was regarded to lie at the heart of the corporate failures as considered in Chapter 1. Section 406 of the Act and the new NYSE listing standards require organisations to have an effective compliance and ethics programme that is necessary to 'promote honest and ethical conduct, including ethical handling of actual and apparent conflicts of interest between personal and professional relationships'. Section 406 is particularly focused on the provision of assurance by requiring each public listed company 'to disclose whether or not, and if not, the reason therefor, such issuer [the company] has adopted a code of ethics' as well as 'any change in or waiver of the code of ethics'.[5]

Unlike Sections 302 and 404, Section 406 does not specify a code of ethics but refer to the setting of standards of behaviour. In practical terms, compliance with Section 406 involves the development and publication of a statement such as a code for business conduct and ethics, not just for its senior financial officers but for all directors, officers and employees as well as its business partners. More importantly, the organisation is required to provide training on the code and ensure that there is individual accountability for compliance with the code.

The UK's equivalent for the assessment and reporting of internal controls for public listed companies is provided by the Financial Reporting Council's UK Corporate Governance Code (the Code) and guidance on internal control, which is commonly referred to as the Turnbull Guidance.[6] It should be noted that the Turnbull Guidance is being reviewed to integrate the FRC's earlier guidance issued for directors on going concern and liquidity risk.[7] It is also worth noting that the Code and Turnbull Guidance are also frequently adopted by unlisted companies in the UK.

Unlike SOX, the Code and its supporting Turnbull Guidance have a *comply or explain* requirement which involves organisations explaining any deviations from the Code. The principles and code provisions provided in Section C of the Code that refers to accountability are broad and wide reaching. For example Main Principle C1 states that the board is required to 'present a fair, balanced and understandable assessment of the company's position and prospects'. This refers to the board's responsibility for providing public reports that includes a formal statement of the board's accountabilities for such reports as well as explanation of the basis on which the organisation sustains the business model for the long term and delivers its strategic objectives.

Turnbull's Main Principle C2 that refers to Risk Management and Internal Control specify the board's responsibilities for determining its risk appetite and maintaining 'sound risk management and internal control systems'.[8] The proposed changes arising from the current review of the Turnbull Guidance are expected to ask the board to 'carry out a robust assessment of the principal risks facing the company including those that would threaten its solvency or liquidity'.[9] This involves the need for the board to review the effectiveness of these systems with particular reference to how the principal risks are being managed or mitigated and to report on them to shareholders. The current Code Provisions in Section C are also explicit in stating the requirements for set up, composition and responsibilities of the board's audit committee and risk committee.

The Turnbull Guidance for the board advocates a risk based approach to establishing a sound system of internal control and reviewing its effectiveness. The system of internal control is expected to be integral to the organisation's management and governance processes. The Turnbull Guidance provides a useful definition of an internal control system, which is one that encompasses the policies, processes, tasks, behaviours and other aspects of a company that, taken together:

- facilitate its effective and efficient operation by enabling it to respond appropriately to significant ... risks to achieving the company's objectives;

- help ensure the quality of internal and external reporting;

- help ensure compliance with applicable laws and regulations, and also with internal policies with respect to the conduct of business.[10]

In summary, the accountabilities of senior officials, the board and its committees together with the provision of assurance through formal disclosure and reporting are common features of current regulatory standards and governance codes. For organisations to function effectively, they are required to integrate their assurance frameworks into their day to day management and governance processes. To achieve this, organisations' responsibility frameworks should include a clear definition of the terms of reference for boards and their committees as well as personal responsibilities and levels of authority. To promote personal and corporate accountability further, responsibility frameworks do well to be linked to the organisations' personnel performance management.

Regulatory Spotlight on Personal and Corporate Accountability

Every job role has a level of delegated authority for decision making and therefore accountability. Organisations promote personal accountability through a number of means. For a start, every organisation expects the individuals they employ to act in accordance with their contractual agreement to perform an agreed service, job role or function, and to be accountable for their performance. These expectations are supplemented by job descriptions, mandates, charters and policies. The existence of such documents does not guarantee the right sort of behaviours but their absence is likely to impede the development of the required ones. In addition, these documents play a significant role in setting the tone and influencing the corporate culture and ethics of the organisation, a quality that is not always recognised and often underestimated.

Regulatory regimes are not taking chances with holding organisations to account where required. This is most evident in the UK financial services regulatory regime. In addition to regulating corporate responsibility, the UK financial services authorities have a unique tool through their *Approved Persons* regime that holds individuals accountable at a personal level. The Approved Persons regime requires directors and individuals performing *designated control functions* – in the language of the regime – to comply with the authorities' *Statements of Principle and Code of Practice for Approved Persons* (which resemble a professional code of conduct) and to ensure that the organisations they work for comply with the *Principles for Businesses*.[11]

This regime was first introduced as part of the Financial Services and Markets Act (2000)[12] which was influenced by lessons from the fall in 1995 of the UK's oldest merchant bank, Barings, when the regulator could hold no person accountable for the bank failure. The regime requires regulated organisations to identify individuals to be held accountable for each control function as defined by the regulators, each of whom must be formally registered and approved by the respective regulatory authority. As part of the approval process, individuals are vetted to confirm that they are *Fit and Proper* under the following criteria:

- honesty, integrity and reputation;

- competence and capability: and,

- financial soundness.

The organisation is responsible for ensuring that relevant individuals are approved by the regulators and that they remain *fit and proper*. The organisation is also expected to formalise the requirements for such individuals to comply with the regulatory standards and codes of practice in their employment contracts by including the organisation's right to suspend or dismiss the individual in the event of a breach of the regulator's rules.

Following lessons from the 2008 financial crisis, the Approved Persons regime was extended in 2010 to include persons of *significant influence* such as those individuals operating at the group level (where the group is not UK regulated) or who are performing certain trading activities. Under this new *Approved Persons and Significant Influence* regime, the financial services regulators take a more interventionist approach by requiring certain individuals to be interviewed prior to approval. There are three potential outcomes as part of this vetting process: individuals may be approved without conditions; approved with certain conditions such as a second interview and/or confirmation of specific training or development; or, not be approved.

It is clear that the regulators are serious about assuring themselves that individuals who have *significant influence* and/or are performing key activities are suitable and sufficiently competent and capable. To reinforce the importance of personal and corporate accountability under the new regulatory regime, sanctions and fines reached record[13] levels in 2012.

To Conclude this Chapter …

Responsible organisations share the same concerns as the regulators about the competency and capability of those they employ. Many already invest heavily in training and developing their staff as well as their executive and non-executive directors, with board development featuring prominently in current board evaluations. Continual development of directors helps to extend their contribution in the boardroom '… beyond meeting the basic legal requirements and fiduciary responsibilities inherent in board service'.[14] At staff level, organisations should ensure they do not over emphasise the technical aspects of training that focus on *doing things right*; to gain broader benefits of personal accountability, training and development programmes should consider the decisions making culture of the organisation that promotes *doing the right things* for the organisation. This in turn encourages individuals to avoid being complacent and to challenge the status quo to achieve the right outcomes for the organisation.

It pays for organisations to understand that rules and contractual agreements are limited in their ability to regulate behavior or enforce responsible decision making and accountability. People with an appropriate sense of accountability can compensate for weak structures and processes, but without accountability even well designed systems cannot make people work better. Organisations need their key people to be able to assess situations and determine actions that are appropriate, including timely escalation of matters without a need for a rule to be in place for every eventuality. This is particularly pertinent for managing uncertainty, which is inherent in any risk management process.

In summary, organisations need to demonstrate their accountability across the business by taking steps to ensure that they, and their people, understand and are discharging their responsibilities appropriately. Directors and managers can delegate some of their responsibilities but cannot be absolved from their accountabilities. Assurance is the process by which the boards, and those to whom they have delegated responsibilities across the organisation, demonstrate accountability. I borrow the words of my learned colleague, Kathryn Morgan, a Fellow and Council Member of the Institute of Actuaries, to conclude this chapter:

> It is not enough to rely on good people doing the right things – we all have different views of what the right things are, and the transparency and accountability provided by a good control system means that a company can be managed on information not assumptions. Managing risks cannot happen by accident but require a conscious governance framework that takes into account the human factor.[15]

Key Points from this Chapter

1.   Accountability refers to a sense of responsibility, integrity and duty.

2.   Accountability if imposed rather than accepted at a personal level is more likely to encourage boiler plate compliance.

3.   Organisations can gain more value from its people when promoting personal and corporate accountability by taking into account the human factor and giving more emphasis on *doing the right things* than *doing things right*.

4.   Accountable people are more likely to encourage healthy challenge and help make even poor structures and processes work better.

5.   Accountability helps to drive appropriate debate in the boardroom in the search for insight to the risks and the effectiveness of the organisation's risk mitigation strategies.

6.   An assurance framework supports a conscious and objective process by which an organisation can assess and confirm the proper discharge of individual's accountability for managing risks.

Endnotes

1   Andreas Schedler, Larry Diamond and Marc F. Plattner, (eds). *The Self-Restraining State: Power and Accountability in New Democracies* (Boulder, Colorado and London, Lynne Rienner Publishers, 1999) Chapter 2 *Conceptualizing Accountability*, 13–28.

2   Eversheds LLP, *The Eversheds Board Report: Measuring the impact of board composition on company performance* (London, Eversheds LLP, May 2011), The report involved a study of 241 companies headquartered in the UK, continental Europe, the USA and the Asia-Pacific region that was supplemented by 50 in depth interviews with directors. The Report ranked challenge as the third most important ingredient for an effective board after composition of the board and an effective chair. 48.

3   U.S. Government, Sarbanes-Oxley Act 2002, 'Public Law No. 107–204', formally known as the 'Public Company Accounting Reform and Investor Protection Act and Corporate and Auditing Accountability and Responsibility Act' (Washington DC, U.S. Government Printing Office, 2002), Section 302.

4   Ibid., Section 404.

5   Ibid., Section 406.

6   Financial Reporting Council (FRC), *Internal Control: Revised Guidance for Directors on the Combined Code 2005*, commonly known as 'Turnbull Guidance', which at November 2013, was under review by the FRC (London, FRC, 2005).

7   Financial Reporting Council (FRC), *Going Concern and Liquidity Risk: Guidance for Directors of UK Companies* (London, FRC, 2009). This paper is under review alongside the Turnbull Guidance to create more integrated guidance under the UK Corporate Governance Code in 2014.

8   Financial Reporting Council (FRC), *The UK Corporate Governance Code* (London, FRC, September 2012), Section C: Accountability.

9   Financial Reporting Council (FRC), *Consultation Paper: Risk Management, Internal Control and the Going Concern Basis of Accounting,Consultation on Draft Guidance to the Directors of Companies applying the UK Corporate Governance Code and Associated Changes to the Code* (London, FRC, November 2013).

10   Financial Reporting Council (FRC), *Internal Control: Revised guidance for directors on the Combined Code 2005*, commonly known as 'Turnbull Guidance', which at November 2013, was under review by the FRC (London, FRC, 2005), Section 2, Paragraph 19.

11   Prudential Regulation Authority and Financial Conduct Authority, *Handbook*. Accessed 28 December 2013. http://fshandbook.info/FS/html/PRA/PRIN and http://www.fshandbook.info/FS/html/FCA/D3.

12   UK Parliament, *Financial Services Act 2012* which updates the Bank of England Act 1998, the Financial Services and Markets Act 2000, which include changes in the UK regulatory regime that includes the breakup of the Financial Services Authority to form the Prudential Regulation Authority and Financial Conduct Authority (London, *The Stationery Office*, 2012).

13   Reynolds Porter Chamberlain LLP, 'FSA hands out record breaking fines against individuals in 2011', 19 December 2011. 'The FSA handed down £12.9 million in fines against individuals in 2011 (to December 16), breaking the record it set last year of £8.8million by 47 per cent.' Retrieved 03 August 2013. http://www.rpc.co.uk/index.php?option=com_flexicontent&view=items&cid=130:insuranceandreinsurance&id=15822:fsa-hands-out-record-breaking-fines-against-individuals-in-2011&Itemid=27

14   George William, 'Board governance depends on where you sit'. This article dated February 2013 is an adaptation of a chapter George contributed to 'The Future of Boards: Meeting the Governance Challenges of the Twenty-First Century', edited by Jay W. Lorsch (Boston, MA, *Harvard Business School Publishing*, July 2012). George William is a professor of management practice at the Harvard Business School, a board member of ExxonMobil, Goldman Sachs, and the Mayo Clinic and previously served on the boards of Novartis AG and Target, among others. From 1991 to 2001, he was the CEO of Medtronic, whose board he chaired from 1996 to 2002. Retrieved 16 March 2013. http://www.mckinsey.com/insights/leading_in_the_21st_century/board_governance_depends_on_where_you_sit.

15   Morgan, Kathryn, in a private communication, September 2013.

Chapter 6

Rethinking Assurance

The lessons from corporate failings we considered in the first five chapters of the book placed the spotlight on the foundations of good governance that include risk oversight, openness in information flows and accountability. The earlier chapters also alluded to the implicit quality of assurance in the governance process; assurance being taken for granted without much conscious reflection contributed to blind risk taking. In this chapter we re-examine the concept of assurance and its integral role in facilitating good governance. By taking a fresh look at assurance, we can apply it more consciously and effectively in the governance process.

Assurance – Fact or Emotion

We usually assume *assurance* is happening until something occurs to tell us otherwise. This sense of being secure or insecure usually only becomes evident when things go wrong as was illustrated in the aftermath of corporate crises we considered in the earlier chapters. So, before we consider the concept of *integrated assurance* and what it could mean, there is merit in re-examining the principles of assurance and its role in supporting corporate governance (more) effectively.

It would seem that, especially in a corporate environment, we all begin with a base level of trust in people or in a system until events cause us to question our belief and erode our confidence. In other words, the need for assurance as an emotion can be latent only to be unleashed when triggered by something that shakes our state of understanding. This could be because everyone working in the organisation is assumed to be competent in the role they are given and that it would be socially unacceptable to question trust without reason. It takes a confident person, particularly in a boardroom environment, to question the quality of trust in others without apparent basis. So, it is usually through experience that we learn and feel confident enough to seek facts required to support the foundations upon which we have formed our trust.

Assurance, according to a number of dictionaries including Cambridge and Webster's, is used commonly to refer to a state of mind such as 'confidence' or a 'promise'.[1] To provide assurance is an act or statement '*to inspire confidence*' *or to create a 'state of being assured; firm persuasion; full confidence or trust; freedom from doubt; certainty'*.[2] Assurance that can inspire confidence and sense of trust is a good outcome.

Confidence, however, refers to an emotional state of mind. To achieve a sense of confidence or trust depends on the individual's need that is influenced by a number of complex factors including personal experience, academic, social and economic background as well as personal risk compass (as discussed in Chapter 3). For some people, trust that is broken as a result of unexpected events can be hard to regain. Having been let down, they are more likely to require a higher quality of assurance in the future. For others, trust and confidence can be restored with more and/or independently validated information, that is, facts.

For the purpose of this book it is sufficient for us to acknowledge these human factors and to be aware that the provision of assurance can be as much about satisfying an emotional state of mind as it is about facts. In a corporate environment, we require assurance to be based on facts – including an understanding of the limits of our knowledge – on the basis that no organisation can survive if it is run solely by intuition and on emotion. These facts we refer to are based on the organisation's systems of internal control, risk management and reporting processes. It is not a coincidence that these are the areas that tend to occupy much of our boards' agenda and organisations' time. Yet, we do not seem to be doing enough as regulators increase their need for *more* assurance.

The *weight of compliance*, felt by many non-executive directors, can distract the board from the strategic agenda and issues that lay beneath. To minimise this risk, boards are seeking to adopt a different approach to demonstrating compliance that is integrated with the board's strategic agenda. The assurance that boards are required to provide to regulators needs to evolve from one that is focused on the existence and conformance with required processes to one which places more emphasis on the *so what* question, that alludes to the effects and outcomes of those processes. In other words, assurance should focus on the integrity and effectiveness of an organisation's system of risk management and control as *risk assurance*.

The notion that assurance in organisations has perhaps been missing the mark is supported in the King Code and Report on Governance for South Africa (King III), which noted that the provision of assurance is 'different from verification', whereby the 'process of verification confirms the existence of stated facts – it confirms data. Assurance is a broader term that refers to the integrity of certain processes and systems'.[3] This means that information provides a basis for the assurance process but the process is incomplete if it does not inspire confidence over the effectiveness of the underlying systems. To reinforce the qualitative nature of assurance, more than one non-executive director has said in the course of my research for this book that assurance is not always about what is on paper but the reliability and integrity of the source.

On this basis, the assurance process potentially begins with the level of trust and confidence the board has in the source of the information. Perhaps assurance could be better described as a statement or indication that inspires confidence, based on an appropriate level of facts from a trusted source. A trusted source, by implication, sets an expected level of integrity and assurance against which information received will be assessed. Let us consider the implicit nature of trust and expectation in the assurance process in the next section.

Aligning Assurance with Expectations

Whenever we place trust in someone or in some process, we set an expectation – for ourselves and for those we trust. When something bad happens, that is not within our expectation, our confidence is dented. We feel let down by the person or the system we have trusted or relied upon. We feel our trust is broken. We may seek blame (which is seldom helpful) and also assurance that it will not happen again. Promises are made and hope is regained – until the next incident. Promises are however made by people and the problem is that people are not infallible. Promises, like assurance which are not based on sound foundations or understanding of expectations are likely to be empty.

SETTING EXPECTATIONS

Let us consider this simple example where a board approves a major IT transformation plan costing nearly £20 million with a target to complete in 24 months' time to support the roll out of its strategy for a single global network connecting all its offices. The executive keeps the board informed that the project is on schedule. Under two years later, the board is informed by the executive that the project had indeed been completed on time; the final cost was 30 per cent above plan and the development of a number of lower priority functionalities was moved to the second phase of the plan. The board was surprised. An extra spend of 30 per cent was significantly more than it had expected while the executive thought this was a reasonable overrun for a major strategic development. The project was, after all, substantially completed on time. Clearly, the expectations and tolerances (risk appetite) of the board were different from that of the executive. The board is likely to feel that their trust in the executive management was misplaced.

Let's suppose a more positive scenario where the board's expectations and risk tolerances are clear; the executive understands that the board expects to be alerted to overruns in time and budgets greater than 10 per cent. In this second scenario, the executive kept the board informed of the timeliness of the project as well as the reasons for the changes in expenditure against the budget. The executive also provided an outline of the plan for phase two of the project. While the implementation of the project in the second scenario was not flawless, the quality of the assurance given by the executive made a difference; it instilled confidence in the board of the capability and integrity of the executive. The board's expectations in this scenario were being managed appropriately.

Incidentally, the example in the first scenario is not as unrealistic as it appears. A very similar event occurred in a large organisation where a multi-million pound IT project that involved the deployment of over 50 external contractors was largely handled by the executive outside the boardroom until it was queried during a visit by its regulators. The executive's view was that having gained the approval of the board, it could just get on with the job. The approach implicitly assumed that any risks that may arise will be well within the Board's tolerances.

A TRANSACTION TO INSPIRE CONFIDENCE

By use of this simple example, we can see that the assurance process resembles a transaction that involves an understanding or agreement between the *stakeholder* (who is the recipient of assurance) and the *provider* of assurance where:

- The *stakeholder* has a set of objectives, needs or expectations (of things that are expected to go right and things that are not expected to go wrong).

- The *provider* of the assurance is required to supply information that is necessary to satisfy the expectations of the stakeholder.

- The *assurance transaction* is the exchange of expectations and assurance between the stakeholder and the assurance provider, which in equilibrium will result in shared objectives of the assurance required. A summary of the *assurance transaction* is provided diagrammatically in Figure 6.1.

In practice, the agreement between the stakeholder and assurance provider is often unwritten; expectations of the stakeholder are typically communicated informally with reliance on common sense and an assumption that all parties have a common understanding of the expectations and requirements. Most of the time, these assumptions are reasonable, particularly where there is an abundance of underlying formal rules and regulations for defining assurance requirements such as those governing financial reporting or the role of the audit committee. When stakeholder expectations are unclear, however, assurance providers are likely to misinterpret the level as well as the frequency of the assurance required.

Stakeholder expectations and objectives for assurance are broadly influenced by three main sources. The first is from legislation, regulation and other external requirements including professional standards as considered in Chapter 4. The second source of influence is derived from the organisation's own strategic goals, vision and policies including job specifications and required performance standards. The third source of influence emanates from the individual's attitude to risk and personal threshold for unwanted surprises and standards of performance, which we discussed in Chapter 3. We summarise in Figure 6.2 the three main sources of influence for determining the objectives in the assurance transaction.

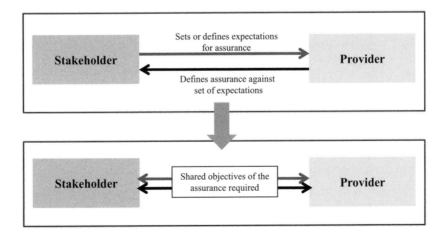

Figure 6.1   The Assurance Transaction

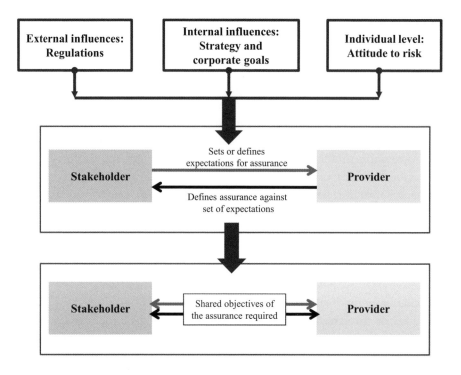

Figure 6.2   Three Main Sources of Influence in Objective Setting in the Assurance Transaction

In summary, to encourage a greater common understanding and shared objectives between the assurance stakeholder and provider, it would help to consider assurance in governance as:

> *a transaction between at least two parties to inspire and maintain confidence. The assurance transaction involves the assurance stakeholder and provider sharing common understanding of the nature of the actions and information required to affirm the status and effectiveness of a system of control and risk management.*

Good communication between the assurance stakeholder and provider is vital to ensure that expectations and objectives of the assurance are understood; this is especially important when the objectives are internally driven and thus could evolve with changing strategic goals and risks of the organisation. Managing changing expectations of stakeholders is part of maintaining the assurance transaction which we shall consider in the next section.

Maintaining Confidence in the Assurance Transaction

Like trust, confidence can be eroded by poor management of expectations of stakeholders in the assurance transaction. As discussed earlier, the better the expectations are managed, the greater the assurance provider's ability to inspire confidence; misunderstandings and surprises arising in the transaction are also minimised. For assurance to be effective, active engagement between all parties is essential to ensure the assurance transaction remains current and relevant.

CONSCIOUS RISK TAKING REQUIRES A CONSCIOUS ASSURANCE PROCESS

Providing assurance with absolute certainty is not always realistic. Communication and feedback between parties help to minimise the expectations gap. Both positive and negative feedback adds value to the assurance transaction. A manager once commented that it was like shooting in the dark without feedback from his stakeholders (his manager and the board) for whom he was seeking to do the right thing; for him, no feedback was worse than negative feedback. Time was wasted trying to fill the void by second guessing the needs of his stakeholders.

In a similar example, we consider a case where a CEO (the assurance stakeholder) does not give feedback to its internal audit team (the assurance provider). As a consequence, the internal audit team second guesses the CEO but inevitably gives more emphasis to those areas where the expectations from other stakeholders such as the audit committee are clearer. In this case, the CEO should not be surprised if the audit plans do not cover the risks as he sees them.

Let us consider a positive example where a board (the assurance stakeholder) queries the choice and quality of the assumptions underpinning a proposed strategic plan; the query triggers an assurance process whereby the executive (as the assurance provider) prepares an improved set of analysis and rationale for the proposed plan. The result is a board that feels more assured and informed to approve the plan; the executive knows from the feedback that providing the rationale with all future proposals will support more confident and efficient decision making in the boardroom.

In brief, these simple examples help to illustrate that the assurance process is richer if both parties engage to share common understanding of the requirements in order to help manage expectations and any inherent uncertainties and imperfections in the assurance process. Figure 6.3 summarises the interplay between the stakeholder and the provider of assurance and the importance of the feedback loop.

As principal stewards of the organisation, the board is expected to engage proactively with external stakeholders, including investors, regulators and government bodies, in order to understand their expectations and to meet their assurance needs. The availability of governance codes and regulation, as discussed in the earlier chapters, minimises second guessing the expectations of external stakeholders in the assurance transaction. However, to assure others, the board must first assure themselves. It would serve boards well to view assurance as a conscious process that needs to be nurtured and evolved with the changes in the risk environment as well as the needs of the organisation and its stakeholders.

ANATOMY OF THE ASSURANCE FOOD CHAIN

Viewed consciously, assurance transactions are pervasive and exist silently to connect every individual in the organisation. At the most basic level, employment and service contracts serve to specify the expectations of individuals whose performance is assured through regular feedback and appraisal with their managers as stakeholders. At the highest level, governance involves two main assurance transactions: firstly, between the board and the external stakeholders (such as customers, investors as well as regulators); secondly, between the board and the executive management.

To satisfy the board's assurance requirements, further assurance transactions are set up by the executive management with other assurance providers deeper within the organisation. By joining up these assurance transactions we create an *assurance food chain*. Within the organisation, the board resides at the top of

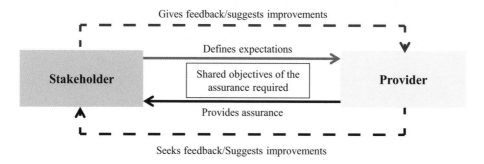

Figure 6.3   Maintaining the Assurance Transaction

the assurance food chain in its relationship with the executive management as the immediate assurance providers. The assurance food chain is illustrated in Figure 6.4. From an external perspective, the board will assume the role of assurance provider on behalf of the organisation to its external stakeholders.

ASSURANCE IS EVERYONE'S RESPONSIBILITY

By virtue of being assigned a responsibility, every individual in the organisation has a role to play in the assurance food chain. The individual is expected to be able to demonstrate sound execution of their responsibilities to assure the assigner of the role; this would be expected to take place as part of the organisation's performance management process. Also, their manager whose role involves delegating and supervising staff is expected to seek and give assurance up the chain over the proper discharge of their duties.

Managers form part of the assurance chain as they (as assurance stakeholders) seek assurance from those they supervise (the assurance providers). The assurance process may manifest itself in several ways from informal confirmations of a completion of a task to more formal reporting on the status of a multimillion dollar projects.

Like the blood vessels feeding each cell in a body, assurance is provided and gained silently throughout the organisation by emails and reports darting around the organisation, supplemented by continuous monitoring of dashboards and balanced scorecards. The assurance process does indeed touch everyone in the organisation. As a result, the *assurance food chain* is clearly not limited by structural or functional boundaries. Assurance that is constrained by organisational boundaries will be unable to provide a reliable picture of the risks being managed across the organisation.

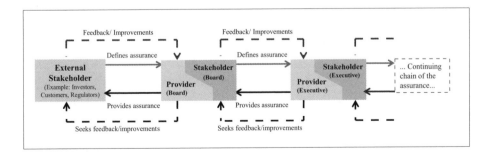

Figure 6.4   The Assurance Food Chain

To Conclude this Chapter ...

Assurance is implicit in the governance process. Lessons from corporate failures, however, indicate that this approach to assurance allows blind trust to prevail to the detriment of the organisations. A more conscious approach to seeking and discussing the assurance requirements of boards is emerging as a necessary step to strengthening corporate governance. Rethinking assurance in this light means that assurance should be viewed as a transaction between at least two parties – the assurance stakeholder and provider of assurance. Clear understanding of the expectations of the assurance stakeholder is essential for the assurance provider to be effective in delivering the assurance required and to inspire confidence.

At the fundamental level, every individual with an assigned responsibility will have a role to play in the assurance food chain to seek and/or provide assurance regarding their assigned responsibilities. The board sits at the highest level of the assurance food chain within the organisation and ensures that its assurance needs are satisfied to enable it to assure external stakeholders of the organisation. To be reliable and free of blind spots, the assurance food chain must be able to work across organisational and functional boundaries. To support effective governance across the organisation, boards need to develop an approach to seeking and providing assurance across functional boundaries at a more conscious level than ever before.

Key Points from this Chapter

1. Assurance should be viewed consciously as a transaction involving at least two parties – the *stakeholder* and the *assurance provider* – to inspire and maintain confidence against a set of expectations.

2. Understanding the relationships within the *assurance food chain* helps to improve the quality of assurance across functional boundaries.

3. Assurance should not only confirm compliance with policies but the integrity of the organisation's risk management and systems of control.

4. The giving and seeking of assurance is everyone's responsibility.

Endnotes

1 Cambridge Dictionaries Online, s.v. 'assurance'. Accessed 03 August 2013. http://dictionary.cambridge.org/dictionary/british/assurance_2.

2 Webster's Online Dictionary, s.v. 'assurance'. Accessed 03 August 2013. http://www.websters-online-dictionary.org/definition/assurance.

3 King Committee on Corporate Governance and Institute of Directors in Southern Africa (IoDSA), *King Code and Report on Governance for South Africa* ('King III'). (Johannesburg, *IoDSA*, 2009), Principle 9.

PART II
RISK ASSURANCE BEYOND BOUNDARIES

Chapter 7

Seeking the Holistic Risk and Assurance Picture

In Part I of the book we considered the lessons from the financial market crisis since 2008 to illustrate the challenges facing directors as the soundness of corporate governance systems is scrutinised. The management of risks, and assurance of its effectiveness, was shown to be disjointed and did not support effective risk governance. We concluded Part I with a call to rethink the nature and the role of assurance in corporate governance. We move the discussion forward in this chapter by understanding the challenges facing boards in gaining a clear and holistic risk picture as they cut through the clutter of information they are given in the name of assurance.

A Plan to Inspire Confidence across the Assurance Food Chain

Non-executive and executive directors alike are constantly under the microscope – more so since the financial crisis. Their ability to discharge their responsibilities appropriately is open to question. The quality of their judgment and of the information upon which their decisions are based are also subject to challenge. As a result of the 2008 financial crisis, directors and their boards in many financial services organisations were told that they were either taking too much risk or were unaware of the risks their organisations were running. Surprises in the boardroom questioned the quality of the assurance provided over the effectiveness of the organisation's risk management. Corporate governance was evidently not working to expectations of the governments, regulators, as well as the general public. Confidence in the boardroom needed to be restored.

In reexamining assurance in corporate governance it would be fair to state that such a rethink was probably overdue; the lessons from the financial crisis have merely provided a catalyst for our analysis. To all intents and purposes the responsibilities of directors have been reinforced rather than changed by the harsh lessons of the financial crisis. The crisis highlighted areas where better or increased attention was required, for example, the skills and effectiveness of the boards as well as their focus on risk oversight over a wider range of issues. The crisis raised questions about the diligent execution of corporate governance rather than the absence of policies within organisations.

As discussed in earlier chapters, this renewed focus is reflected in the UK Corporate Governance Code (2012) and Guidance on Audit Committees (September 2012) issued by the UK Financial Reporting Council in response to lessons from the financial crisis. The provisions of these new codes have sought to expand, and clarify further, the nature of the responsibilities of directors, including the assurance they should receive in relation to the organisation's system of risk management and control, particularly in an environment of change.

Management is responsible for supporting the work of the directors in the boardroom by providing assurance to the board that appropriate systems are in place for 'the identification, assessment, management and monitoring of risk, for developing, operating and monitoring the system of internal control'.[1] In providing the assurance required by the directors, management may seek the support and advice of various specialist functions within the organisation such as legal, health and safety, compliance, information security and internal audit as well as other external sources of objective advice.

Where an organisation does not have an internal audit function, the audit committee is required to consider annually the appropriateness of the total arrangements in place to provide the level and type of assurance it requires in relation to the organisation's system of risk management and control. In carrying out this assessment, the audit committee is expected to consider a number of factors that include the 'scale, diversity and complexity of the company's activities and the number of employees, as well as cost/benefit considerations'.[2] Additionally, the Guidance states that the audit committee should:

> also consider whether there are any trends or current factors relevant to the company's activities, markets or other aspects of its external environment that have increased, or are expected to increase, the risks faced by the company. Such an increase in risk may also arise from internal factors such as organisational restructuring or from changes in reporting processes or underlying information systems. Other matters to be taken into account may include adverse trends evident from the

monitoring of internal control systems or an increased incidence of unexpected occurrences.[3]

For corporate governance to work effectively, the total effect of assurance activity in respect of the risks facing an organisation cannot be taken for granted. Assurance activity in respect of each risk needs to be carried out consciously and explicitly if it is to inspire confidence in the boardroom. This means it needs to be planned and anticipatory in its approach. As part of the *assurance food chain*, directors are expected to seek assurance that the risk taking within the organisation is within the limits they have specified. This involves obtaining a consistent view and *one truth* about the risks they are running without which their ability to exercise sound and balanced judgment could be impaired.

For those working in financial services, it is worth reiterating that directors' judgment is expected to be judged as part of the regulatory risk assessment process. Additionally, directors sitting on boards of those organisations listed publicly on stock exchanges are required to answer to their wider group of stakeholders as part of the *assurance food chain*.

Perhaps the board's statement of internal control[4] as provided by the Turnbull Guidance for directors could be better used to communicate the organisation's holistic approach to risk management and internal control rather than to merely demonstrate its compliance with the listing rules. At the time of writing, the Turnbull Guidance is being reviewed by the Financial Reporting Council[5] who is seeking to integrate the main principles of risk management and control, and to promote more open disclosure of effective risk management.

For those in central government, the UK National Audit Office's guide for audit committees[6] sets out clear requirements for a similar statement of internal control to demonstrate to parliament and the public the responsible use and management of resources through sound risk management, control and governance within the organisation.

We considered in the last chapter that directors and the board of an organisation operate at the highest level of the *assurance food chain*. While management, which includes the executive members of the board are responsible for providing appropriate information for the purpose of assuring the board, as principal stewards of the organisation the board cannot be passive in seeking such assurance. The respective relationships that exist between the board and management as well as the external stakeholders of the organisation are akin to contracts that require the seeking and provision of assurance.

To inspire confidence consistently across the *assurance food chain*, the board requires a plan – a dynamic one to reflect the changing circumstances of the organisation; this includes the evolving expectations particularly of external stakeholders who may be influenced by specific events in the media and press. That plan is an assurance plan that is aligned with the risks of the organisation.

The Need for a Joined Up and Holistic Risk Picture

The challenge of sitting at the top of the internal *assurance food chain* – at the helm – is determining how each piece of the risk picture is identified, escalated, filtered and aggregated to provide a complete and meaningful picture of the risks facing the organisation. In Part I, we considered the instances where boards were seen to be either unaware of the risks they were taking or that excessive risks were being taken that ultimately led to the demise of their organisations. With hindsight, the assurance they had received appears empty. The board's need for a joined up and holistic picture of the risks and mitigation plans is paramount in order for it to discharge its responsibilities effectively.

As a reminder, the role of the board as summarised by the Turnbull Guidance for directors is to:

> *set appropriate policies on internal control and seek regular assurance that it will enable it to satisfy itself that the system is functioning effectively. The Board must further ensure that the system of internal control is effective in managing those risks in the manner which it has approved.*[7]

Turnbull goes on to state that management is accountable to the board for monitoring the system of control and for providing the assurance needed by the board. At the helm, the board is therefore required to know, and should actively seek to know, two main things:

- Whether or not the ship is indeed on course, that is, that the systems of internal control are sound and working as expected.

- If there are any *icebergs* that could sink the ship, where they might be and how they can be avoided, that is, being preemptive of the principal risks that could impact its key stakeholders and which could threaten the strategic goals and viability of the organisation.

To satisfy each aspect of its assurance needs, the board should seek and be provided with assurance at two main levels:

- At a specific process, area of business, risk, project or portfolio level.

- At an aggregated view that provides the big picture of the organisation's principal risks.

Also supporting a holistic approach to assurance and risk oversight is the King Code and Report on Governance (King III). In fact, King III is very direct in its support for integrated reporting, which permeates throughout the Code. Its rationale is that 'Strategy, risk, performance and sustainability have become inseparable'. King III advocates the importance of integrated reporting that places emphasis on more holistic consideration of risks in respect of an organisation's financial performance as well as its sustainability by disclosing both positive and negative impacts that the organisation's strategy and operations have on its stakeholders. King III states clearly in its Principle 3.5 that 'The audit committee should ensure that a combined assurance model is applied to provide a coordinated approach to all assurance activities'.[8] King III is the clearest yet for specifying a code for integrated assurance.

The board has a challenging role in balancing its need for information that is necessary to assure itself of the sound running of the business as a whole – too much is as bad as too little. In addition, *silo* information can also obscure the big and real picture which the board needs to inform decision making. Achieving the *big and real picture* must lie at the heart of our system of integrated assurance. King III advocates an integrated report for boards in respect of the organisation's performance across the *triple context* which refers to economic, social and environmental factors. This also covers strategy, risk and financial management.

Combined assurance as stated in King III refers to the coordination of internal and external assurance over these dimensions of performance and is a formal requirement of the audit committee for its oversight responsibilities. King III acknowledges the challenges facing the leadership in the boardroom in seeking and implementing this holistic picture. Recognising its value to modernising governance, King III emphasises the social and moral obligations of the board as *responsible corporate citizens* to provide integrated reporting.

The intense focus on corporate governance and on the apparent lack of risk oversight must, however, be baffling for some boards. According to the Eversheds Board Report,[9] which is based on a comprehensive survey of 241 leading global companies and which was complemented by 50 indepth interviews of directors, there was overwhelming agreement (93 per cent overall compared with 100 per cent for bank directors) amongst the directors that the board should be involved with risk management and a similar majority of 88 per cent confirming that risk is already on the agenda.

Unsurprisingly, only 8 per cent of the directors in the study thought that the financial crisis has had any transformative effect on their agenda. Having said this, the directors could not agree on the content of their risk remit. Directors in the study were also split in their understanding of the primary role of the board as *minder* and *strategist* and what each entailed; 67 per cent of bank directors thought that the board's role as *minder* is to provide oversight in a supervisory or monitoring capacity compared with only 17 per cent of directors from other industries whose corporate directors thought that safeguarding shareholder value was the more important function.

Perhaps it is appropriate for us to revert to first principles in considering how assurance is delivered to stakeholders in the name of corporate governance. Governance codes and regulations in the UK believe that a principles based approach remains appropriate for allowing boards to *comply or explain* or *apply and explain* their chosen strategy for compliance. The board and its directors at the top of the internal *assurance food chain* are responsible for defining the approach and the assurance plan it needs to discharge its responsibilities in accordance with the relevant governance codes.

Clearly a principles based approach relies on the judgment of the board and its management. It involves determining compliance systems that are both appropriate and proportionate for the organisation. Determining proportionality typically requires management to take into account the size or scale, diversity, nature and complexity of the organisation as well as the associated costs and benefits such compliance systems are expected to deliver. This proportionality principle which is adopted by both the financial services regulators and the UK Financial Reporting Council is pragmatic and sensible.

The challenge for boards and management remains in exercising the *right* judgment. Post reform, the financial services regulators' approach to supervision of regulated organisations will judge the judgment of the boards and management. It is early days yet in terms of how this approach will exactly play out in the boardroom in the coming years. Some early indications are that directors are being challenged on the robustness of their decisions, particularly in new business and strategic developments; the financial regulators are clearly taking a more preemptive and interventionist approach to supervising firms. The rationale for their approach is the broad link between corporate success or failure and the firm's strategy. By the strength of regulatory focus on the key decisions that set the direction of an organisation, it is hoped that bad decisions can be averted.

Seeking Risk Intelligence – When More is Less

Boards are usually not short on the volume of information they receive. Board packs averaging 50–100 pages are generally accepted to be the *norm* and even *good* in some organisations. I have also come across some boards where the norm is a board pack that runs between 200–300 pages per sitting, which could double depending on the cycle of reporting in the year. At the other extreme, I have come across a board where the pack was not circulated beforehand but was walked through and discussed by the executive management at the board meeting; needless to say the ability of the non-executive directors to prepare for discussion or to challenge the executive was greatly impaired. I understand the executive management of that organisation has since been replaced.

The board agenda is not decreasing and neither are the board packs. The introduction of electronic board packs for a more sustainable solution, to *save the trees* as well as the administrative burden, is not a coincidence. With increased regulation in corporate governance, board agendas are largely influenced by mandatory items such as statutory and regulatory developments, and related reporting. The agenda of the board's sub-committees, such as the audit committee, risk committee, remuneration and nominations committees, are of course determined by their specific areas of focus and terms of reference.

Information that constitutes assurance on the sound operation of the relevant system of risk management and control is typically embedded in the board packs in various guises; they can also be provided on an ad hoc basis when requested by the board or its sub-committees or as part of an agreed plan as determined by the functional area such as compliance, health and safety or internal audit. In addition to the reporting of financial and strategic performance of the organisation, some typical examples of standing reports of a compliance nature, which the board may receive from various assurance providers, include:

- anti-financial crime including the Money Laundering Reporting Officer's report;

- Bribery Act compliance report;

- customer complaints analysis;

- report of external auditor independence and provision of non-audit services;

- fund and investment management auditors' report;

- health and safety report;

- information security and Data Protection Act compliance report;

- litigation report;

- health checks on key outsourcing arrangements;

- management letters from external auditors;

- audit report of quality standards such as International Organisation for Standards;

- Sarbanes-Oxley Act sections 302 and 404 certifications;

- sustainability and corporate social responsibility report;

- annual report on whistle-blowing and Public Interest Disclosure Act.

Additionally, the board and its relevant sub-committees may receive functional reports from the risk, compliance, finance and internal audit functions that cover similar areas of interests. The list of reports and papers that constitute assurance to the board is clearly long. It is easy to see how directors and management could have different understandings of the residual risks and issues pertaining to the same subject.

It is also easy to understand how disparate information can only serve to confuse rather than to clarify the risk picture – like pieces of a jigsaw which do not join up. Borrowing the perception of Professor Thomas Malone, Founding Director of the MIT Center for Collective Intelligence at the MIT Sloan School of Management, boards and their organisations need *collective intelligence*[10] that is built on the benefits of shared knowledge. This is achieved by having an aggregate understanding of what is and what is not working. To gain risk intelligence, boards therefore require a process that help them to sew together the disparate information they receive from the organisation.

Working Beyond Functional Boundaries to Gain Collective Intelligence

Effective assurance at an integrated level cannot just happen; it requires a degree of design and coordination of resources to minimise waste, duplication of effort and collation of knowledge. To lay the foundations for considering the design and coordination of assurance, we must first identify the respective responsibilities in the assurance food chain, particularly in those principal areas of the business that could make or break the organisation.

A survey,[11] published by the Chartered Institute of Internal Auditors for the UK and Ireland in 2010 of 62 of its members from both the private and public sectors, showed that there was an average of six principal assurance providers in their organisations. Some organisations listed up to 14 sources. Only 8 per cent had any form of *combined assurance* plan showing the sources of assurance provided. The duplication of the information appears to be arising for three main reasons in that the information is provided:

- to demonstrate board oversight and compliance with regulation or trade standards;

- because it is an important area of risk which the board may have asked or expected to consider; and/or,

- because it is part of an established cycle of management review.

It is unsurprising that directors and assurance providers alike have started to question the approach to providing assurance in the boardroom. Increased regulation and standards of governance have contributed to the rise and focus on assurance functions, such as compliance, risk and internal audit. With their particular areas of professional focus, together with the wide implications of the principles based approach adopted by regulation and governance codes, it was inevitable that the assurance functions found their mandates overlapping.

A more joined up and conscious approach across functional boundaries to gaining assurance seems logical as well as necessary if organisations are to benefit from the collective and shared knowledge of their assurance providers. To summarise, directors and organisations have started to challenge the *silo* approach by assurance functions as well as the quality of the assurance for four main reasons:

1. Variations of the *truth* that could obscure the real view of the risks.

2. Risk of gaps in the overall assurance of risks.

3. Duplicated effort and cost of compliance at both management and board levels, including increased pressure on the board agenda.

4. Increased need to direct with confidence especially under the scrutiny of external stakeholders that include investors, regulators and the public.

To Conclude this Chapter ...

It is my reading that the changes in risk governance did not arise directly but indirectly from the financial crisis, as a result of increased regulatory requirements for more overt demonstration of risk oversight and the resultant growth of assurance functions and activity. Without coordination and collaboration, assurance functions find themselves duplicating and overlapping in their activities, with some organisations reporting the rise of *turf wars* between the assurance functions. The financial crisis has undoubtedly led to fiscal constraints and reduced availability of resources in all sectors of the economy such that inefficiency becomes more noticeable and less acceptable.

For organisations not in financial services, it is the need for more efficient and effective corporate governance and management of risks that appears to be the motivation for a more coordinated and joined up approach to satisfying the assurance needs of the board and its sub-committees. Recognising that overlaps and duplication are unsustainable, a number of organisations including professional bodies have started to explore and define what *integrated assurance* may mean from their respective positions.

In defining *integrated assurance* in Chapter 10 of this book we will seek to address the challenges facing the boards in gaining holistic assurance, taking into consideration their *wish list*.

Key Points from this Chapter

1.   Increased scrutiny of the quality of judgment at board and management levels requires organisations to adopt a more efficient and conscious approach to seeking and providing assurance.

2.   Joined up and coordinated assurance across functional boundaries is necessary to minimise gaps and overlaps in providing a holistic view of risk taking and effectiveness of the organisation's systems of control.

3.   Silo management and narrow focus of assurance over risk management leads to gaps in governance, and increases duplication and cost of compliance.

4.   Shared and collective knowledge drives better value from the governance process by focusing on what matters to the sound running and viability of the business.

5.   The need for a holistic risk and assurance picture lays the path for developing integrated assurance.

Endnotes

[1]   Financial Reporting Council (FRC), *Guidance on Audit Committees* (London, FRC, September 2012), 4.9, Internal controls and risk management.

[2]   Ibid., 4.12, The internal audit process.

[3]   Ibid., 4.13, The internal audit process.

[4]   Financial Reporting Council (FRC), *Internal Control: Revised Guidance for Directors on the Combined Code 2005*, commonly known as 'Turnbull Guidance', which at November 2013, was under review by the FRC (London, FRC, 2005).

5   Financial Reporting Council (FRC), *Consultation Paper: Risk Management, Internal Control and the Going Concern Basis of Accounting, Consultation on Draft Guidance to the Directors of companies applying the UK Corporate Governance Code and Associated Changes to the Code* (London, FRC, 2013).

6   National Audit Office (NAO), *Financial Management and Governance Practice – The Statement on Internal Control: A Guide for Audit Committee* (London, NAO, January 2010).

7   Financial Reporting Council, *Internal Control: Revised Guidance for Directors on the Combined Code 2005* (London, FRC, 2005), 15, Section Two on responsibilities of the board.

8   King Committee on Corporate Governance and Institute of Directors in Southern Africa (IoDSA), *King Code and Report on Governance for South Africa* ('King III') (Johannesburg, *IoDSA*, 2009), Principle 3.5.

9   Eversheds LLP, *The Eversheds Board Report: Measuring the impact of board composition on company performance* (London, Eversheds LLP, May 2011), 29, 59.

10 Massachusetts Institute of Technology, 'Collective Brainpower. Using new technologies to amplify human intelligence' (Boston, MA, *MIT Spectrum*, Summer 2010). Article retrieved 25 May 2011, http://scripts.mit.edu/~cci/HCI/index.php?title=Main_Page. See also definition in the Handbook of Collective Intelligence, MIT Centre for Collective Intelligence.

11 Chartered Institute of Internal Auditors – UK & Ireland, *Professional guidance for internal auditors: Coordination of assurance services* (London, IIA-UK & Ireland, 2010).

Chapter 8

Assurance in a Three Lines of Defence Model

In the last chapter we highlighted the increasing number of assurance providers in an organisation. As organisations seek to coordinate and gain a holistic view of their risk management and assurance activities, a method for recognising the sources of assurance – generally referred to as the *three lines of defence* model – began to emerge through common practice over recent years. It is, however, also a term that has been open to interpretation. Unsurprisingly, I am often asked by individuals at the board level what the three lines of defence *actually mean*. Given its relevance to the development of an integrated framework for assurance, I thought it helpful to dedicate this chapter to discussing the principles of the three lines of defence model and to provide practical guidelines for its use.

Key Principles of the Three Lines of Defence Model

The concept of the three lines of defence probably emerged to help organisations distinguish the main layers of control for managing risks in the business. In simple terms, the first line of defence refers to front line management who are directly accountable for a risk or business process. The second, and third, lines of defence refer to activities by resources which are not owners of the risk under consideration but which provide an additional safety net to the first line of defence, such as a monitoring or advisory activity. Activities from the third line of defence are those that are most independent from the risk or business process.

Essentially, there are two basic principles for allocating a control process or risk mitigation activity to any particular line of defence. These are:

- The purpose or nature of the responsibilities, for example, whether the activity is a front line operation for the direct delivery of goods and services to the customer or a monitoring role that is removed from the front line.

- The degree of independence of the person carrying out the activity from the ownership and accountability of the risks associated with the process under consideration.

In other words, the more independent a function or an activity is from owning or operating the process in question, the more likely it is acting as second or third line of defence. Conversely, the closer a function or an activity is to being accountable for operating a particular process in question, the more likely it is acting as the first line of defence. The first, second and third lines of defence refer effectively to the layers of protection from harm an organisation has.

The depth of defence required depends on the significance of the risks. This simple principle underpins an organisation's risk based approach to designing control processes and risk mitigation plans, and to providing assurance. Precise allocation of a control to a line of defence is less important than its significance in managing the risk effectively. The three lines of defence model is not quite the military phalanx formation used by Alexander the Great and his father Philip II of Macedon, but its objectives are arguably similar. With a record of undefeated battles, perhaps there are lessons to learn from Alexander the Great and his Macedonian phalanx formation!

Returning to present times, as a term, the three lines of defence model is used most often to explain the independent role of internal audit and where it fits in the organisation's governance framework. It is not surprising that the profession has taken opportunities as they have arisen to define the model and to raise the awareness of the role of internal audit. In late 2010, the European Confederation of Institutes of Internal Auditing (ECIIA) in conjunction with the Federation of European Risk Management Associations (FERMA) published joint Guidance for boards and audit committees on the implementation of Article 41 of the 8th European Company Law Directive. Article 41 refers to the requirement of the board 'to monitor the effectiveness of risk management and control systems within a firm…' and in particular section 2.b of the Article refers to the requirement of the audit committee to '… monitor the effectiveness of the company's internal control, internal audit where applicable, and risk management systems …'.[1]

In the joint Guidance, FERMA and ECIIA set out the respective roles and responsibilities of the board, executive and senior management, operational management and where the risk and internal audit functions would fit in the three lines of defence model. In a nutshell, the Guidance indicates that the responsibilities of operational management fall under the first line of defence while the risk and internal audit functions fall under the second and third lines of defence respectively. In December 2012 the ECIIA went on to issue a complementary report in collaboration with the European Confederation of Director's Association entitled – *Making the most of the internal audit function,*[2] which provides guidance to boards and governing bodies with particular reference to assurance in respect of the organisation's risk management and systems of internal control.

The definition of three lines of defence in the aforementioned publications has been adapted by the UK Chartered Institute of Internal Auditors (IIA) and Institute of Directors in a paper entitled *What every director should know about internal audit,* issued jointly in Spring 2013. In this paper, the three lines of defence model, which emphasises the role of internal audit in the third line of defence is described as follows:

Under the first line of defence, operational management has ownership, responsibility and accountability for directly assessing, controlling and mitigating risks.

The second line of defence consists of activities covered by several components of internal governance (compliance, risk management, quality IT and other control departments). This line of defence monitors and facilitates the implementation of effective risk management practices by operational management and assists the risk owners in reporting adequate risk-related information up and down the organisation.

Internal audit forms the organisation's third line of defence. An independent internal audit function will, through a risk-based approach to its work, provide assurance to the organisation's board of directors and senior management. This assurance will cover how effectively the organisation assesses and manages its risks and will include assurance on the effectiveness of the first and second lines of defence. It encompasses all elements of an institution's risk management framework (from risk identification, risk assessment and response, to communication of risk-related information) and all categories of organisational objectives: strategic, operational, reporting and compliance.[3]

Clearly, the definition provided by the IIA above is designed to communicate the role of internal audit in the third line of defence. When used more broadly, as seen in organisations' annual statements and governance reports, the term three lines of defence is particularly helpful in conveying an organisation's approach to organising its system of risk management and internal control. It instils a degree of confidence that there is depth in the organisation's defence system against risks to its business.

With the proliferation of monitoring and assurance activities across the organisation, as discussed in the last chapter, the definition of the three lines of defence would benefit from further guidance to help organisations determine whether or not there is sufficient level of objective and independent assurance being provided. This assessment is particularly pertinent for organisations which do not have an internal audit function and are required to assess the adequacy of their assurance arrangements across the three lines of defence. In the next section, we expand on the definition of the three lines of defence model by considering a wider range of assurance activities beyond the risk or internal audit functions.

Interpreting the Three Lines of Defence Model

Building on the definition provided in the joint paper from the UK Chartered Institute of Internal Auditors and Institute of Directors, we flesh out the definition of the three lines of defence (LoD) model to include the principal responsibilities and functions typically found in organisations within each line of defence. The detail is provided diagrammatically in Table 8.1.

Table 8.1   Three Lines of Defence model (LoD) in an Integrated Assurance Framework

---

The Board and its Sub-Committees

Sets standards of conduct and overall risk appetite in line with the organisation's strategic goals.

Oversees the effectiveness of the executive's risk management and control through appropriate integrated assurance reporting across all LoD.

Executive governing body

Ensure appropriate risk and control strategies are implemented in 1st LoD and front line activities.

Ensure 2nd and 3rd LoD are joined-up and effective in supporting the organisation's strategy and risk governance.

Retains overall accountability for decisions in taking and accepting risks and related strategies.

1st **Line of Defence**	2nd **Line of Defence**	3rd **Line of Defence**
All front-line and operational management and their system of controls in entirety that comprise of policies, strategies, systems, and processes for day to day running of the business that include managing risks in their areas of responsibilities. Retains responsibility for compliance and decisions in the course of managing risks and considering advice and recommendations from other LoD or external sources.	Functions, subject area experts and systematic activities primarily to provide advice and support risk management and control. To provide a 2nd pair of eyes over the effectiveness of controls and mitigation established particularly by management in 1st LoD. Retains responsibility for the advice they give and effectiveness of their monitoring policies and frameworks.	All forms of independent assurance activity of the effectiveness of the whole or specific system of risk and control management within or across all LoD. The scope of the activity is usually determined by the board and/or management as guided by statutory, regulatory or professional guidance. Retains responsibility for the methodologies deployed, their execution and management reports.
Typical 1st LoD functions include: customer services, sales and distributions, premises and facilities, technology, media and communication, aspects of human resources, finance and asset management and investment functions.	Typical 2nd LoD functions and activities include risk, legal, QA, compliance, information security, parts of finance, accreditation and performance monitoring or reporting activities including programme and change offices.	Typical 3rd LoD functions include internal audit as well as external sources of independent audits and reviews engaged as part of a management need or system of control and risk management.

The definition follows the two main principles identified earlier in relation to the nature of the responsibility and degree of independence from the ownership of the risk or business process. While it is important to understand how each type of activity fits in the three LoD model, its real importance lies in its context and how it coexists with the other lines of defence for the purpose of managing a particular risk. We illustrate this point by considering the example of the risk of making invalid or incorrect payments to suppliers and other creditors:

- A control activity that takes place in the first LoD is the authorisation of the payment (in accordance with an authorisation policy) and input checks into the supplier payments system which triggers the payments. The controls in the first LoD help to protect against the risks of errors in individual transactions.

- At the aggregate level, the control in the form of bank reconciliations of the payments is conducted to help confirm that all individual transactions from the bank account are valid and accounted for. The bank reconciliation control, assuming that it follows good principles of 'segregation of duties' means that the activity does not also reside in the first LoD with access to the payments system. The bank reconciliation control provides a second LoD by helping to pick up on any erroneous transactions from the first LoD.

- An additional activity carried out by people independent of the first and second LoD, for example, to verify the sound working of these controls by the first and second LoD, would be deemed third LoD.

To provide further guidance on interpreting the three LoD model, it is useful to consider the typical challenges or known common debates relating to the model. This is covered in the next section.

Common Debates in Applying the Three Lines of Defence Model

In this section, we consider three common questions or areas of debates in the three LoD model.

WHAT HAPPENS WHEN THE FIRST LOD BEHAVES LIKE SECOND LOD OR THIRD LOD?

We have all come across functions which reside in the first LoD carrying out monitoring activities, self checks or self audits that resemble activities normally carried out by a second LoD function, and sometimes even regarded as an independent activity under the third LoD. By and large, in these situations where these self checks or audit activities are integral to the first LoD management process and have been carried out by staff accountable to the first LoD management then these activities should be considered part of the first LoD system of internal control. On the other hand, audits or reviews by external and more independent sources, which have been commissioned by management in the first or second LoD, would count as third LoD activities. The degree of independence from the first LoD management is the determining factor in these scenarios.

Another scenario that may arise is when functions appear to be carrying out both first and second LoD activities, for example, an accounts function that has operational responsibilities for procurement (first LoD) as well as preparing the statement of accounts (second LoD) for the organisation. Another example in this scenario is where the personnel function has line responsibility for car fleet management (first LoD) as well as monitoring and reporting (second LoD) on employee turnover and other personnel related performance management trends.

The third example that is worth mentioning refers to the risk function which is generally assumed to fall under the second LoD. This depends however on the nature of the risk function's activities and responsibilities. While most risk functions carry out predominantly a support and monitoring role within the organisation, there are many that have also been assigned operational line responsibilities (first LoD) such as implementation of the organisation's credit risk and liquidity risk policies on a day to day basis. Referring again to the two principles of the three LoD model, it is the nature or purpose of the activity rather than the department or functional structure which determines the line of defence in which it sits.

Clearly, organisations do not structure themselves around the three LoD model but in a manner that they believe would enable them to run their businesses efficiently and effectively. When determining which LoD an activity lies in, it is best to consider the two principles mentioned earlier – the nature of the activity and the independence of those carrying out the activity from the owners of the risk or the process. This means that one particular function or department can contribute to more than one line of defence arising from different control activities.

IN WHICH LOD DO THE BOARD AND THE EXECUTIVE COMMITTEE RESIDE?

The next common area of discussion relates to where management committees, executive boards and company boards and their sub-committee should reside in the three LoD model. Given its accountability for governance, system of risk management and control, the board of an organisation is required to reside across all lines of defence. Taking the standpoint of the shareholder as external stakeholder, some argue that the board should assume the first line of defence while others might regard that the board, as stewards of the organisation, is the only line of defence. This debate illustrates the limitations as well as the intended use of the three LoD model. We would suggest that the three LoD model be applied from an internal perspective for supporting the effective discharge of the board's responsibilities to its external stakeholders in the assurance food chain.

From an internal perspective, we can consider the question in two ways: one, in respect of the personal responsibilities of an executive, and, two, in respect of the collective responsibilities of the executive committee. An executive would reside in the relevant LoD depending on the nature of his or her responsibilities; for example, the sales director who is responsible for managing the sales channels will reside in the first LoD in respect of those responsibilities. At the committee level, we show in Table 8.1 that the responsibilities of the executive committees and company boards straddle across all LoD. The rationale for this lies in the nature of the governance responsibilities of these committees across the organisation.

Some may only recognise the role the executive committee play in the first and second LoD, arguing that its activities would not count as sufficiently independent. Some would place the board in the third LoD because of its oversight role at the top of the internal assurance food chain, although the board's accountability for setting risk appetite and strategy would suggest that it sometimes operate in the first line of defence and would therefore operate in all three LoD.

These arguments, however, disregard the role of the board as well as the executive management in the third LoD when challenging or overseeing the effectiveness of the efforts of the first and second LoD for managing the risks facing the organisation. In brief, the executive committee and board carry out responsibilities that could be recognised as being first, second or third LoD. When mapping assurance across the lines of defence, it is helpful to be clear about the risk or activity in question and its ownership.

This principle also applies to determining whether some committees, project boards and other working parties at the operational level of the organisation's governance structure fall within the first or second LoD. The terms of reference of these groups, responsibilities, nature of their activities and also sources of the information they receive should help determine whether or not they are carrying out front line business management (first LoD) or predominantly oversight and monitoring of risks and controls (second and possibly third LoD).

The membership of the groups is also another indicator of the line of defence in which they operate. For example, a project committee established by the sales management team in the first LoD to implement a new sales system would be regarded to be an integral part of that management team's process in the first LoD. On the other hand, a project board that consists of a wide representation of the organisation to oversee the delivery of a major project or projects and which forms part of the organisation's governance at the executive or board level would be regarded to operate at least in the second LoD.

DO EXTERNAL AUDITORS RESIDE IN THE THIRD LOD?

The final question to cover in this chapter refers to the assurance activities of the external auditors of the company financial statements and other third parties of assurance providers. The common debate is whether or not these activities fall within the third LoD or even a fourth LoD. In fact, some discussions have even suggested that the supervisory reviews of the regulators could be assigned the fourth LoD.

On the basis that regulator activity is not optional, voluntary or an integral part of the organisation's risk and control framework, it would be inappropriate for it to be recognised as a form of armoury in the organisation arsenal of defence. While the outcome of regulatory activity is an authoritative source of feedback on the organisation's risk and control capability, it is unlikely that any organisation would rely on a regulatory review to help it complete its assurance requirement. In respect of the external auditors and other independent third party assurance providers, they should be recognised appropriately as activities in the third LoD as shown in Table 8.1. The introduction of a fourth LoD is probably an unnecessary complication.

In brief, in addition to internal audit – on the assumption that it is independent and operating according to the Institute of Internal Auditors *International Professional Practices Framework*,[4] we would classify any audits and reviews carried out by persons or parties who are independent of those responsible for the risks or processes in the first or second LoD to be a third LoD activity. Examples include independent reviews commissioned by management in the other lines of defence and sometimes in conjunction with internal audit where specialist and technical expertise is required such as information security audits on complex and global platforms, major change management reviews and highly technical stochastic risk and capital modelling.

To Conclude this Chapter ...

The three LoD model helps us to understand the different layers of control in our organisations. It helps us to identify control activities for managing a risk from an end to end perspective. It is the nature of the control activity and the independence of the person(s) from the risks under consideration that determines the LoD a control activity would be allocated. In this respect, the three LoD model can be fluid and it is more important to understand the significance of the control activity than its precise allocation to a line of defence. The three LoD model is particularly useful in providing a basis for challenging the significance of each assurance activity for the purpose of managing risks effectively in the organisation. For these reasons the model lends itself well to be used in the integrated assurance framework.

Key Points from this Chapter

1.　With the proliferation of assurance activities in organisations, the three lines of defence model is increasingly used to help organisations describe their systems of internal control and accountability for managing its risks to the organisation.

2.　The three lines of defence model helps the organisation to peer through the layers of risk management and control processes in order to determine their respective relevance and importance in managing risks to the organisation.

3.   The allocation of a risk mitigation, control process or assurance activity in the first, second or third line of defence is determined by reference to two main principles – the nature or purpose of the activity and independence of the resources carrying out that activity from the ownership of the risk.

4.   Precise allocation of a control and assurance activity to a line of defence is less important than understanding the significance of its role in mitigating the risk in question.

5.   Ability to identify risks and map related assurance activities across the three lines of defence is central to developing an integrated approach to assurance.

Endnotes

[1]   Federation of European Risk Management Associations (FERMA) / European Confederation of Institutes of Internal Auditing (ECIIA) *Guidance on the 8th EU Company Law Directive, Article 41 – Guidance for boards and audit committees* (Brussels, FERMA/ECIIA, September 2010), 6.

[2]   European Confederation of Institutes of Internal Auditing (ECIIA) / European Confederation of Directors' Association (ecoDa), *Making the Most of the Internal Audit Function: Recommendations for Directors and Board Committees* (Brussels, ECIIA/ecoDa, January 2013).

[3]   Chartered Institute of Internal Auditors (IIA-UK and Ireland) / Institute of Directors (IoD), *What every Director should know about Internal Audit – Essential Information for Boards and Audit Committees* (London, IIA-UK and Ireland, April 2013).

[4]   Institute of Internal Auditors (IIA), *International Professional Practices Framework* (IPPF) (Orlando, FL, IIA, 2009). The IPPF consists of authoritative guidance developed by the IIA international technical committees that include mandatory and highly recommended practices that refer to the IIA's Code of Ethics and the International Standards for the Professional Practice of Internal Auditing ('The Standards').

Chapter 9

The Current Faces of Integrated Assurance

In this chapter we pick up the discussion from Chapter 7 in search for a more holistic risk picture with the proliferation of risk management and risk assurance activities in response to increasing regulatory and governance requirements. We will explore the current approaches that embody the characteristics of integrated assurance for supporting a coordinated view of risks and assurance. The aim is to inform the development of a framework for integrated assurance, which we will consider in the next chapter.

Different Interpretations of Integrated Assurance

There is, as yet, no universally agreed definition for the term *integrated assurance* either as a concept, process or methodology. The term is used to serve different and specific needs for integrating assurance and risk management. It can be applied in varying scope, depth and purpose. Two other terms with similar integration aims which we should mention are *integrated governance, risk and compliance* (GRC) and 'The Enterprise Risk Management (ERM) – Integrated Framework'[1] as defined by the Committee of Sponsoring Organisations of the Threadway Commission (COSO).

GRC is a term sometimes used to highlight the link and coordination required between the respective assurance providers in governance, risk, compliance and internal audit with regulatory compliance as the common driver. GRC is not a proprietary term but a generic acronym which started to emerge around the mid 2000s, introduced by technological solution providers as the regulatory burden in financial services intensified. A GRC programme seeks to align risk and compliance processes at every level in the organisation. An integrated approach to risk management that is supported by technology seems sensible for organisations to help them demonstrate their compliance with regulatory requirements.

The COSO Enterprise Risk Management (ERM) – Integrated Framework, on the other hand started from an internal control[2] perspective which was broadened to encompass the principles of risk management across every entity of the organisation on the premise that every entity has the potential to add value to the organisation's stakeholders. Both *GRC* and COSO ERM are good labels for their respective purposes, each of which is clearly relevant to supporting the aims of *integrated assurance*.

Other terms which we may have come across include *total assurance, coordinated assurance* and *combined assurance,* all of which have been used interchangeably and in similar context to *integrated assurance.* The term *combined assurance* is most associated with the *King Code and Report for Governance in South Africa* (King III Code) where it is defined as 'integrating and aligning assurance processes in a company to maximise risk and governance oversight and control efficiencies, and optimise overall assurance to the audit and risk committee, considering the company's risk appetite'.[3] King III Code emphasises the coordination of all assurance activities, in particular those of the external and internal assurance providers. While King III Code's definition of combined assurance places emphasis on supporting the oversight duties of the audit and risk committee, the definition is closest to what we are looking for in respect of a holistic and aggregate view of an organisation's risks and its control environment. Professor Mervyn King, the inspiration behind the King III Code, cites other benefits of coordinated assurance which include preventing the overload of assurance or assessment fatigue in the boardroom.[4]

Considering the roots of these labels and the drivers behind their creation, we will explore the different ways in which the concept of *integrated* assurance is being used under the following three categories:

- *Integrating assurance for a particular portfolio of risk*

Integrated assurance in this context is focused on a particular type or portfolio of risks such as regulatory risks, major project risks and change management risks.

- *Integrated assurance for risks across the enterprise*

Integrated assurance in this context is concerned about the view of assurance for all risks, which we shall presume to be principal risks, across the whole organisation.

- *Integrated assurance from the perspective of an assurance provider*

Integrated assurance in this context is focused on the roles and standards for working together with other assurance providers.

Integrated Assurance for a Particular Portfolio of Risk

In January 2011, UK Prime Minister David Cameron stated in a letter supporting the mandate of the Major Projects Authority (MPA) his concerns that there was no 'cross-governmental understanding of the size and cost of the Government's Major Projects portfolio, nor of the cost and viability of the individual projects within it...'.[5] To protect against further common failings in projects and to promote greater efficiency in public spending, the Cabinet Office MPA was established in April 2011. Its mandate included setting and adopting an integrated assurance and approvals framework which involves building on and developing the relationships between the MPA, internal audit and other assurance providers in the management of major projects and change programmes.

The integrated assurance and approvals approach at the MPA does not mean joint reviews but sharing of information between internal and external providers of assurance to ensure proper coverage and to minimise duplication of efforts. The other key aspects of the framework include:

- An Assurance Strategy at a Portfolio level,

- All programmes and projects being required to have an Integrated Assurance and Approvals Plan,

- Assurance activity that is a risk-based and end-to-end process, from change concept (policy development) through to benefit delivery.

- Project assurance activities that are linked to financial approval and key milestones.

- Assurance providers, including internal audit, being required to continually coordinate their work to avoid duplication or omission.

- Results of assurance reviews that are shared and escalated appropriately to enable intervention action to be taken where projects are failing.

It is too early for the framework to have been fully tested but the rationale for an integrated approach at the Cabinet Office MPA is clear and pragmatic. Central Government's major projects are inherently high risk due to their scale, innovation, cost and their reliance on a diverse set of stakeholders working together.

According to the National Audit Office in an earlier report, managing assurance effectively is essential for 'reducing the financial risk to the public purse and increasing the chance of achieving value for money for the taxpayer'. The report recognises that assurance in itself does not deliver a project but provides necessary information on the potential risks to its successful delivery. As a result, assurance helps '... those that sponsor, govern and manage ... [projects to] ... make better informed decisions which reduce the causes of project failure, promote the conditions for success and increase the chance of delivering the required outcome cost-effectively'.[6]

Integrated assurance for the management of projects and change programmes has probably been in place for most organisations, through established project governance processes that include change policies and project management boards. The coordination of delivery across subcontractors at a consistent professional level is clearly critical for the success of major and strategic projects although the term *integrated assurance* is not always used.

For example, when the British Airports Authority (BAA) was appointed to build the new Terminal 5 at London Heathrow, it too adopted a unified approach across a complex network of suppliers and business partners to deliver an integrated and assured system to all its stakeholders involved in the strategic programme that spanned over 20 years from planning to its delivery in 2008. The integrated system of assurance covered people, process and product assurance. This involved continuously updating of plans to reflect the progress and status of all the projects in the programme and the issue of system assurance certificates following the testing and commissioning of the projects.

At a cost of £4.3 billion and an urgent need to address an accelerating capacity risk at London Heathrow, the risk of failure according Sir John Egan, CEO at BAA between 1991 and 1999, would have been 'an alarming prospect for any PLC board.'[7] Assurance from across all teams against such a risk seems highly sensible. The integrated teams, says T5 and Heathrow HR and Change Director Doherty, is one of three key ingredients that ensured the success of the project; the other two ingredients are 'an intelligent client and courageous and determined leaders'.

Another example is the NASA Kennedy Space Centre's (KSC) Integrated Design and Assurance System (IDAS) whose aims include identifying *best-in-practice* tools and harnessing collective knowledge. By sharing information on 'finding, developing, learning, debugging, and verifying the method to do each analysis…' time is not wasted, allowing 'the design, sustaining, and assurance engineers to "work smarter instead of harder"…'. While there are challenges in its implementation, the vision of the IDAS is to be:

> *For all NASA Centers and Programs, an integrated and comprehensive system that enables design, sustaining, safety, reliability, maintainability, quality, logistics, cost, human factors, and risk engineers to collaboratively design and model systems, track changes, and provide performance feedback over the systems' entire life cycle.*[8]

The integrated aspect in the IDAS approach relates to a coordinated strategy for ensuring there is confidence in managing across all work goals, problem solving, innovation, training and development. Assurance is integrated in the project life cycle in the IDAS approach.

Integrated assurance at a specific risk or portfolio level is also evident in the coordination of quality assurance (QA) activities, for example in compliance with health and safety standards across all sites within an organisation. A comprehensive example can be found in the approach by the U.S. Department of Energy's (DOE) Office of Science at the Fermi National Accelerator Laboratory (Fermilab) located in Illinois which undertakes scientific research 'at the frontiers of high energy physics and related disciplines'. The scope, infrastructure and multi disciplinary nature of such research necessitates a 'single, integrated, effective quality assurance program'. Fermilab implemented its Integrated Quality Assurance (IQA) program in 2010:

> *to limit duplication of effort and ensure both integration and consistent application throughout the laboratory, a single lab-wide implementing procedure (e.g. corrective and preventive actions, graded approach) is used whenever that procedure can be extended beyond individual divisions/sections/centers without detriment to its intention, compliance, or effectiveness.*[9]

The principle that underpins Fermilab's IQA program is the maintenance and compliance with standards across all levels of work including those provided by subcontractors. At the highest level, the IQA enabled Fermilab to demonstrate that it is meeting the requirements of the DOE – a key stakeholder in the *assurance food chain*. At the operational level, the IQA is implemented through a graded approach to the application of preventative and corrective actions and controls that are based on an analysis of risks in the respective area under consideration.

The benefits of integrated assurance and reporting at a specific risk or portfolio level can also help drive value not previously identified. We consider the case of Novo Nordisk, a global healthcare company headquartered in Denmark with over 36,000 employees in 75 countries, which manufactures and markets to about 180 countries. Novo Nordisk had been publishing its environmental reports since 1994 which was further extended to cover social issues in 1998. Recognising its business philosophy as one that strives to make balanced decisions across three primary considerations – financial, social and environmental – which Novo Nordisk refers to as its *Triple Bottom Line*[10] principle, an integrated assurance approach was established to support a more integrated report particularly to its external stakeholders.

With growth, innovation and ambitions to be a leader in its field, the company felt that such integrated assurance that could be viewed by external third parties was necessary to help the organisation demonstrate its accountability in a transparent manner. Additionally, the process of achieving integrated assurance that was aligned to its philosophy and business objectives enabled Novo Nordisk to increase internal accountability for performance.

The notion that the responsibility for sustainability is not limited by function but one which must be owned by everyone in the organisation is noted by COSO in its thought leadership and research paper 'Demystifying sustainability risk'.[11] It is also not a coincidence that the paper recognises the significance of the triple bottom line as a holistic approach to managing sustainability risks of an organisation. Appropriately, the paper advocates the integration of the concept of the triple bottom line which covers social, environmental and economic performance in an organisation's enterprise risk management programme.

Integrated Assurance for Risks across the Enterprise

To illustrate the second type of approach to integrated assurance, we consider the UK National Health Service (NHS) *Integrated Governance* model and *Assurance Framework* for executives and non-executives in the NHS. The aim of the model is to provide a 'journey towards optimal governance' by moving governance out of silos towards a more holistic approach in the face of an increasing governance agenda. The governance agenda of each healthcare organisation in the NHS is wide and includes clinical, research, infection prevention, people, information, risk and financial as well as corporate governance. Implementing the Integrated Governance model in healthcare organisations (Trusts) within the NHS involves the development of:

> *Systems, processes and behaviours by which trusts lead, direct and control their functions in order to achieve organisational objectives, safety and quality of services and in which they relate to the wider community and partner organisations.*[12]

Central to supporting the Integrated Governance environment is an Assurance Framework as defined in an earlier report by the Department of Health in 2003 entitled 'Building the Assurance Framework – A Practical Guide for NHS Boards'. The Assurance Framework refers to 'a simple but comprehensive method for the effective and focused management of the principal risks to meeting their objectives. It also provides a structure for the evidence to support the Statement on Internal Control',[13] which the chief executive officer of a NHS trust is required to certify as part of the statutory accounts and annual report.

The Statement on Internal Control is expected to cover the totality of risks, both clinical and nonclinical. In this regard, by comparison with the requirement of Sections 404 and 302 of the Sarbanes-Oxley Act (2003) whose focus is on the controls relating to financial reporting, the NHS's model is potentially more onerous. To deliver such a Statement on Internal Control, the board of each NHS trust is required to demonstrate that they have been informed of the totality of the risks.

The Assurance Framework is expected to help boards achieve this requirement by providing the evidence required through a systematic process that brings together otherwise fragmented risk management activities, performance management arrangements and clinical governance reporting and other sources of assurances. The Assurance Framework involves the following key processes:

- Identification of the board's *principal objectives* and related *principal risks*; this helps to set the expectations of assurance required

- Identification of the controls for managing those principal risks and mapping them against valid sources of assurance providers.

- Review of assurance reports against principal risks.

- Review of the Assurance Framework document which summarises the nature of the assurances being provided against the board's principal objectives and risks including gaps, for the purpose of supporting the board's Statement on Internal Control.

- Remedial action as required.

Like the other models we have outlined earlier, the coordinating principle is central to the NHS Integrated Governance model and Assurance Framework. The holistic approach for integrating assurance across all portfolios of risks is one which this book advocates, and which is the basis used for defining the framework for *integrated assurance* in the next chapter.

Integrated Assurance from the Perspective of an Assurance Provider

To illustrate the third approach, we refer to a key assurance provider in the *assurance food chain* – the internal audit function. The Institute of Internal Auditors global Standard 2050 on coordination states that 'The chief audit executive [CAE] should share information and coordinate activities with other internal and external providers of assurance and consulting services to ensure proper coverage and minimise duplication of efforts'. This Standard, according to the Practice Guide issued by the global Institute of Internal Auditors in March 2012, explains that this coordination responsibility:

> requires the CAE's inclusion and participation in the organisation's assurance provider framework. This framework can consist of internal audit, external audit, governance, risk management, or other business control functions/disclosures performed by the organisation's management team. Inclusion and participation in this framework helps

ensure that the CAE is aware of the organisation's risks and controls in relation to organisational goals and objectives.[14]

The Practice Guide reinforces the importance of risk management and assurance in the corporate governance arrangements by setting out the expected practices and standards for working with other assurance providers for supporting the goals of the organisation. The Practice Guide expands on an earlier professional guidance issued by the Chartered Institute of Internal Auditors – UK and Ireland (IIA) in 2010 following a survey of practices amongst its member organisations on the 'Coordination of assurance services'.

The professional guidance recognises the growth of the number of assurance providers within organisations and the need for more effective assurance of risk management across a diverse set of stakeholders. In its survey, the IIA listed no less than 17 assurance providers in organisations of which the top 10 were:

- Internal audit (90 per cent)

- Management – self-assessments (71 per cent)

- External audit (63 per cent)

- Management – Key Performance Indicators and performance reports (60 per cent)

- Risk management function (55 per cent)

- Health and safety auditors (45 per cent)

- Compliance functions (37 per cent)

- Quality auditors (36 per cent)

- Regulatory bodies (29 per cent)

- Information security auditors (26 per cent)

- External inspection agencies (19 per cent)

From the list, it is easy to understand why some boards may feel overwhelmed by its oversight needs. Recognising the merit of each assurance that an organisation may require, the IIA suggests grouping these sources within a single model to 'provide the basis for a better understanding and organisation of assurance, while creating a platform for coordination'.

The IIA survey however found that only 8 per cent of respondents stated that their organisations have a combined assurance plan that is agreed by the board and which showed all assurance providers; most organisations appear to be limiting the coordination of assurance to the board agreeing the internal and external audit plans while 22 per cent of audit committees would also agree the work of other assurance providers.

The IIA professional guidance states that coordination can refer to the internal audit function working jointly with another assurance provider while preserving its right to carry out its own assurance activity 'freely and independently in order to meet its obligations'.[15] The guidance includes three examples to illustrate the main methods for coordinating with other assurance providers:

- Example 1: Internal audit relies (where it is appropriate to do so in accordance with the IIA standards) on the compliance function to perform clinical audits within a National Health Service environment and conducts a review of the compliance function and it operational frameworks periodically.

- Example 2: Internal audit works jointly with another assurance provider (such as Health and Safety) in the organisation with mutual benefits in sharing approaches and experience.

- Example 3: Internal audit leverages the assurance work carried out by management, for example, through management self assessments, and other assurance providers to reduce the scope of its own assurance activity in respect of those areas.

The professional guidance has clearly been developed for internal audit functions as they define their place in the *assurance food chain* and the role they play in enhancing risk governance as efficiently as possible. The guidance goes some way in recognising the holistic approach required to coordinate assurance across all lines of defence as covered in the last chapter. The guidance from the IIA however stops short of providing a definition for *integrated assurance* within the organisation. It provides, instead, a stance for the role of internal auditors for working with other assurance providers. The guidance on the coordination of assurance from the global and UK based Institute of Internal Auditors reflects the nature of the internal audit profession and its work with all sources of assurance providers. Such a need seems less for other professions which is evident in the limited guidance available in respect of coordination.

To Conclude this Chapter ...

A universal common framework for integrated assurance may not yet be defined but the seeds for one can be found in the various assurance models discussed in this chapter. Each model may have presented itself differently based on the practical assurance needs of the organisation such as governance oversight of a major project risk or risks across the organisation. There is, however, commonality in the way coordination and collaboration of teams run through each model for the purpose of making informed decisions in risk management without wasting resources. In summary, the integrated approach to providing assurance has emerged from the practical needs of three main parties in the *assurance food chain*:

- those who are responsible for governing including directors, boards and their subcommittees;

- those who are accountable to the governing bodies for delivering the strategy and objectives of the organisation; and,

- those whose primary role is to provide assurance to those governing bodies.

Poor experiences arising from gaps and duplication that have resulted in increased effort and costs without necessarily increasing the effectiveness of risk oversight and governance have led to the need for more collective intelligence through coordination and integration. Indeed, the apparent high level of risk and control activity at times resulted in boards being potentially overladen with information such that gaps and real exposures to risks were obscured. To enable them to direct, with more confidence, governing bodies and boards alike needed to rethink the assurance they were getting in a more integrated way.

In defining a common framework for integrated assurance in Chapter 10, we have taken these drivers into account to ensure that the definition is universally applicable and adaptable to meet different levels of risk oversight required.

Key Points from this Chapter

1.   The combined effects of higher regulatory standards for risk management and the proliferation of assurance providers have led to the need for an integrated approach to providing assurance, particularly at the board level.

2.   A universal common framework for integrated assurance is not yet defined but practical models are being developed to meet specific needs within organisations.

3.   The principles of coordinating or integrating assurance can be found within different approaches, models and labels such as enterprise risk management, combined assurance and coordinated assurance.

4.   A common thread in current integrated approaches is the effective management of risk and its governance at the specific as well as the enterprise wide level.

5.   The development of current approaches for integrated assurance has emerged through practical reasoning for successful delivery of goals by effective coordination of risk governance and assurance.

Endnotes

[1]   Committee of Sponsoring Organizations of the Treadway Commission (COSO) *The Enterprise Risk Management – Integrated Framework* (New Jersey, American Institute of CPAs, 2004).

[2]   COSO, *Internal Control – Integrated Framework* (New Jersey, American Institute of CPAs, 1992 and updated in 2013).

[3]   Institute of Directors in Southern Africa (IoDSA) and the King Committee on Governance, *King Code and Report on Governance for South Africa* (Johannesburg, IoDSA, 2009), Glossary of Terms.

[4]   European Confederation of Institutes of Internal Auditing, 'Spotlight on global assurance' (Brussels, *European Internal Audit Briefing*, July 2009 Issue 15), 2.

[5] H.M. Treasury, *Major Project Authority – Integrated Assurance* (London, HM Treasury, 2012), Annex A.

[6] National Audit Office (NAO), *Assurance for High Risk Projects* (London, NAO, June 2010), Overview.

[7] Doherty, Sharon, 'Terminal 5 comes alive', *Director*, March 2008, accessed 16 July 2013, http://www.director.co.uk/MAGAZINE/2008/3%20March/terminal5_61_8.html

[8] NASA John F. Kennedy Space Center, 'IDAS Challenge, Vision, Mission and Goal', May 2007. Retrieved 10August 2013 http://kscsma.ksc.nasa.gov/Reliability/Documents/IDAS/7_IDAS_Challenge_Vision_Mission_and_Goal.pdf.

[9] Fermi National Accelerator Laboratory (Fermilab), *Integrated Quality Assurance*. Number 1001, Revision 001. (Batavia, IL, Office of Quality and Best Practices Fermi National Accelerator Laboratory), 2010, 8.

[10] Novo Nordisk, *Annual Report 2011*. Retrieved April 2013. http://annualreport2011.novonordisk.com/web-media/pdfs/Novo-Nordisk-AR-2011-en.pd, 11.

[11] Committee of Sponsoring Organizations of the Treadway Commission (COSO), *Demystifying sustainability risk – Integrating the triple bottom line into an enterprise risk management program*, a research commissioned and published by COSO (New Jersey, American Institute of CPAs, May 2013).

[12] UK Department of Health, *Integrated Governance Handbook – A handbook for executives and non-executives in healthcare organisations* (London, Department of Health, 2006), 10.

[13] UK Department of Health, *Building the Assurance Framework: A Practical Guide for NHS Boards* (London, Department of Health, 2003), 3.

[14] Institute of Internal Auditors (IIA), *Global Practice Guide: Coordinating Risk Management and Assurance* (Orlando, FL, IIA, March 2012), 1.

[15] Chartered Institute of Internal Auditors (IIA-UK and Ireland), *Professional Guidance for Internal Auditors: Coordination of assurance services* (London, IIA-UK and Ireland, July 2010), 8.

Chapter 10

Defining a Framework for Integrated Assurance

In the last chapter, we considered the different approaches to integrating assurance for facilitating more effective risk management as part of the governance process. A universal common framework for integrated assurance may not yet be defined but the principles of coordinating assurance across functional boundaries can be found within each of the different approaches and models in use. Taking into account the lessons from Part I and the strengths of current practice, we will proceed in this chapter to define a framework for integrated assurance.

What Good Looks Like from the Lens of the Board

In the last chapter, we showed how the need for joined up – *integrated* – assurance has largely emerged as organisations sought to enhance performance by improving risk oversight and governance. We considered the different approaches for promoting joined up assurance of risks at a specific and enterprise wide level. Without exception, each approach champions integrated team working in order to share knowledge and coordinate resources towards a common goal – embedded systems of risk management and control. Driven by the practical need to enhance performance and improve governance of risks, the concept of *integrated assurance* has emerged despite the absence of a common definition.

The same practical reasons led me to develop an *integrated assurance* framework some years ago, in my role of directing the three key assurance functions – risk management, compliance and internal audit – in the UK arm of a global financial services company. The role provided me with a vantage position to see the significance of a coordinated approach to managing risks and providing assurance over its effectiveness, that is *risk assurance*. Developing a framework that provides a joined up view of the risks and performance of the organisation's risk management systems seemed a natural step for enhancing the governance process in the organisation.

Rolling forward several years, the framework continues to be refined with practical use and new lessons arising from the events of the 2008 financial crisis. The key lesson gained from more recent events is the need for an integrated assurance framework to be wholly consistent with the aims of good risk governance. In other words, *integrated assurance* should focus with the lens of the board and its sub-committees, particularly the risk and audit committees.

So, what does *good* integrated assurance look like? Taking into account the wish list we have collected so far in the earlier chapters, let us check off those items which we believe boards do not want or need to experience in the boardroom:

- ☑ Blind risk taking.

- ☑ Risk taking exceeding the board's risk appetite and tolerances.

- ☑ Obscured view of evolving risks and their potential speed to crystallisation.

- ☑ Unnecessary distraction from things that really matter such as strategy.

- ☑ Different *truths* that serve to confuse rather than inform.

- ☑ Uncoordinated view of risk management and controls.

- ☑ Silo approach to risk assessment, mitigation, assurance and reporting.

- ☑ Duplication of effort and costs, assurance overload and fatigue.

- ☑ Inability to provide consistent reporting to external stakeholders.

With the addition of an overriding objective of promoting confidence in the board room, we set out a definition of a framework for integrated assurance below.

Defining the Integrated Assurance Framework

With the overall aim of supporting effective corporate governance in the boardroom and the organisation, a framework for integrated assurance could be described as follows:

> *Integrated assurance refers to a structured approach for gaining a holistic picture of the principal risks and the level of residual exposure an organisation is required to manage. It involves aligning and optimising the organisation's assurance over the management of those risks and the core business activities in line with the board's risk appetite and exists to support the board's risk oversight and risk taking. It promotes shared risk intelligence and accountability with a common goal to strengthen the organisation's risk management and oversight.*

As a process, integrated assurance involves an organisation-wide systematic assessment of the relevance as well as the strengths of assurance activities in relation to the organisation's principal risks and core business processes. The assessment focuses on obtaining a clear view of risks to the organisation for the purpose of satisfying the risk oversight and governance needs of the board, and for optimising the level of risk management and assurance activities across all lines of defence. The assessment is aligned with the organisation's risk appetite, policies and risk assessment approach, and is facilitated by an integrated risk assurance mapping process.

The assurance mapping process is a methodical approach for identifying and assessing the nature, validity and interconnectivity of the sources of assurance across all lines of defence for managing the principal risks and core business processes in the organisation. Risk assurance mapping promotes clarity throughout the assurance food chain of the organisation by identifying the needs of the stakeholders and the enhancements required for effective risk assurance.

The assurance map, as an output of the risk assurance mapping process, is not an end in itself but an aid for determining the optimal level of risk assurance activities required in each line of defence. The value of the assurance map is in the discussion it facilitates between stakeholders and assurance providers beyond the functional boundaries in which they operate, for example, at *risk surgeries* or *black swan*[1] meetings. An embedded integrated assurance process will not only promote greater collaboration between functional areas but gain collective intelligence for identifying risks as they evolve and emerge, and for determining any additional assurance required.

Integrated assurance can be applied at three main levels. At the fundamental level of implementation, integrated assurance enables the organisation, in particular the audit and risk committees, to direct and confirm the assurance activities required of the key assurance providers. At the highest level of implementation, integrated assurance enables the organisation to gain a holistic picture of the risks and the level of residual exposure it is required to manage in line with the board's risk appetite. As a result, the board is better supported in its risk and governance oversight for the purpose of directing and delivering the organisation's strategic goals and business plans. An assured board is also better equipped to assure its external stakeholders.

The degree of formal certification and attestations required of the key outputs of the integrated assurance process can vary according to the expectations of the board as well as the organisations' external stakeholders. The structured approach of an integrated assurance framework gives the board options for providing balanced and transparent reports to its external stakeholders while demonstrating, with confidence, appropriate discharge of its accountability. Furthermore, for organisations without an internal audit function, integrated assurance provides a structured approach for audit committees to assess the need for having an internal audit function.[2]

In brief, integrated assurance enables the board to translate its assurance requirements in respect of principal risks from an intuitive to a practical process, facilitating effective debate and discussion in the boardroom. As noted by Glen Moreno, an eminent non-executive director, who chairs one of UK's top 100 public listed companies and is deputy chairman of the UK Financial Reporting Council, 'Assurance is often intuitive among experienced non-executives, but boards require an effective process to maximise the benefits of their experience'.[3]

Applying Integrated Assurance at Three Levels

Integrated assurance can be applied at one of three main levels. We provide an outline of each level of application in this section followed by fuller explanation in Chapters 12–14. The case studies in Part IV of the book help to illustrate how integrated assurance is being applied to meet different assurance needs of organisations.

LEVEL 1 – RISK ASSURANCE PLANNING

Integrated assurance applied at Level 1 is focused on identifying coverage, that is, the availability and contribution of assurance over controls for managing particular risks across the three lines of defence. The main purpose of assurance mapping at this level is to assist the planning of assurance required particularly by the organisation's audit and risk committees. At its most basic level, integrated assurance at Level 1 provides a map of risk assurance that exists from each line of defence with no comment on the quality of that assurance.

Many internal audit functions today carry out a form of assurance mapping, either intuitively or formally as part of their audit planning cycle, with more functions starting to include principal risks in the scope of their mapping process. This is helping to address concerns that some internal audit planning was not sufficiently risk based. On the other hand, some internal audit plans that switched their focus wholly to the organisation's risk registers have omitted oversight of core business activities particularly where management had not identified any potential risks in those areas.

With rising standards of governance, audit committees are increasingly expecting to see more formal assessment of the basis of internal audit plans and how they are aligned to risks and the assurance provided by other parts of the organisation. For organisations where there are no internal audit functions, assurance mapping (even) at Level 1 offers the audit committees[4] with a structured and risk based approach for assessing the availability of assurance across the business and the need for an internal audit function.

LEVEL 2 – ENHANCING RISK ASSURANCE

Level 2 application of integrated assurance builds on the information gathered at Level 1 by assessing the quality of risk assurance from each line of defence. Quality in this context refers to the relevance, formality and integrity of the approach to providing assurance over the effectiveness of controls for managing a particular risk. By considering the quality, and not just its existence, integrated assurance at Level 2 enables the organisation to enhance and optimise risk oversight across the organisation. In other words, the use of Level 2 assurance mapping extends beyond supporting the internal audit plan. Optimising risk oversight and assurance at Level 2 can take place in three main scenarios:

1.   There is 'too much' assurance, which is usually another way of saying that there is duplication of effort and unnecessary overlaps and, more importantly, that the board and its audit and risk committees are not gaining any more insight into the risk or control environment of the organisation.

2.   The level of confidence in the board's risk oversight and assurance is low, which is usually attributable to the absence or insufficiency of the right kind of assurance rather than to simply 'too little' assurance.

3.   The organisation does not have an internal audit function and its audit committee is required to determine objectively if one is necessary. The insights gained from the qualitative analysis of risk assurance across all lines of defence lend themselves well to supporting the role of audit committees in this respect.

In the course of mapping and assessing risk assurance at Level 2, the organisation is able to gain clarity of ownership and accountability of the risks as well as the assurance that it requires. While we see long term benefits of embedding integrated assurance as part of an organisation's risk governance framework, Level 2 mapping of assurance can be applied initially as a one-off exercise – to jump-start management's improvement plan. Subsequent reviews should be less revolutionary and provide enhancements to the organisation's risk assurance arrangements on an incremental basis.

It is worth reiterating here that Level 2 is focused on assessing the quality of assurance provided and not the underlying effectiveness of risk management. The assessment of quality of assurance is distinct from reporting on the results of the assurance, that is, the residual risk and by implication the effectiveness of risk management. The latter is the focus at Level 3. In other words, before we can gain confidence in our risk management through the assurance we are getting, we need to be satisfied that the assurance itself is reliable, relevant and of appropriate quality. This is the object of Level 2.

LEVEL 3 – INTEGRATED RISK OVERSIGHT AND ASSURANCE

Integrated assurance at Level 3 aims to harness the shared and collective intelligence of risk owners and assurance providers to determine the level of confidence the organisation has from its risk management activities. It collates the high level conclusions from all the assurance providers, taking into account the quality of assurance determined at the prior level of assessment, that is, Level 2.

At Level 3 application, risk assurance mapping across all lines of defence not only seek to identify the coverage and quality, but also the results of assurance. The assurance map at Level 3 provides the basis for producing an aggregate risk assurance report as well as facilitating integrated risk and assurance discussions, for example, at 'Black Swan' meetings.

In addition to delivering the benefits of Levels 1 and 2, integrated assurance at Level 3 supports a holistic risk oversight by providing an overall view of the level of confidence the organisation has in its risk management and systems of control. More importantly, integrated assurance at Level 3 promotes collective intelligence for advancing more effective risk management across the organisation. We provide a summary of the three levels of application in Figure 10.1.

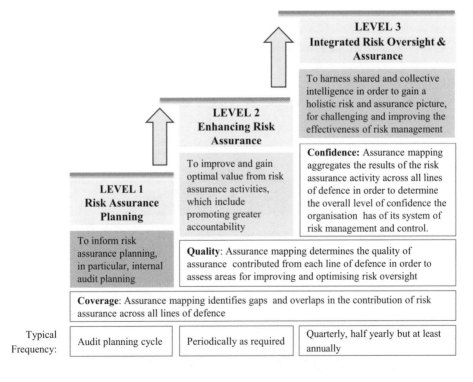

Figure 10.1   Integrated Assurance – A Summary of the Different Levels of Applications

Key Components of an Integrated Assurance Framework

Having determined the design principles and vision of an integrated assurance framework, we identify four main components that involve effective communication and shared intelligence:

1.   Ownership, roles and responsibilities.

2.   Integrated assurance map and mapping process.

3.   Integrated assurance reporting.

4.   Methodology including policies and procedures.

This is shown diagrammatically in Figure 10.2 and refers to the board and executive management as key internal stakeholders of the integrated assurance framework. A high level description of each component is provided in this section to provide context for the next part of the book, which expands on the implementation of the framework.

I. OWNERSHIP, ROLES AND RESPONSIBILITIES

Like any programme that is expected to be sustainable in an organisation, establishing and embedding the integrated assurance framework requires

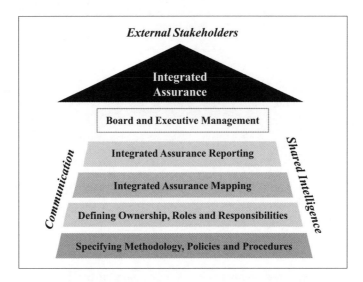

Figure 10.2   Components of an Integrated Assurance Framework

people who can champion its cause. The support of the players listed below – all occupying key roles in the assurance food chain – is necessary to provide the framework with the best chance of success. Depending on the size of the organisation, some roles may be carried out by the same individuals or delegated to individuals with equivalent authority.

- *Executive board*

    The executive board collectively owns and approves the integrated assurance framework and the appropriateness of the alignment of assurance activities across the organisation. The executive board is accountable at the individual level for the risk and control strategies operating in their respective areas of control.

- *Executive owner*

    The executive owner is the champion at the *top table* in the organisation whose role is to provide visible support for integrated assurance in order to obtain buy-in at the outset and to ensure its implementation on a sustainable basis. The executive owner is the natural sponsor of the implementation project of the integrated assurance framework.

- *Operational owner*

    The operational owner is the custodian of the integrated assurance framework who leads its development, implementation and ongoing maintenance. The individual has delegated authority from the executive to work across entities and assurance providers at all levels of the organisation. The operational owner is also responsible for collating and producing the integrated assurance reports at the enterprise or organisational level, which depending on the size of the organisation may require reporters at the entity level to be appointed.

- *Risk assurance providers*

    These are individuals who own the risk or control process for which assurance is being required or provided. These are usually not new roles, the exception being where the risk or business process has no owner in which case the assurance food chain is broken and the gap needs to be fixed. Assurance providers are usually confirmed by the integrated assurance mapping process.

- *The board*

   The board and its sub-committees play a significant role in supporting and encouraging such a framework to be established and continually improved. Their accountability to external stakeholders and wider role in corporate governance requires them to ensure that the executive develop, install and maintain effective systems of governance, risk management and control. The board, and in particular its audit and risk committees, are well placed to state their risk assurance requirements and influence the design and ongoing development of the framework.

The roles outlined above relate to *steady state* of the integrated assurance framework. During first implementation of the framework, project related roles may be required such as a project team consisting of key stakeholders in the assurance food chain and facilitators for initialising the integrated assurance map.

2. INTEGRATED ASSURANCE MAP AND MAPPING PROCESS

The integrated assurance map is the output of the assurance mapping process. It charts the assurance that exists or is expected to be provided against the organisation's principal areas of risks and core business activities across the three lines of defence. We refer to the charting of the assurance across the three lines of defence simply as the *mapping* process. The assurance map and the mapping process is essential to understanding the nature, validity, as well as the interconnectivity of the sources of assurance across the organisation.

More importantly, the mapping process provides the basis to gain collective intelligence over the changing risk and assurance picture. Fundamentally, the mapping process enables the organisation to optimise the level of risk assurance and risk mitigation required for managing risks in accordance to the board's risk appetite. A fuller description of the integrated assurance mapping process is provided in Chapter 11.

For context, it is worth stating that the charting of the assurance map is dependent on a number of processes being in place which we identify as enablers or foundations for implementing integrated assurance:

- *Three lines of defence model*

  The mapping of assurance refers to the three lines of defence model, which is explained in Chapter 8. As it is a model for identifying and allocating the different layers of risk management and internal control, it should not hamper organisations which do not already use such a model.

- *A statement of responsibility and accountability*

  Underpinning the mapping of assurance across the organisation is the allocation of accountabilities and responsibilities in respect of key areas of risks and core processes. The board, its subcommittees and executive management can be identified as key internal stakeholders of the assurance mapping process. The organisation's framework for identifying and allocating accountability for risks and assurance over their sound management provides a key source of information for the integrated assurance map. Unclear ownership and accountabilities on the other hand will be exposed by the mapping process and will need to be resolved before the mapping can be completed.

  The combined effects of heavier regulation, the proliferation of assurance activities, and risks that transcend functional boundaries, demand greater clarity in the way accountabilities are organised. The mapping process helps to identify gaps and overlaps, and facilitates the appropriate allocation of accountabilities across functional boundaries.

- *Risk management framework*

  The assurance mapping process refers to many key aspects of the organisation's risk management framework which includes risk appetite, risk identification, assessment of risk and controls as well as risk mitigation policies and risk reporting. In particular, the principal risks – which hopefully are already identified in the organisation's risk register or database – provide the basis of the analysis in the assurance map. The integrity of the integrated assurance mapping and the resulting integrated assurance report relies on the soundness of the identification of risks and core business processes. For example, a risk management approach that is not sufficiently forward looking will hamper the risk mitigation strategies and system of controls, which in turn would affect the assurance being required and provided for governance. The old adage *garbage in, garbage out* unfortunately applies here.

3. INTEGRATED ASSURANCE REPORTING

The integrated assurance report is the second key output in the integrated assurance framework. It is based on the results and conclusions derived from the mapping of risk assurance across the three lines of defence. The exact format, content and level of detail it contains will depend on three main factors:

1.   The level of application of integrated assurance (see Chapters 12–14);

2.   The objectives of the assurance mapping; and

3.   The style of corporate reporting in the organisation.

For example, where the assurance map is applied at the most basic level for the purpose of internal audit planning, the report could consist of the resulting audit plan and its rationale that is supported by an appropriate summary of the assurance map.

Depending on the size of the organisation, the integrated assurance reports may be produced at both entity and group levels. The frequency of these reports and underlying risk assurance mapping is also dependent on the needs of the board and objectives of the assurance mapping. Where integrated assurance is part of the planning process of assurance activities and other formal signoff processes, such as the year end reporting, they can be timed to suit the planning cycles of the organisation. In other words, integrated assurance reporting should be adapted to the objectives and assurance requirements of the stakeholders.

4. METHODOLOGY INCLUDING POLICIES AND PROCEDURES

This component of the framework refers to the policies, processes and procedures for operating and implementing assurance mapping and reporting. It refers to all aspects of the specification and documentation of the other components of the framework. The documentation of the overall framework is necessary for communicating to the board as well as external stakeholders as part of external reporting of the organisation's system of risk and internal control.

A pragmatic approach should be adopted to determine the level of detail required as the value is in the practical lessons from implementing the framework and the discussions that it supports. Key areas where it is useful to maintain appropriate documentation include:

- Roles and responsibilities including the terms of reference of the integrated teams who work together in the assurance mapping and reporting process.

- Criteria for the assessment of risk assurance that are aligned with the organisation's risk management approach.

- Format and nature of any formal attestations and reporting required.

To Conclude this Chapter ...

Integrated assurance should be viewed as an approach for supporting the holistic risk oversight and assurance requirements of an organisation. The framework is designed to address the shortcomings arising from a disparate and silo approach to providing assurance over the effectiveness of the organisation's risk management and systems of control. A board that is armed with a joined up and holistic view of the risk and assurance picture is able to conduct its affairs with greater confidence. Confidence, in turn, provides a sound foundation for effective decision making and instils trust in others. Implementation at the third and highest level promotes value within integrated assurance through shared and collective intelligence for sharpening risk management and oversight across the organisation.

In Part III of the book, we explain further the practical implementation of integrated assurance. We also provide some case studies in Part IV to help illustrate the different ways integrated assurance is being implemented to support the risk and assurance oversight of organisations and their boards.

Key Points from this Chapter

1.   Integrated assurance refers to a structured approach for gaining a holistic picture of the risks and the level of residual exposure an organisation is required to manage by aligning and optimising the

organisation's assurance over the management of principal risks and business processes in line with the board's risk appetite.

2.   Integrated assurance supports the board in its risk and governance oversight for the purpose of directing and delivering the organisation's strategic goals and business plans. An assured board is better equipped to assure its external stakeholders.

3.   Integrated assurance provides the board with an effective and practical process for maximising the benefit of their experience through the discussion and debate it encourages by providing a holistic risk and assurance picture.

4.   Integrated assurance provides a methodical and objective process for audit committees to review the need for internal audit functions in those organisations that do not have one.

5.   There are three main levels at which integrated assurance can be applied:

       – Level 1 – Risk Assurance Planning
       – Level 2 – Enhancing Risk Assurance
       – Level 3 – Integrated Risk Oversight and Assurance

6.   An embedded, integrated assurance process will promote greater collaboration between functional areas as well as accountability for risk oversight and assurance.

7.   The Integrated Assurance Framework consists of four key components:

       – Ownership and responsibilities
       – Methodology including policy and procedures
       – Integrated assurance map
       – Integrated assurance reporting

8.   The assurance map is not an end in itself; its value lies in the discussion it facilitates between stakeholders and assurance

providers in the assurance food chain – within the organisation and between the board and external stakeholders.

9.   The board and executive play key roles in championing the successful implementation of integrated assurance as well as shaping its design.

Endnotes

1   Nassim Nicholas Taleb, *The Black Swan – The Impact of the Highly Improbable, Rev. Ed.* (London, Penguin Books Ltd, July 2011). The term Black Swan refers to an outlier, extreme event that is unpredictable.

2   Financial Reporting Council (FRC), *Guidance on Audit Committees* (London, FRC, 2010), Paragraph 4.10: 'The audit committee should monitor and review the effectiveness of the company's internal audit function. Where there is no internal audit function, the audit committee should consider annually whether there is a need for an internal audit function and make a recommendation to the board, and the reasons for the absence of such a function should be explained in the relevant section of the annual report.'

3   Moreno, Glen, Chairman of Pearson plc, Deputy Chairman of the UK Financial Reporting Council and Director at Fidelity International chairing its audit committee, in a private meeting, June 2013.

4   Financial Reporting Council (FRC), *Guidance on Audit Committees* (London, FRC, 2010), Paragraph 4.10: 'The audit committee should monitor and review the effectiveness of the company's internal audit function. Where there is no internal audit function, the audit committee should consider annually whether there is a need for an internal audit function and make a recommendation to the board, and the reasons for the absence of such a function should be explained in the relevant section of the annual report.'

PART III
IMPLEMENTING INTEGRATED
ASSURANCE

Chapter 11

Integrated Risk Assurance Mapping

Having considered the case and vision for integrated assurance in parts I and II of the book, we now turn our focus on its implementation. We concluded Part II of the book in Chapter 10 with a description of the integrated assurance framework. This chapter kicks off Part III of the book by considering one of key components of the integrated assurance framework – risk assurance mapping. We will describe the principles and key steps for mapping risk assurance for application at one of the three levels described in Chapter 10. To avoid tedious repetition, I will not reintroduce the concepts from Chapter 10.

As a reminder, the terms *integrated assurance mapping* and *assurance mapping* and, *risk assurance* and *assurance*, are used interchangeably in this book.

Introduction

We identified in the last chapter the central role played by the assurance mapping process within integrated assurance. As discussed, assurance mapping is a methodical approach for identifying and assessing the nature, validity and interconnectivity of the sources of assurance across the three lines of defence. Assurance mapping promotes clarity in the organisation's assurance food chain by identifying the needs of the respective stakeholders and the enhancements required for effective risk assurance.

It is important to remember that the assurance map is not an end in itself but an aide for supporting effective risk oversight and finding more value in the organisation's risk governance. The value of the assurance map is in the discussion it facilitates between stakeholders and assurance providers in the assurance food chain, beyond the functional boundaries in which they operate. The success of the integrated assurance framework is reliant on effective collaboration between functional areas and their shared and collective intelligence for identifying risks as they evolve and emerge in the business.

Put simply, the assurance mapping process involves charting the risk assurance being provided against the organisation's principal areas of risk and core business activities for which assurance is expected or being provided across the three lines of defence. The information required in the mapping process depends on the level at which integrated assurance is applied, which is considered in Chapters 12–14.

Key Steps to Mapping Risk Assurance

The level of application of integrated assurance will dictate the depth and type of information required to be gathered from the assurance mapping process. Regardless of the level of application, the process of mapping assurance across the three lines of defence involves four key steps:

- *Step 1 – Scoping of Risks for the Assurance Map*

This step involves identifying the risks for which assurance is required or expected. Risks in this context refer to principal risks and core business processes for which the organisation requires oversight in order to ensure the sound running of the business. This step refers to the scoping within the assurance map; there is a wider question that relates to the extent of which integrated assurance should be implemented across the organisation, for example, subsidiary level within a large group. We will consider this broader question at the end of this chapter under options for scoping integrated assurance as it is helpful to first understand the processes involved in the assurance mapping process.

- *Step 2 – Identifying the System of Control for Assurance and Risk Oversight*

In respect of each risk that is in scope, this step identifies the area of risk control requiring assurance – that is, specific systems of control and risk mitigation processes for which assurance is provided or expected in respect of the risk identified from Step 1. This step clarifies and refines the scope for charting the risk oversight and assurance required.

- *Step 3 – Identifying the Owners of the Risks and Risk Assurance*

This step confirms ownership of the risks and the related systems of control and risk mitigation required.

- *Step 4 – Charting Risk Assurance across the Lines of Defence*

This step identifies the different layers of assurance that exists in respect of each risk across the three lines of defence, and analyses them. The detail of the analyses depends on the specific need of the organisation which determines the level at which integrated assurance is applied.

Figure 11.1 provides a summary of the four key steps of assurance mapping for application at one of the three levels. Each of these four steps is explained below. To illustrate each step of the mapping process, we will be referring to Figure 11.2, which provides an example template of an assurance map.

STEP I – SCOPING OF RISKS FOR ASSURANCE MAPPING

The scoping of the risks against which assurance is charted is guided by three key factors – principal risks, core business processes and those processes that underpin material financial items in the report and accounts of the organisation. A principal risk refers to an existing, evolving or emerging risk that could fundamentally threaten the successful delivery of the strategy of

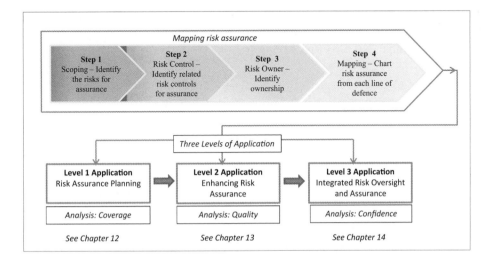

Figure 11.1   Four Basic Steps in the Assurance Mapping Process

the organisation and which includes potential threats to the business model and sustainability of the organisation; while core business processes refer to fundamental or essential activities for operating the business as determined by the business model and its operating environment. The additional consideration of those processes that underpin the reporting of material financial items aim to capture any control activities omitted by the identification of risks and core business activities.

These factors are clearly not mutually exclusive. The rationale for using all three factors is to minimise omission and gaps when identifying risks requiring oversight and assurance. In particular, on the premise that the identification of risks can be subjective and limited by imagination, the consideration of core business activities, as determined by the business model and strategy, provides an objective perspective for scoping risks for assurance oversight. Take for example an organisation where its outsourced customer administration system is a key feature of its operating model but due to the absence of any recent bad experience, the outsourcing arrangement is not identified as a principal risk. To ensure that the customer administration system remains reliable and does not disrupt business operations, assurance over the robustness of the outsourcing arrangements would be highly sensible.

Finally, the consideration of key processes that support the most material numbers in the financial statements is to provide the last safety net for identifying control processes that require risk assurance. The principles underpinning this factor are similar to those advocated by Section 404 of the Sarbanes-Oxley Act and lessons from the 2008 financial crisis that include the limitations of the work of the external financial auditors in providing assurance over the broader controls against excessive risk taking.

This book advocates, as a minimum, the use of two factors – in particular, principal risk and core business process as determined by the organisation's operating model. An example of the scoping of the risks is shown in columns 1(a), 1(b) and 1(c) of the sample assurance map in Figure 11.2, which shows the use of all three factors.

In the example assurance map, the organisation has identified the risk that its strategy does not deliver the growth it needs as a principal Risk #1; the strategic planning process is also recognised as a core business activity and that the delivery of its strategy (which includes expansion plans and new investment in technology) will be a material item in its financial statement.

[1] Reason for Assurance			[2] Area of Assurance	[3] Exec Owner	[4] Assurance across the Three Lines of Defence								
					1st Line	2nd Line Functions					3rd Line Sources		
[1A] Principal Risk	[1B] Core Activity	[1A] Material Financial Reporting			Front line management	Planning	Risk	Compliance	Legal	Health & Safety	Internal Audit	Other independent assurance	External Audit
■ #1	■	■	Strategic planning	A.Name	■	■						■	
■ #2	■	n/a	Health & safety management	N.Brown	■		■		■	■	■		
■ #3	■	■	Remuneration & bonus schemes	K.Smith	■		■	■	■		■	■	■
n/a	■	n/a	Product Development	D.Fally	■	■	■		■	■			

Key:
■ = relevance or applicability

Figure 11.2   Integrated Assurance Mapping – Example Template of an Assurance Map

Let us also assume in the example that the organisation has recognised the significant threats of non-compliance with health and safety regulations (Risk #2) that could result in manslaughter claims; it also recognises that safety management is a core activity across the organisation but the activity is not a material item in the financial statements of the organisation.

The other example areas in scope for risk assurance mapping refer to the Risk #3 of the organisation's remuneration and bonus arrangements incentivising risky behaviours, and Risk #4 in respect of product development, which is a core business activity although it is not recognised as a risk to the organisation.

STEP 2 – IDENTIFYING RELATED SYSTEMS OF CONTROL FOR ASSURANCE MAPPING

Having determined the risks that require oversight and assurance, the next step in the process is to identify the specific systems of control and risk mitigation processes for managing those risks. The rationale for this step is to clarify the specific area of assurance – that is, the nature of the control process for which assurance is to be provided. This is best illustrated by an example.

Referring to the example assurance map in Figure 11.2, the strategic planning process is identified as the area of assurance required in respect of

Risk #1. As mentioned in Step 1, Risk #1 refers to the risk that the strategy of the organisation does not deliver the growth required. The related control process, or area of assurance, of this risk is the strategic planning process, which is noted in Column 2 of the example assurance map.

Let us also consider the example Risk #2, where the organisation has identified the threat of manslaughter liabilities arising from non-compliance of its health and safety policies. The area for assurance in respect of this risk is the organisation's system of health and safety management. A similar analysis is applied to the remaining examples in the assurance map in relation to remuneration and bonus policies, and product development.

STEP 3 – IDENTIFYING OWNERS OF THE RISK AND RISK ASSURANCE

The assurance map identifies ownership of the area of assurance. This is critical for securing accountability and for championing the actions required. This is shown in Column 3 in the example assurance map in Figure 11.2. Ownership should be captured at a sufficiently senior level in the organisation to demonstrate accountability for the risk and assurance required.

STEP 4 – CHARTING RISK ASSURANCE ACROSS THE LINES OF DEFENCE

Step 4 in the mapping process could be described as the gateway step for applying integrated assurance at any of the three levels of application, each of which dictates the nature of information and analysis required. In this section, we will be describing how the information is collected and reserve the description of the analysis required for each level of application in their respective chapters. At the base level, Step 4 involves identifying the different layers of assurance that exists in respect of assuring against each risk or core activity across the three lines of defence.

The type of information collected is illustrated in Columns 4a-c in the example assurance map Figure 11.2. In the example template, assurance that is derived from the first line of defence, in which the risk owner would typically reside, is checked against Column 4a, while assurance provided by functions in the second line of defence is checked against the relevant function in Column 4b. The various functions operating in the second line of defence, which typically include compliance, risk and some specialist areas can be identified separately in this column. Any independent assurance from functions such as Internal Audit in the third line of defence is checked against Column 4c.

Taking the first item in the example template which relates to strategic planning, the mapping identifies that there is no assurance activity provided by the first line of defence but that assurance (of some form) is available from the Planning and Risk functions in the second line of defence, as well as from Internal Audit in the third line of defence. The example template in Figure 11.2 shows only the basic information of the mapping process by indicating the existence of assurance from each line of defence. Step 4 is completed with the analysis required depending on the level at which integrated assurance is to be applied:

- Application at Level 1 – Risk Assurance Planning

At Level 1, the analysis at Step 4 is concerned primarily with the coverage, that is mere existence and contribution of risk assurance from any particular source of assurance.

- Application at Level 2 – Enhancing Risk Assurance

At Level 2, the analysis at Step 4 is not only concerned about the existence but the nature and quality of the risk assurance from each source of assurance.

- Application at Level 3 – Integrated Risk Oversight and Assurance

At Level 3, the analysis at Step 4 aims to assess the level of confidence the organisation can have in the effectiveness of risk management, as concluded by the risk assurance activities across the lines of defence.

As a process, assurance mapping can become all consuming. There is a risk that in the process, we lose sight of its objectives. It is therefore worth stressing that the assurance mapping process is not an end in itself but a route for gaining better insights into the organisation's risk governance and into finding more value in the assurance food chain.

To Conclude this Chapter ...

We described in this chapter the four main steps to mapping risk assurance – a key process for supporting integrated assurance for application at one of three levels. It is worth emphasising that the risk assurance mapping process is not an end in itself but a platform for enriching risk assurance activities in order to optimise risk oversight in the boardroom and improve the effectiveness of risk management across the organisation. The process can be applied at one of three levels; each level builds on the last. In the following chapters, we expand on each of the three levels at which integrated assurance can be applied and in Chapter 15 we consider the options for implementation and getting started.

Key Points from this Chapter

1.   Integrated assurance mapping is a core component of the integrated assurance framework which involves identifying the existence, quality as well as results of the relevant risk assurance activities.

2.   Areas for inclusion in the assurance map are the principal risks of the organisation and the core business activities that represent the organisation's business model.

3.   The four main steps to assurance mapping are:

   – Step 1 – Scoping of risks for the assurance map.
   – Step 2 – Identifying the system of control for assurance and risk oversight.
   – Step 3 – Identifying the owners of the risks and risk assurance.
   – Step 4 – Charting risk assurance across the lines of defence.

4.   Assurance mapping is not an end in itself but a process for gaining better insights in the organisation's risk governance and for finding more value in the assurance food chain. Its ultimate aim is to support the board's risk oversight and to increase the overall effectiveness of risk management across all functional boundaries throughout the organisation.

Chapter 12

Integrated Assurance at Level 1

In Chapter 10, we introduced the three main different levels at which integrated assurance can be applied. The key steps for mapping risk assurance were discussed in Chapter 11. To avoid repetition of the concepts, it is assumed that these chapters have been read before continuing with this chapter, which explains the first level of application of integrated assurance.

Introduction

At Level 1, integrated assurance is focused on identifying the coverage, that is, the availability and level of contribution each line of defence provides to assurance against a particular risk or business activity for the purpose of informing assurance plans. Implementing integrated assurance at Level 1 begins with the four key steps described in the assurance mapping process in Chapter 11. A summary of the steps is shown in Figure 12.1. It is information collected at Step 4 of the mapping process that distinguishes the different ways in which integrated assurance mapping is applied. Level 1 application involves defining the criteria for assessing the contribution that each identified assurance activity makes to the overall risk assurance picture. The main aim of the assessment is to enable appropriate assurance plans to be determined for addressing any gaps and overlaps identified in respect of the risk under consideration. In the next section, we discuss the approach for rating the contribution each line of defence makes to assurance against risks at Level 1 implementation.

Defining the Assessment Criteria at Level 1 Application

Level 1 application of integrated assurance is primarily concerned with the coverage of assurance in respect of a risk or core business process, as identified on the assurance map. Information is captured by the assurance map as to whether or not assurance is being provided against a particular risk or core business process. To assess the contribution of risk assurance from each

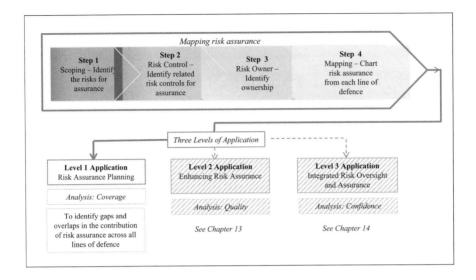

Figure 12.1   Four Basic Steps to Implementing Integrated Assurance at Level 1

identified assurance provider, the rating criteria can be as simple or complex as appropriate.

For example, if the aim is merely to obtain a high level overview of gaps and overlaps of assurance in respect of risks identified for assurance mapping, we can adopt a simple rating criterion such as the one shown in Table 12.1. The rating would merely aim to indicate three simple states of assurance – 'comprehensive' risk assurance, 'partial' risk assurance or 'no' risk assurance.

The information in this criterion is limited to simply indicating the existence or availability of risk assurance. It could, however, be lifted by adding additional ratings to also express the level of the contribution. Such an example is shown in Table 12.2.

Table 12.1   Level 1 – Example of a Simple Rating Criterion for Assessing Contribution

Level I Rating	Brief description
Green/Yes	Comprehensive assurance is being provided against the risk
Amber/Partial	Partial assurance is being provided against the risk
Red/No	There is no assurance being provided against the risk
n/a	Not expected or not applicable

Table 12.2   Level 1 – Example for Rating the Level of Contribution to Risk Assurance

Level I: Rating	Brief description
0	Unknown/insufficient information/negligible contribution of assurance in respect of the risk or business activity under consideration
1	Minor contribution to assurance of < less than 25% coverage of controls in respect of the risk or business activity under consideration
2	Moderate contribution to assurance up to 75% coverage of controls in respect of the risk or business activity under consideration
3	Significant contribution to assurance >75% coverage of controls in respect of the risk or business activity under consideration
n/a	Not expected or not applicable

In the second example criterion, the rating aims to determine the level of contribution from an assurance provider, that is, the degree of coverage of the controls in respect of the risk or business activity under consideration. The degree of coverage includes a qualitative assessment of relevance of the assurance activity. The percentages in the example criterion are not intended to offer precision but an estimate of the significance of the assurance activity for the purpose of assessing if more or less assurance is required. The percentages can be varied to reflect the individual preference of the organisation. For practical application, the precision in measuring the coverage is not significant as the aim at Level 1 is to assist with the planning of assurance activity after considering obvious gaps and duplication.

Both examples show that the rating criteria can be expressed by colour and/or rating (such as a number or a letter). It is the description of the rating that is important. Having defined the rating criteria, we can proceed to mapping the assurance across the three lines of defence for each of the risk or business activity on the integrated assurance map.

Assurance Mapping at Level I

To illustrate how the assessment of the assurance at Level 1 flows from the mapping process, we refer to the example assurance maps used in the last chapter. In Figure 12.2, we show how assurance could be mapped using the example rating criteria defined in Table 12.2.

[1] Reason(s) for Assurance			[2] Area of Assurance	[3] Executive Owner	[4] Assurance across the Three Lines of Defence									[5] Analysis of Assurance Activity
					[4a] 1st Line Functions	[4b] 2nd Line Functions Sources of assurance					[4c] 3rd Line Independent Sources of assurance			Actions and Recommendations
[1a]	[1b]	[1c]			Front line management	Planning	Risk	Compliance	Legal	Health & Safety	Internal Audit	Other independent assurance	External Audit	
[1a] Principal Risk	[1b] Core Activity	[1c] Material Financial Reporting												
• #1	•	•	Strategic planning	A.Name	n/a	3	2	0	0	n/a		0	0	Optimal level of risk assurance – no further actions required
• #2	•	n/a	Health & safety management	N.Brown	3	0	3	0	1	3	2	0	n/a	Significant overlaps. Potential for rationalising assurance across all lines of defence.
• #3	•	•	Remuneration & bonus schemes	K.Smith	1	0	2	3	1	n/a	1	3	0	Overall high level of activity accepted this year to reflect the risk identified
n/a	•	n/a	Product Development	D.Fally	3	0	1	2	0	n/a	0	0	n/a	Assurance underweight particularly with new product strategy; consider assurance from internal audit

Key	Rating of level of contribution of assurance
0	Unknown/insufficient information/negligible to assurance
1	Minor contribution to assurance (less than 25% coverage)
2	Moderate contribution to assurance (up to 75% coverage)
3	Significant contribution to assurance (more than 75% coverage)
n/a	Not expected or not applicable

Figure 12.2   Integrated Assurance Mapping at Level 1 – Example Assurance Map

Let us consider the first item identified on the example assurance map that relates to strategic planning (shown in Column 2, which results from Step 2 of the mapping process). Using the criterion defined in Table 12.2, the contribution of assurance is assessed to be:

- From the management in the first line of defence, there is no assurance being provided in respect of the risk or process, particularly if the risk owner is supported by the Planning Department in the second line of defence as it is assumed in this example.

- From the second line of defence, the Planning Department provides significant assurance that covers over 75 per cent of the controls in relation to the risk under consideration; the Risk function also provides moderate assurance of up to 75 per cent of the risk through its reporting of risk indicators.

- From the third line of defence, independent assurance of the risk is being provided from the Internal Audit function with up to 75 per cent coverage of the controls in relation to the risks through its consideration of the strategic planning approach for the group's top five strategic projects.

The conclusion in respect of the risk or business process under consideration is determined by the total coverage of controls provided by all the relevant assurance providers, considering any gaps or duplications. The conclusions are recorded in Column 5, which in this example, are considered to be optimal – that is, there are no material overlaps or gaps in the risk assurance in respect of the strategic planning – and that no further actions are required. It is important to stress that the conclusion expresses an assessment of the coverage of the underlying controls for managing the risks rather than the average score of the coverage. The assessment is repeated for the rest of the risks and core business activities identified for assurance mapping. Clearly, the assessments are not intended to be precise but provide indicative levels of risk assurance that is available or are required.

In respect of the second item on the example assurance map, referring to health and safety risks, assurance of the risks is assessed as being covered very well, with probably unnecessary overlaps in the second line of defence. In respect of this risk, the assessment concludes that there is opportunity for reducing and rationalising the assurance the organisation is receiving.

In the third example risk that refers to remuneration and incentive schemes, the assurance mapping highlights a high level of assurance, particularly from the second and third lines of defence where external expertise was used. In respect of this risk, the assessment accepts that the high level of assurance activity is necessary to reflect the current focus of regulators and other external stakeholders.

The assurance map is completed by working through the risks methodically to assess the level of contribution available from the organisation's assurance food chain. A completed assurance map can provide a form of dashboard showing, at a glance, the level of assurance each line of defence contributes to a particular risk or business activity. The amount of information that is collected during the mapping process varies depending on the level of detail required for the purpose of analysis and reporting. Focussing on the decisions that the integrated assurance mapping are expected to help inform should ensure a pragmatic approach.

Analysis and Reporting at Level 1

Once the assessments are completed, the assurance map can be analysed for the purpose of framing the assurance plans across the organisation. At Level 1, the analysis includes decisions relating to whether or not:

- Management assurance from the first or second lines of defence is providing the expected or appropriate level of assurance over the underlying controls in respect of the risk under consideration.

- Gaps in risk assurance are attributable to a lack of risk ownership or definition of responsibilities.

- More or less independent assurance is required, for example, by internal audit in respect of a particular risk or business activity.

- The organisation's risk assurance arrangements are at an optimal level, and if not, what actions are required to redress the balance.

At Level 1, the proposed actions are limited to determining an appropriate internal audit plan, taking into consideration the assurance that is being provided by the other lines of defence. Actions for enhancing the assurance provided by the other lines of defence would refer to Level 2 application of integrated assurance.

Depending on the specific purpose of implementing integrated assurance at Level 1, the resulting report to the organisation's executive management and/or audit and risk committees could include a paper summarising the conclusions of the assurance mapping together with the completed assurance map, such as the one shown in Figure 12.2 and the proposed internal audit plan. The report may include recommendations for further qualitative analysis that is akin to applying integrated assurance at Level 2, for example, where assurance activities have been identified to have limited relevance or provide limited value to managing the risks of the organisation. Where the integrated assurance mapping process is used to help an organisation assess whether or not an internal audit function is required, the report will clearly cover the conclusions and recommendations as appropriate.

The frequency of mapping and reporting at Level 1 is clearly dependent on the degree of change in the risk landscape, business model and resulting core business activities within the organisation. Typically, the frequency is aligned with the assurance planning cycle, which is usually annually.

To Conclude this Chapter ...

In summary, Level 1 application of integrated assurance aims to provide a view of the availability or contribution of assurance in respect of a set of principal risks and core business activities. The availability of assurance is rated to help determine whether or not the organisation is receiving an appropriate level of assurance across all lines of defence. While Level 1 application is typically used to help support the assurance plans in internal audit, mapping the availability of assurance will provide the basis for the next level of application, which we will cover in the next chapter.

When deciding on the outputs of the Level 1 assurance map, it is worth considering the potential questions which the organisation and/or its boards may ask, such as:

Q1. Do the gaps or overlaps identified by the Level 1 assurance mapping present any surprises and do the resulting proposed actions help to optimise the assurance activities across the three lines of defence?

Q2. Are there any key areas of risk or business activity that have not been considered in the assurance map?

Q3. Are there significant gaps in the assurance being provided to the board or senior management that should be rectified and at what timescales?

Q4. Are there assurance activities which appear to be redundant, or have limited relevance, that are outside the remit of Level 1 application but nonetheless require further understanding?

Q5.   Do the internal audit plans complement the organisation's assurance activities by ensuring that the appropriate risks and core business activities are covered without unnecessary duplication?

Q6.   If the organisation does not already have an internal audit function, does the assurance mapping identify the need for one or confirm that the assurance arrangements from the first and second lines of defence remain sufficient?

Key Points from this Chapter

1.   Integrated assurance at Level 1 is focused on identifying the level of contribution each line of defence provides to assurance against a particular risk, or business activity, for the purpose of informing assurance plans particularly in the third line of defence.

2.   Level 1 application of integrated assurance mapping is commonly used to inform internal audit planning in the third line of defence and provide a basis for communicating the rationale of the plan to the board and the audit committee.

3.   Where an organisation has no internal audit function, integrated assurance at Level 1 provides the organisation and its audit committee with a methodical approach for assessing the adequacy of risk assurance within the organisation and if an internal audit function is required.

4.   Identifying gaps and overlaps is integral to Level 1 application. It provides a foundation for enhancing risk assurance at the next level of application – Level 2.

Chapter 13

Integrated Assurance at Level 2

This chapter describes integrated assurance application at Level 2, which focuses on enhancing risk assurance across all lines of defence with the aim of achieving optimal risk oversight and assurance. It builds on the foundations provided at Level 1. The assessment of the coverage of assurance from Level 1 is an essential input for Level 2. To avoid repetition, we will not repeat the concepts of Level 1 in this chapter unless it is helpful to do so.

Introduction

Level 2 application of integrated assurance builds on the information gathered at Level 1 by assessing the quality of risk assurance from each line of defence identified at Level 1. By also considering the quality, and not just its existence, integrated assurance at Level 2 enables the organisation to enhance and optimise risk oversight across the organisation. With these aims in mind, the analysis of risk assurance at Level 2 requires determination of an appropriate quality assessment criterion at Step 4 of the assurance mapping process. Figure 13.1 provides a reminder of the four key steps of the assurance mapping process.

Level 2 seeks to understand the quality and degree of relevance each assurance activity contributes to risk oversight of a particular area; the analysis goes beyond determining gaps and overlaps. We consider in the next section how such an analysis is carried out.

Characterising Quality of Risk Assurance Activity

To optimise risk oversight across all lines of defence in the organisation, integrated assurance at Level 2 involves an appropriate level of understanding of the nature and quality of the assurance. Before we define the criteria for conducting such an analysis, let us examine the three main characteristics by

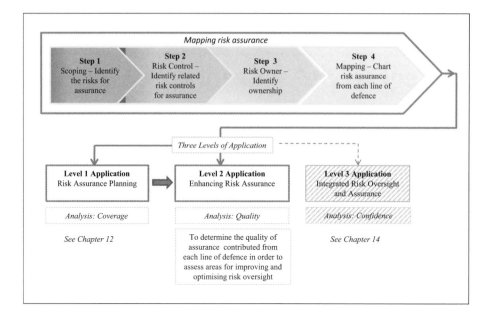

Figure 13.1   Four Basic Steps to Implementing Integrated Assurance at Level 2

which the quality of risk assurance can be assessed – relevance, formality and integrity of approach.

RELEVANCE

Assurance activity can be directly or indirectly relevant to the management of a risk. Taking fraud risk as an example, assurance activity that has direct relevance would include any assessments carried out on the robustness of the organisation's anti-financial crime policies and controls in managing the risks arising from fraud, theft as well as money laundering. Using the same example, indirect relevance or contribution of an assurance activity to the management of fraud risks could be derived from the reporting of key fraud risk indicators to the audit or risk committee of the organisation. In other words, assurance is regarded to be indirect if it is only obtained by inference from performance or management indicators, or non-specific reports in relation of the risk or business activity under consideration.

FORMALITY

Formal assurance follows a defined process or procedure that is evidential and auditable. Conversely, assurance is regarded to be informal if it is not based on a defined process but on the word of an individual. An assertion, or verbal affirmation, of the effective management of a risk or business activity that is not based on a defined process designed to provide assurance, even where a record of the statement has been retained, for example, in minutes of a meeting, is regarded to be informal.

Assurance that is formal is provided in a written form that is auditable. Formal assurance includes reporting that is part of an established governance cycle or as a result of a request or need identified by the board or management of the organisation. Examples of formal assurance reporting that are part of the governance cycle include strategic planning, annual financial and operating reports, periodic capital and solvency reports, risk indicators and analyses, annual anti-money laundering reporting, whistle-blowing policy, other compliance reports as well as internal audit reports.

Management self certification of compliance and risk mitigation activities is also an example of formal assurance where it forms part of the organisation's system of governance and internal control. Self certification is not the preserve of the first or second lines of defence; it can apply to all lines of defence, for example, for gaining assurance in respect of compliance with policies that are applicable to all parts of the organisation such as information security, anti-bribery, money laundering as well as mandatory corporate training and awareness programmes in relation to these policies.

INTEGRITY OF APPROACH

Integrity refers to the credibility and robustness of the approach by which assurance is provided. This, in turn, promotes confidence in assurance in respect of a risk or business activity. Integrity of the assurance process is partly correlated with the formality by which risk assurance is provided and reported to the board, that is, formal assurance is more likely to be supported by processes that are designed and subject to review.

Defining the Assessment Criteria at Level 2 Application

To assess the overall quality of risk assurance activity, we require a rating criterion that embraces the key characteristics as discussed above. An example of an assessment criterion is shown below in Table 13.1. The descriptions can be adapted to suit personal circumstances, for example, by varying the percentages by which the risk is covered by the assurance activity.

**Table 13.1   Level 2 – Example criterion for Rating the Quality of Risk
Assurance**

Level 2: Rating	Brief description
0	Low or undetermined quality, where assurance activity is informal or indirect, or is less than 25% of the expected coverage of key controls in respect of the risk or business activity under consideration.
I	Limited quality, where formal and direct assurance activity provides at least 50% of the expected coverage of key controls in respect of the risk or business activity under consideration.
2	Reasonable quality, where formal and direct assurance activity provides at least 75% of the expected coverage of key controls in respect of risk or business activity under consideration.
3	High quality, where formal and direct assurance activity provides more than 75% of the expected coverage of key controls in respect of the risk or business activity under consideration.

The example criterion shows that the assessment of the nature and quality of the assurance methodology can be expressed by colour and/or rating (such as a number or a letter). As discussed in the last chapter, it is the description of the rating that is important. When describing the criteria, it is important to remember that Level 2 assurance mapping assesses the quality of approach of the assurance – that is, relevance, formality and integrity of the assurance activity – rather than the quality of the organisation's system of risk management and internal control. The assessment of the latter is the result of an assurance activity. It is important to stress this distinction here to avoid confusion later when assessing assurance at Level 3, which focuses on the results of the assurance activity.

The assurance map in Figure 13.2 illustrates how the above example criterion is applied. For continuity, the assurance map is based on the examples discussed in Chapters 11 and 12, in particular Figure 12.2, which illustrates the assurance map applied at Level 1. As in Level 1, the mapping at Level 2 of the quality of assurance against each risk or core business activity follows a methodical approach. For each risk or core business activity identified in line with steps 1–3 in the assurance mapping process (Figure 13.1), assurance is assessed for quality and any improvements required to gain optimal risk oversight.

The rating and assessment of the quality of the assurance activity involves judgement; any attempt to achieve precision in what is a qualitative assessment would outweigh the benefits that could be derived from the process. In other words, whether an assurance activity is rated to be of 'limited' or 'reasonable'

| [1] Reason(s) for Assurance | | | [2] Area of Assurance | [3] Executive Owner | [4] Assurance across the Three Lines of Defence | | | | | | | | | [5] Analysis of Assurance Activity |
| [1a] Principal Risk | [1b] Core Activity | [1c] Material Financial Reporting | | | [4a] 1st Line Functions: Front line management | [4b] 2nd Line Functions Sources of assurance | | | | | [4c] 3rd Line Independent Sources of assurance | | | Actions and Recommendations |
					Front line management	Planning	Risk	Compliance	Legal	Health & Safety	Internal Audit	Other independent assurance	External Audit	
#1	•	•	Strategic planning	A.Name	0	3	2	0	0	0	2	0	0	Quality of risk assurance activity is appropriate – no enhancements required
#2	•	n/a	Health & safety management	N.Brown	3	0	3	0	1	3	2	0	0	Overall high quality of assurance activity. Assurance by Legal is formal but limited to litigation. Potential to reduce level of 2nd line of defence assurance activity.
#3	•	•	Remuneration & bonus schemes	K.Smith	1	0	2	3	1	1	1	3	0	High quality and level of assurance activity this year to reflect the risk identified. Expect reduced activity next year in Compliance and by external independent assurance (formal/limited) while risk indicators could be enhanced.
n/a	•	n/a	Product Development	D.Fally	3	3	1	0	0	0	3	0	0	Overall quality of assurance is high with potential for removing duplication across all lines of defence.

Key — **Rating of quality of assurance**

0 Low or undetermined quality, where assurance activity is informal or indirect, or, is <25% expected coverage of key controls in relation to the risk

1 Limited quality, where formal and direct assurance activity provides at least 50% of the expected coverage of key controls in relation to the risk

2 Reasonable quality, where formal and direct assurance activity at least 75% of the expected coverage of key controls in relation to the risk

3 High quality, where formal and direct assurance activity provides >75% of the expected coverage of key controls in relation to the risk

Figure 13.2 Integrated Assurance Mapping – Example Template at Level 2 Application: Enhancing Integrated Assurance

quality is less important than the resulting decisions and actions that may be required to improve assurance in the underlying controls for managing a particular risk or business process.

We should not underestimate the documentation that will be required when assessing each risk or business activity on the integrated assurance map. Additional spreadsheets or notes may be necessary to record the type of risk assurance activity and resulting decisions of the evaluation process. A pragmatic approach to documentation is, however, necessary to avoid losing sight of the goal, which is to identify improvements required in order to gain optimal value from assurance activities across the organisation. For example, it may be worth focusing on documenting those areas where assurance is informal or indirect for the purpose of framing appropriate actions.

We illustrate in Figure 13.3 the underlying information that may be recorded during the mapping process. We expand on the information recorded against two of the risks from Figure 13.1 in relation to strategic planning (Risk #1) and remuneration and bonus schemes (Risk #3). The information recorded is selective and focused on evaluating risk assurance with regard to the level of formality, integrity and relevance to the risk under consideration. As it would be impractical to attempt to fit such additional information on the same assurance map, it is recommended that a 'shadow' assurance map (a table or spreadsheet) is used to support the evaluations. The 'shadow' assurance map is retained in the details of the working file while the main assurance map can be used, for example, to accompany the evaluation report without overwhelming the audience.

Evaluation and Practical Application of Level 2 Assurance Map

One of the direct outcomes of the analysis and assessments of assurance at Level 2 is a potential set of actions for enhancing the quality of assurance provided by a particular line of defence. The aim of such enhancements – in case we should forget – is to help the organisation achieve an optimal level of assurance of its principal risks and core business activities. With this focus in mind, it is useful to consider some pertinent questions to help confirm the evaluations arising from the assurance mapping process that include:

Q1.   Would an increase in the formality of an existing informal or indirect risk assurance activity have the potential to add significantly more value to the overall assurance food chain across the organisation?

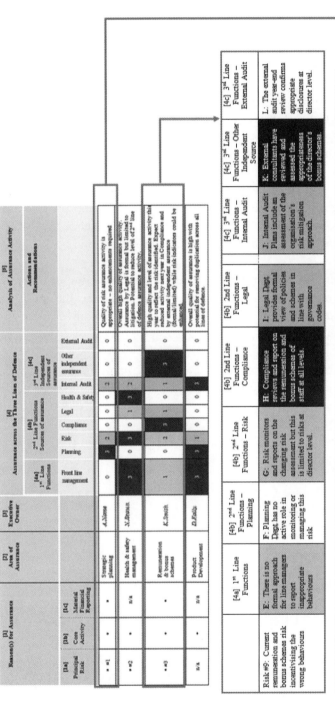

Figure 13.3   Integrated Assurance Mapping at Level 2 – Example for Recording Underlying Information

Q2.   Could enhancing the informal or indirect risk assurance currently provided by the first and second lines of defence help reduce the level of assurance required from the third line of defence without diluting its overall contribution to risk oversight of the organisation?

Q3.   Where there is apparent duplication of assurance activities between the lines of defence, how can duplication of effort be removed without eroding the ownership of the risk? What additional actions are required to guard against such a risk?

Q4.   Where the level and quality of assurance for a particular principal risk or business activity appear to be optimal, and no enhancements are being proposed, is the risk potentially volatile to warrant additional assurance for a limited period?

In addition to helping us to frame the conclusions of the assurance mapping and recommendations for consideration by the organisation, the questions also help ensure that we do not lose sight of the board's risk governance and oversight responsibilities.

As in Level 1, the frequency of Level 2 assurance mapping and reporting is largely dependent on the degree of change in the risk landscape of the organisation and the number of actions arising from the last report. Broadly speaking, the re-mapping at Level 2 can be carried out on a need basis, or at least annually, if it is to help inform the optimal organisation of risk assurance activity in line with the organisation's changing risk profile or landscape.

To Conclude this Chapter …

In summary, integrated assurance mapping and reporting at Level 2 helps us to identify areas in the assurance food chain that could be enhanced for the purpose of achieving optimal risk oversight across the organisation. Ultimately, it helps to raise confidence in the organisation's internal system of risk management and controls and to support the proper discharge of responsibilities with regard to risk governance. The organisation and its boards may consider that no enhancements to its assurance food chain are necessary if the gaps are insufficient to dampen their confidence in their ability to discharge their oversight responsibilities.

Being reasonably satisfied with the quality of the assurance an organisation has in place provides the foundations for implementing integrated assurance at the next level – Level 3 – which is concerned with aggregating the results of the organisation's risk oversight and assurance.

Key Points from this Chapter

1. Integrated assurance at Level 2 is focused on enhancing the quality of risk assurance in order to optimise risk oversight across the organisation, while promoting accountability in the process.

2. Quality of assurance is assessed by three main characteristics – relevance, formality and integrity of approach of risk assurance.

3. Application at Level 2 helps to identify opportunities for coordination and collaboration across the three lines of defence to gain more efficient risk assurance and oversight for the organisation.

4. The assurance mapping process at Level 2 begins with defining appropriate criteria for assessing the nature and quality of risk assurance in terms of its expected relevance, formality and integrity of its approach.

5. Maintaining focus on the purpose of assurance mapping helps to ensure that the process remains pragmatic and does not take on a life of its own, diverting attention from the importance of evaluating the quality of assurance.

Chapter 14

Integrated Assurance at Level 3

This chapter describes the application of integrated assurance at the highest level defined in our model. Integrated assurance at Level 3 promotes and harnesses collective intelligence to gain a holistic risk and assurance picture of the organisation, thereby enabling more effective risk management of the organisation. Application at Level 3 builds on the foundations covered by levels 1 and 2.

Introduction

At Level 3, integrated assurance helps the organisation strengthen its risk management by means of a two stage process which, in practice, will exist concurrently. The first stage helps the organisation determine the overall level of confidence it has in its systems of risk management. The second stage refers to promoting the sharing and collective use of intelligence in managing risks to the organisation.

Level 3 integrated assurance helps the organisation determine the overall level of confidence it has in its systems of risk management by considering the quality of the controls and mitigations as reported by the risk assurance activities in respect of the organisation's principal risks and business activities. We refer to the reported quality of the controls and mitigations as the result or outcome of the risk assurance activity, or *result of assurance* for short.

The overall level of confidence depends on two factors: firstly, a judgement of the quality of the controls and mitigations (and therefore residual risk) as reported by the risk assurance activities, that is, the *result of assurance*, and secondly, trust in the reliability of the assurance activity itself, that is, the *quality of assurance*. In this chapter, we will refer to making this combined assessment as *assessing assurance* and to the overall level of confidence as *confidence in the risk assurance.* It is important to keep in mind that we use these phrases as a convenient abbreviation for assessing the system of risk management and for confidence in the system of risk management.

The aforementioned assessments help to support the second stage of integrated assurance at Level 3 which refers to harnessing and promoting shared and collective risk intelligence across the organisation. Together, they enable the organisation to gain a holistic picture of risks in order to improve the effectiveness of the organisation's system of risk management. We will discuss each of the two stages in turn below.

Stage One – Assessing Confidence in Risk Assurance

As mentioned earlier, our confidence in risk assurance is based on the combined assessment of two factors – the *result of assurance* and the *quality of assurance*. To prepare this combined assessment, there are three key steps:

Step 1   Determine initial criteria for assessing the level of confidence in the risk assurance by aligning the results of assurance to the organisation's risk ratings prior to factoring in the quality of assurance.

Step 2   Determine the combined rating criteria for assessing assurance at Level 3 that takes into account the risk-aligned ratings from Step 1 and quality of assurance.

Step 3   Apply the combined rating criteria for assessing the overall confidence in the risk assurance in the assurance map at Level 3.

Clearly, the steps are described here as discrete processes for illustrative purposes. Once they are set up, the steps will merge to become a single continuous process. We describe each step in turn below.

STEP 1 – DETERMINING AN INITIAL RISK-ALIGNED RATING FOR ASSESSING CONFIDENCE OF RISK ASSURANCE MAPPING AT LEVEL 3

To provide context for this preliminary step, we refer to Figure 14.1 for a reminder of the four key steps of the assurance mapping process. In particular, we pick up in Step 4 of the assurance mapping process and the determination of appropriate assessment criteria, at which integrated assurance is being applied.

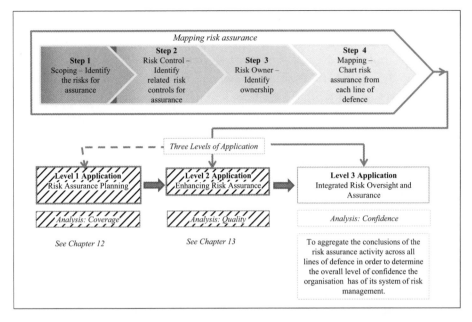

Figure 14.1   Four Basic Steps to Mapping Assurance at Level 3

We begin Step 1 by considering the assessment criteria of the results of assurance for the initial assurance map. To ensure the assessment criteria is aligned to the organisation's risk management policies, we take into account the organisation's approach to risk assessment in two main ways:

- *The organisation's approach to evaluating results of assurance*

   A consistent approach to evaluating results of assurance is necessary to ensure that there is a common interpretation of what a 'good' or a 'bad' risk assurance outcome means for the organisation. As assurance is intrinsically linked to risk, it makes sense for the evaluation of the assurance over the appropriateness of an organisation's systems of internal control and risk mitigation strategies to be also aligned with its risk management framework. Without a consistent evaluation basis, mapping the results of risk assurance would make the aggregation of the results more challenging and potentially misleading.

•   *The organisation's risk appetite and tolerances*

> Implicit in the assessment of the effectiveness of risk management is the organisation's ability to manage its risks in line with risk appetite and tolerance that have been agreed with the board. Underpinning the organisation assessment of risks and the effectiveness of its controls is the board's tolerances for risks. As explained in Chapter 6, Rethinking Assurance, assurance is provided within the context of the risk appetite of the stakeholder. Excessive risk taking or ineffective risk management is therefore relative to the board's risk taking policies. Where the board's risk appetite is clear and has been communicated across the organisation, it is more likely that the triggers and thresholds for escalation are determined and embedded in the management processes which include risk assurance reporting. Consistent application of the organisation's risk tolerances therefore facilitates appropriate and uniform assessment of the confidence the organisation can have in its systems of internal control and risk mitigation effort.

An example of a rating criterion with a description of its alignment with the organisation's risk assessment approach is provided in Table 14.1, the process by which the rating criterion is derived is explained with an illustrative example in Figure 14.2.

The rating criterion in Table 14.1 provides an example for describing how confidence in an organisation's controls and risk mitigation can be assessed and aligned with the organisation's risk assessment approach, the example for which is shown in Table A in Figure 14.2. Clearly, each organisation has its own approach for scoring risks – that is, for assessing different types of risk factors (such as financial, reputation and operational risks) and rating them against a set of likelihood and impact scores. As explained earlier, a consistent approach for assessing the residual risks and results of assurance provided by all sources helps in the process of aggregating a view of the level of confidence we could have in the organisation's system of risk management and control.

Table 14.1   Level 3 – Example Criterion for Risk-aligned Rating of Confidence in the Results of Assurance

Rating	Brief Description of the Rating Criterion	Detailed description that is aligned with the organisation's risk assessment approach (based on example shown in Figure 14.2)
0	Low confidence in the assurance over the risk or business activity under consideration.	With a residual risk score between 12 and 16, the assurance activity concludes that the systems of internal control and risk mitigation provide no or low confidence in assuring against the risk materialising.
1	Limited confidence in the assurance over the risk or business activity under consideration.	With a residual risk score between 4 and 9 where the impact ≥ 4 and likelihood ≥ 3, the assurance activity concludes that the systems of internal control and risk mitigation provide limited confidence in assuring against the risk materialising.
2	Good level of confidence in the assurance over the risk or business activity under consideration.	With a residual risk score between 3 and 4 where the impact ≥ 3 and likelihood ≥ 2, the assurance activity concludes that the systems of internal control and risk mitigation provide a good level of confidence in assuring against the risk materialising.
3	High level of confidence in the assurance of the risk or business activity under consideration.	With a residual risk score between 2 and 1 where the impact or likelihood is ≥ 2, the assurance activity concludes that the systems of internal control and risk mitigation provide a high level of confidence for assuring against the risk materialising.

Table B in Figure 14.2 illustrates how we can then translate an organisation's approach for assessing or scoring risks into an equivalent system for assessing the results of assurance and the level of confidence the organisation can have over the effectiveness of its controls and risk mitigation. The resulting rating criterion in Figure 14.2 is extracted and shown in Table 14.1 for use in assessing assurance across the three lines of defence at Level 3. If required, an initial assurance map can be produced based on this initial criteria to provide a preliminary picture of the level of confidence of risk assurance the organisation has.

As in the earlier examples discussed at application levels 1 and 2, the criteria can be expressed by colour or a rating number. The most important element of the criteria is clearly the description of the rating. The rating of the assurance map at Level 3 is potentially more complex than at Levels 1 and 2 because, as described above, it is necessary for it to be aligned to the risk assessments and risk appetite of the organisation.

Table B: Aligned assessment of assurance with the organisation's risk assessment (Example in Table A below)

Rating	Risk Aligned Rating Criteria at Level 3	Aligned assessment of assurance
0	Low confidence in the risk assurance over the risk or business activity under consideration	With a residual risk score between 12 and 16, the assurance activity concludes that the systems of internal control and risk mitigation provide no or low confidence in assuring against the risk materialising
1	Limited confidence in the risk assurance over the risk or business activity under consideration	With a residual risk score between 4 and 9 where the impact $\geq$ 4 and likelihood $\geq$ 3, the assurance activity concludes that the systems of internal control and risk mitigation provide limited confidence in assuring against the risk materialising
2	Good level of confidence in the risk assurance over the risk or business activity under consideration	With a residual risk score between 3 and 4 where the impact $\geq$ 3 and likelihood $\geq$ 2, the assurance activity concludes that the systems of internal control and risk mitigation provide a good level of confidence in assuring against the risk materialising
3	High level of confidence in the risk assurance of the risk or business activity under consideration	With a residual risk score between 2 and 1 where the impact or likelihood is $\geq$ 2, the assurance activity concludes that the systems of internal control and risk mitigation provide a high level of confidence for assuring against the risk materialising
n/a	Insufficient information or not applicable for the Assurance Map	Insufficient information for assessing the level of confidence or not applicable for the Assurance Map at Level 3

Table A: Risk Assessment – Illustrative example of a definition for assessing risk in an organisation's risk management framework

Financial	Reputation	Brief Descriptor	IMPACT	Risk Scores			
>35% revenue	Long term damage	Catastrophic	4	4	8	12	16
20%-35% revenue	Up 2 years' bad PR	Significant	3	3	6	9	12
10%-20% revenue	1-2 years' bad PR	Moderate	2	2	4	6	8
<10% revenue	<1 year bad PR	Negligible	1	1	2	3	4
			Rating	1	2	3	4

PROBABILITY			
Extremely unlikely	Unlikely	Possible	Likely
Probability or likelihood of a risk occurring or crystallising in the given period:			
>20 years	Between 10-20 years	Between 2-10 years	Within 1-2 years

Figure 14.2 Defining the Confidence Rating in the Results of Assurance: Alignment with the Organisation's Approach for Risk Assessment

The example used in Figure 14.2 (with the resulting confidence rating criteria in Table 14.1) presumes that a risk management approach is in place and provides a common platform for assessing the organisation's risks and therefore the effectiveness of its systems of internal control and risk mitigation strategies. The absence of a mature risk management approach has been identified by some organisations as a challenge for implementing integrated assurance. The situation is not ideal but the challenge is not unmanageable.

In an organisation where the risk assessments and risk assurance are not fully consistent or aligned with its risk management approach or the board's risk tolerances, the rating criterion could be defined based on common understanding. Moderation by the assessor or reporter of the aggregate assurance map will be required to rationalise the variations of assessments between the different assurance providers. The moderation is likely to involve a degree of judgment or subjective overlay that is inevitable in the absence of a common definition or systematic approach for assessing the results of assurance activities. In practice, these gaps in organisations are usually addressed fairly rapidly when they start to implement an integrated assurance framework as the need for more consistent risk and control assessments become evident. In this regard, the integrated assurance framework has its use in driving consistency and enhancing risk and governance processes within organisations.

STEP 2 – DETERMINING THE COMBINED CRITERIA FOR ASSESSING OVERALL CONFIDENCE IN RISK ASSURANCE

Having determined the risk-aligned rating for assessing the result of risk assurance in Step 1, we now consider the second factor of the quality of assurance. This is taken from Level 2 of the assurance mapping process. To illustrate how the quality of assurance is factored into the assessment of confidence in the results of risk assurance activity, we use the example quality rating criterion shown in Table 13.1 in Chapter 13 and map that against the confidence rating criterion defined earlier in Table 14.1.

Figure 14.3 shows how by considering the quality of the risk assurance activity, the resulting level of confidence that the residual risks are within appetite is appropriately adjusted to provide a simple summary rating such as:

A – High level of confidence that residual risks are within risk appetite.

B – Good level of confidence that residual risks are within risk appetite.

Level 3 Assurance Mapping Risk-Aligned rating of the confidence in the outcomes of the assurance activity (based on example from Table 14.1)		Level 2 Assurance Mapping: Rating of quality of assurance (based on example from Table 13.1)			
Risk Aligned Rating		**0** Low or undetermined quality, where assurance activity is informal or indirect with less than 25% coverage of the risk or business activity	**1** Limited quality, where assurance activity is informal or formal or indirect assurance provides up to 25% coverage of the risk or business activity	**2** Reasonable quality, where assurance activity is primarily formal and direct providing up to 75% coverage of the risk or business activity	**3** High quality, where assurance activity is primarily formal and direct providing more than 75% coverage of the risk or business activity
0	*Low confidence in the assurance over the risk or business activity under consideration*	*C1 – Limited confidence/higher priority*	*C1 – Limited confidence/higher priority*	*D – Low confidence*	*D – Low confidence*
1	*Limited confidence in the assurance over the risk or business activity under consideration*	*C1 – Limited confidence/higher priority*	*C1 – Limited confidence/higher priority*	*C1 – Limited confidence/higher priority*	*C1 – Limited confidence/higher priority*
2	*Good level of confidence in the assurance over the risk or business activity under consideration*	*U – Insufficient information*	*C2 – Limited confidence/Lower priority*	*B – Good level of confidence*	*B – Good level of confidence*
3	*High level of confidence in the assurance of the risk or business activity under consideration.*	*U – Insufficient information*	*C2 – Limited confidence/Lower priority*	*A – High level of confidence*	*A – High level of confidence*
		Level of confidence that residual risks are within risk appetite			

Figure 14.3   Factoring the Quality of Assurance in the Assessment of Confidence in the Results of Risk Assurance Activity

C – Limited level of confidence that residual risks are within risk appetite, where C1 is expected to be given higher priority (over C2 ratings) for follow up.

D – Low level of confidence that residual risks are within risk appetite.

U – Insufficient information to complete the assessment.

With the enhanced and combined rating criteria, we can proceed to applying it in Step 3.

STEP 3 – APPLYING THE COMBINED RATING CRITERIA IN THE ASSURANCE MAP AT LEVEL 3

Applying the combined rating we have derived is best summarised and illustrated by the example in Figure 14.4. For familiarity and simplicity, we have used the same example assurance maps from the previous chapters. Using the same examples also allows us to illustrate the progressive steps through each level of application of the integrated assurance mapping process.

The assurance map on the left in Figure 14.4 shows how the risk-aligned rating of confidence (based on the example ratings shown in Table 14.1 in Step 1) is applied to record the results of the risk assurance prior to considering the quality of the risk assurance activity. We refer to this as the initial assurance map at Level 3 of the mapping process.

On the left of Figure 14.4, we show the Level 2 assurance map from Figure 13.2 in the last chapter. With the combined criteria, as discussed above in Figure 14.3, we show the resulting assurance map at the bottom of Figure 14.4. This is enlarged in Figure 14.5 for clarity.

Given the discussions of the assurance mapping process in the preceding chapters, we have skirted over the details of the mapping process itself in this chapter. It is worth, however, noting some practical issues when assessing the results of risk assurance activity. The results of assurance do not always lend themselves directly to being assessed – by any criteria for that matter – usually because some assurance reports, for example, performance indicators and management information 'dashboards' are broad in their application. Judgment will be necessary for assessing the relevance of these indicators to determine how, and if, they provide any insights into the strength of underlying controls in managing a particular risk or business activity. Performance indicators and

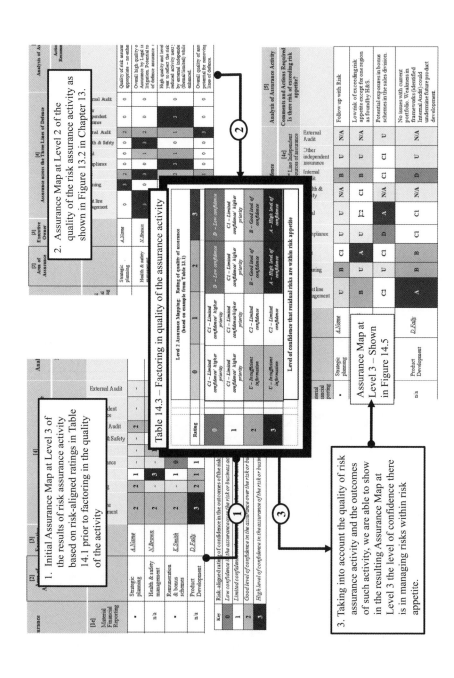

Figure 14.4   Summary of Steps in Mapping Integrated Assurance at Level 3

[1] Reason(s) for Assurance			[2] Area of Assurance	[3] Executive Owner	[4] Assurance across the Three Lines of Defence									[5] Analysis of Assurance Activity
					[4a] 1st Line Functions	[4b] 2nd Line Functions Sources of assurance					[4c] 3rd Line Independent Sources of assurance			Comments and Actions Required. Is there risk of exceeding risk appetite?
[1a] Principal Risk	[1b] Core Activity	[1c] Material Financial Reporting			Front line management	Planning	Risk	Compliance	Legal	Health & Safety	Internal Audit	Other independent assurance	External Audit	
• #1	•	•	Strategic planning	A.Name	U	B	C1	U	U	N/A	B	U	N/A	Follow up with Risk
• #2	•	n/a	Health & safety management	N.Brown	B	U	A	U	U	C1	B	U	N/A	Low risk of exceeding risk appetite except for one region as found by H&S.
• #3	•	•	Remuneration & bonus schemes	K.Smith	C2	U	C1	D	A	N/A	C1	C1	U	Potential exposures in bonus schemes in the sales division.
n/a	•	n/a	Product Development	D.Falby	A	B	B	C1	C1	N/A	D	U	N/A	No issues with current portfolio. Weakness in frameworks (identified Internal Audit) could undermine future product development.

KEY:

Confidence Rating at Level 3 (derivation as shown in Figure 14.3)

Risk Aligned Rating	Level 2 Rating – Quality of assurance			
	0	1	2	3
0	C1 – Limited confidence/priority	C1 – Limited confidence/priority	D – Low confidence	D – Low confidence
1	C1 – Limited confidence/priority	C1 – Limited confidence/priority	C1 – Limited confidence/priority	C1 – Limited confidence/priority
2	U – Insufficient information	C2 – Limited confidence	B – Good level of confidence	B – Good level of confidence
3	U – Insufficient information	C2 – Limited confidence	A – High level of confidence	A – High level of confidence

Level 3 Rating - Level of confidence that residual risks are within risk appetite

Figure 14.5   Example of Integrated Assurance Mapping at Level 3 – Overall Level of Confidence in Risk Assurance

management information dashboards that are aligned with the organisation's risk tolerances and limits reduce the need for interpretation. Where judgement is required, the following questions help provide the required focus:

- Do any of the indicators help assure the board, and senior management, that the risk under consideration is being managed appropriately and, if so, to what level of confidence as defined by the rating criteria?

- Do any of the indicators help assure the board and senior management that the relevant systems of internal control and risk mitigation plans are operating appropriately and, if so, to what level of confidence as defined by the rating criterion?

Like Level 2, the mapping of risk assurance activity against each principal risk and core business activity at Level 3 is carried out methodically by considering the assessments of the relevant risk assurance activity and recorded on the assurance map. The conclusions and noteworthy remarks are captured depending on the particular uses of the assurance map at Level 3, which we consider in the next section.

Stage Two – Promoting Shared Risk Intelligence

We now consider the second element of integrated assurance at Level 3. To a large extent, this stage refers to using the aggregate view of the assessments of the assurance for facilitating and promoting shared intelligence across the organisation. The goal is to increase the effectiveness of organisations' systems of risk management and control and, of course, risk governance.

Stage Two of the implementation process involves using the information gained from the integrated assurance maps as described above for facilitating discussion and promoting shared intelligence. It creates value from the integrated assurance mapping process. By its nature, the process at Stage Two cannot be over prescriptive as it depends on a number of factors that are unique to each organisation. This includes the scope of application, size of the organisation and maturity of its risk management. We provide, however, two useful practices for implementing Stage Two and using the integrated assurance map at Level 3 as part of the organisation's quest to gain holistic risk oversight and assurance.

FORUM FOR COLLECTIVE AND SHARED RISK INTELLIGENCE

The value of integrated assurance lies in the collective and shared knowledge of the organisation's risk picture and effectiveness of its risk mitigation efforts, which includes its systems of internal control. We discussed in Chapter 2 the importance of working across functional boundaries in order to gain such a holistic risk picture of the organisation. To this end, establishing a forum by which risks, and assurance over those risks, are discussed is essential with the following key design features:

- Appropriate membership representing key parts of the organisation and the assurance food chain that include significant business units, main assurance providers such as the risk, compliance and internal audit functions.

- A chair of the forum with appropriate mandate and authority whose main role is to facilitate open discussions, ensure effective follow through of risk mitigation plans and reporting to the relevant boards.

- Typical content and agenda items that include:

  - Horizon scanning of emerging risks and changes in the organisation's risk environment at an enterprise wide level that aims to complements rather than replace the risk management process at the local level.
  - Development of 'black swan' (or 'grey swan') scenarios and events that could stress the organisation's risk profile and business model, including the use of techniques such as reverse stress testing.
  - Assessing the residual risks and the effectiveness of the organisation's risk mitigation strategies and assurance plans, with the aim of optimising risk assurance activities across all lines of defence and addressing areas where the risk appetite of the board is being exceeded, or likely to be exceeded.

The integrated assurance map at Level 3 is a key source of information for discussion, which we consider further below in the second good practice for implementing integrated assurance at Level 3.

A common question I am asked is whether or not the work of such an *integrated risk assurance* forum should be carried out by the risk committee or its equivalent such as the risk and audit committee. The answer is one of practicality. In theory, the risk committee could include the agenda items outlined above but given the typical breadth of the terms of reference of many risk committees, it is often challenging to extend its consideration further. In smaller organisations it could be considered, especially where the likely participants of the forum are already members of the risk committee. By and large, an *integrated risk assurance* forum operates like a working group that supports the work of the risk (and audit) committee. In larger organisations, local *integrated risk assurance* working groups could be established that feed into the forum at group level.

The second common area that is typically mentioned by non-executive directors, when discussing the establishment of a forum for shared risk intelligence, is the skills and experience of its participants. This is unsurprising in view that the non-executive directors often rely on the integrity as well as the skills and experience of those providing risk evaluations. To help instil confidence in the boardroom, the chair of such a forum has the additional responsibility of ensuring continual training and development of members of the forum.

CRITICAL USE OF THE INTEGRATED ASSURANCE MAP AT LEVEL 3

Stage 2 of implementing integrated assurance at Level 3 involves the critical use of the insights provided by the assurance map. The assurance map at Level 3 contains a number of insights that include evaluations of the aggregate level of confidence the organisation can draw from its risk assurance activities and the effectiveness of its systems of risk management and internal control in line with the board's risk appetite. To help extract the appropriate insights for supporting the organisation's collective and shared risk intelligence gathering, it is useful to consider the following key boardroom-level questions as part of the process:

Q1.   What level of confidence does the assessment of the risk assurance suggest that the organisation and its board can have in the organisation's risk management and systems of control, and is this consistent with the views of the board?

Q2.   What, if any, of the principal risks or business activities require more attention, and are any of these a surprise to the board?

Q3.   Are there any discrepancies with the board's annual statement of internal control?

Q4.   What, if any, are the principal risks or business activities where risk assurance can be reduced due to unnecessary duplication or excessive attention compared to the risk appetite of the board?

Q5.   Where aspects of the board's risk appetite are being exceeded, what is the level of exposure and what remedial action is being taken?

Q6.   Is there a continuing increase in the maturity of the organisation's risk assurance, across the lines of defence, such that it is operating at or close to optimal level?

Q7.   Are there any particular areas of risk, or business activities either at group or entity level, which would benefit from a more regular assessment?

It is important to stress that aggregation of the overall confidence of risk assurance on the integrated assurance map is not an end in itself but a form of indicator to help iron out surprises and inconsistent views being provided by each line of defence. Aggregation of the results is not about trying to achieve uniformity in the views of the assurance providers but to understand the different perspectives that each might bring.

The aggregated view of assurance enables the organisation to demonstrate its multi-dimensional perspective of its risk management and the appropriateness of its risk assurance activities. More importantly, this multi-dimensional and holistic risk picture supports more confident decision making in the boardroom. Indeed, confidence in an organisation's risk assurance that is based on a methodical approach, such as that provided by integrated assurance, contributes to the organisation's capability and capacity to take risk.

Other Practical Applications at Level 3

In this section, we highlight two additional applications of integrated assurance at Level 3 which are worth considering as experience is developed in the process.

MATURITY OF RISK-BASED DECISION MAKING

One of the key insights provided by implementing integrated assurance at Level 3 is the maturity of the organisation's risk management. This is demonstrated fundamentally by the way decisions are made, in particular, how the organisation's risk appetite and tolerances are consciously applied in decision-making at the operational and strategic level.

Many organisations mainly measure the maturity of their risk management by the degree in which the risk identification, assessment and reporting is embedded in the organisation. These measurements focus on the processes rather than the resulting effects of the organisation's risk management, which includes the judgement it makes in designing and implementing its controls and risk mitigation plans – the result of which is the level of residual risk. While it is important for the organisation to understand the full potential of a risk, which is usually referred to as *gross risk*, it can be undermined by inappropriate evaluation of the effectiveness its risk mitigation efforts. The insights provided by the integrated risk assurance mapping process, and shared risk intelligence, help to develop the maturity of an organisation's approach to managing risks.

When evaluating the integrated assurance map at Level 3, it is therefore useful to highlight important observations of the maturity of the organisation's risk management and assurance approach. The frequency of the assurance mapping and reporting at Level 3 should reflect the level of change that occurs within the organisation, its use in facilitating discussions and reporting. In this regard, the frequency should be determined by the *integrated risk assurance* forum as discussed earlier.

ADHERENCE TO THE BOARD'S RISK APPETITE

Integrated assurance mapping at Level 3 enables the adherence to the board's risk appetite to be reported implicitly or explicitly. The implicit way of reporting the adherence to the board's risk appetite is embedded in the derivation of the rating or assessment criteria, as discussed earlier and illustrated in Table 14.1 and Figure 14.2. Ratings exceeding certain risk scores would be deemed to be outside the board's risk appetite. Where a board wishes the adherence of risk appetite to be reported more explicitly, the integrated assurance map can be adjusted relatively easily to include such an indicator.

In the example in Figure 14.6, the organisation has defined its risk appetite in relation to three main factors or categories – reputation risk, financial risk and business risk – where business risk includes strategic and operational risks. More granular categorisations could be used, although this would increase the level of complexity of the analysis. There are a number of ways in which risk appetite can be defined, for example, under individual tolerance and limits which have no high level categorisation. In these circumstances, we recommend that some preliminary work is carried out with the organisation's risk function to determine a set of appropriate measures or ratings which can be used to highlight instances where risk appetite has been exceeded.

Where broad categorisations are not used, a single indicator (column) may be used to merely indicate whether or not the board's risk tolerances have been exceeded in respect of the risk or business activity under consideration. The example Figure 14.6 uses a simple red/amber/green rating (or 3/2/1 scoring) to help indicate whether or not the board's risk appetite has been exceeded. The reason being that any areas where the board's risk appetite has been exceeded would require more explanation than could be reasonably provided on the assurance map.

The need to report on the adherence with the board's risk appetite is increasing, particularly at an aggregate level. In a peer review report on risk governance, the Financial Stability Board describes a risk appetite framework as 'an increasingly important tool in centralising the focus on the firm's risk profile and providing a more integrated picture of the firm's risks'.[1] The report highlights gaps in financial institutions in their reporting of an integrated view of the organisations' risks to enable the appropriate actions to be taken on deviations from the risk profile as defined by the boards. The integrated assurance map is one of the tools which can help organisations gain a better view of risk assurance in order to galvanise their defences in a holistic and aggregate way.

To Conclude this Chapter …

Broadly speaking, implementing integrated assurance at Level 3 reflects a higher level of maturity in the organisation's risk management and governance. At Level 3, the organisation is seeking to harness its collective intelligence for managing risks and understand its residual risks – with appropriate level of confidence. The assurance mapping process is seen as a source of intelligence and not an end it itself. If we allow the process to take over, assurance mapping can become more complex than necessary.

Base Assurance Map from the example in Figure 14.5

[1c]	[2] Area of Assurance	[3] Executive Owner	[4] Assurance across the Three Lines of Defence											Adherence to the Board's Risk Appetite in respect of firm's three key risk appetite factors:			[5] Analysis of Assurance Activity — Comments and Actions Required. Is there risk of exceeding risk appetite?
			[4a] 1st Line Functions	[4b] 2nd Line Functions Sources of assurance					[4c] 3rd Line Independent Sources of assurance							
			Front line management	Planning	Risk	Compliance	Legal	Health & Safety	Internal Audit	Other independent assurance	External Audit		Reputation Risk	Financial Risk	Business & Operational Risk	
.	Strategic planning	A.Name	U	B	Cl	U	U	N/A	B	U	N/A		2	2	1	Potentially more risk taking than expected in execution of the strategic plan. Bad PR with business partners has emerged for prompt attention.
n/a	Health & safety management	N.Bro	C2	U	Cl	D	A	Cl	B	U	N/A		1	1	1	Confidence in risk mitigation is high although training in a new division has been delayed. All incidents within tolerances
.	Remuneration & bonus schemes	K.Smith	A	B	Cl	Cl	Cl	N/A	Cl	Cl	U		2	1	3	Limited confidence as residual risks in sales bonus schemes are higher than specified due to delays in rolling out new changes.
n/a	Product Development	D.Folly	A	B	B	Cl	Cl	N/A	D	U	N/A		1	1	2	Overall confidence limited due mainly to weakness in frameworks (identified by Internal Audit) could undermine future product development.

Key	Rating of adherence to risk appetite
1	Risk appetite or tolerances has not been exceeded
2	Risk appetite or tolerances exceeded temporarily with limited consequence
3	Risk appetite or tolerances exceeded with potential material consequences

Figure 14.6   Example of Integrated Assurance Mapping at Level 3 – Explicit Reference to the Board's Risk Appetite

Once started, and with experience, the assurance mapping and rating criteria can be simplified to suit the aims of the organisation. As for application at Levels 1 and 2, it is important that we constantly remind ourselves of the purpose of mapping the assessments of risk assurance. Given the potential for the assurance map to look 'busy' and complex, it is worth reiterating that simplicity in the ratings (indicators) is recommended.

It is also important to give appropriate attention to providing the narrative or commentary in respect of the aggregated assessments. The evaluations and discussions they generate add great value to the process. The ratings and assessments are, after all, only indicators which by definition have their limitations in providing a full picture without an appropriate qualitative commentary. A good report would be incomplete without identifying the assumptions and limitations of its assessments. Assumptions and limitations may include:

- scope of the integrated assurance mapping in respect of entities and business areas of the group;

- particular focus in terms of risks or business activities;

- underlying assumptions in respect of the nature or quality of the assurance providers.

Integrated assurance Level 3 should be used as a tool to help the organisation and its boards optimise the volume of risk assurance activities across the organisation as well as sharpen its oversight of risks in the boardroom. The process supports collective and shared risk intelligence across all lines of defence in the organisation, which is essential to raising confidence in the boardroom that principal risks are being considered both today and around the corner. As one non-executive director would remind us that confidence is about knowledge and trust – that risks are being managed in accordance with expectations – and actions will be taken when expected.

Key Points from this Chapter

1.	The value within Level 3 integrated assurance lies in the collective and shared risk intelligence gained from working across functional boundaries in the review of risks and of the effectiveness of the organisation's risk management and control strategies in a holistic way.

2.   Integrated assurance mapping at Level 3 facilitates the process of shared risk intelligence and the board's risk governance and oversight, which include supporting the organisation's statement of internal control and clear understanding of its residual risks.

3.   Defining the rating criteria at Level 3 assurance mapping involves alignment with the organisation's risk management and risk appetite framework, which enables an evaluation of the level of confidence the organisation can have in the effectiveness of the underlying systems of risk management and control.

4.   Clear focus on the purpose of integrated assurance mapping is critical to avoiding the process becoming a compliance exercise, that can neither be sustained in the long run nor deliver the benefits required in the boardroom.

Endnotes

[1]   Financial Stability Board, 'Thematic Review on Risk Governance – Peer Review Report', February 2013. Retrieved 15 February 2013 http://www.financialstabilityboard.org/publications/r_130212. htm, Section 2.2 on Risk Management Tools.

Chapter 15

Getting Started

Having considered the case and vision for integrated assurance in Parts I and II of the book, and the different levels at which integrated assurance can be applied in the preceding chapters, in this chapter we examine the *key questions* to get started on the path to implementing integrated assurance.

Introduction

If it is not already obvious from the preceding chapters, successful implementation of integrated assurance involves significant commitment by the organisation in terms of time and resources. In particular, we discussed in Chapter 6 the need for organisations to *rethink* the concept of assurance in order to improve the oversight and level of confidence our boards could have in our organisation's system of risk management and internal controls.

The way we seek assurance and give assurance within the assurance food chain requires more conscious thought and action. Ensuring that we have a joined up assurance food chain will affect people, policies and processes across the organisation. For some organisations, implementing an integrated assurance framework could therefore involve significant change. Following the disciplines of an enterprise wide change programme would be sensible. Most organisations will have an established change, and project management, approach. Getting assistance and support from the organisation's change management team should be considered, particularly if implementing integrated assurance in a large organisation on a group wide basis.

To assist organisations in getting started with an approach that is unique to their needs and circumstances, we suggest considering the following five key questions:

- Question 1   What is the nature of the problem?

- Question 2   How mature is risk management in the organisation?

- Question 3   What is the mindset of the organisation?

- Question 4   What resources and expertise are required?

- Question 5   What is the scope of the implementation?

In terms of importance, Question 1 is essential for gaining clarity over the issues or areas of risk governance which integrated assurance could help to address. It prompts the appropriate consideration of Questions 2, 3 and 4 in order that the options for scoping of the implementation can be examined in Question 5.

To provide further clarity for determining implementation options, it helps to also discuss the expected benefits from the process. A clear understanding of the success criteria and reasons for implementing integrated assurance is useful for handling challenges that arise when the objectives of the plan become diluted and blurred through passage of time, especially when implementation spans over a long period, for example, when implementing in a large organisation. We consider the potential benefits organisations can gain from implementing integrated assurance and success criteria in the last two sections of this chapter.

Key Question #1 – What is the Nature of the Problem?

Part I of the book discusses the rationale for integrated assurance which has general application. Each organisation, however, has its particular issues and needs that are unique to its operating model, strategic aims and stage of development. It is therefore essential to gain clarity of the problem within the organisation so that the implementation is framed and started appropriately. This requires looking beyond the initial statement of the problem or symptoms of weak risk governance, for example, insufficient confidence in the effective management of a particular risk or the internal audit plan.

In other words, it is necessary to understand the underlying causes or contributory factors of risk governance, which include the maturity of risk management, risk culture or mindset as well as the skills and expertise available in the organisation. These considerations are covered by Questions 2, 3 and 4. They will influence the way the problem is ultimately defined, including the nature and size of the problem as well as the pace at which integrated assurance can be implemented. This, in turn, affects the implementation approach and how the project is started. For example, where risk management is not well established, some preliminary steps may be required to agree the principal risks against which assurance is required. There may also be resource constraints requiring the implementation to be re-sized or phased in.

To help with this process, it is useful to consult colleagues and key stakeholders by asking them for their opinion on what is, and what is not, working in the organisation, and what good looks like. This will help to ensure that the problems are articulated in the words of the stakeholders while securing buy-in for the project from the outset and during the process. For illustrative purposes we set out, in Tables 15.1–3, three common problems and their associated consequences which could be adapted for preparing the rationale for implementing the framework in your organisation. The three common problems considered are:

- There is duplication of assurance reporting across all lines of defence. This can occur between line management and other key assurance functions such as risk, compliance, internal audit, information security, other quality assurance areas as well as external audit.

- There are gaps in the organisation's management of risks and system of internal controls.

- The executive and/or the board (including its subcommittees such as the risk and audit committees) do not feel sufficiently confident that the organisation's risk management and system of internal controls are as robust as they should be, particularly in the current economic and regulatory environment. Furthermore, in anticipation of changes in the organisation's strategy, the executive and the board may be concerned that the current approach to risk assurance may not be fit for purpose. A fresh look at the organisation's assurance framework is required.

In summary, Question 1 prompts additional questions to be considered to aid better understanding the underlying problems in relation to risk assurance so that the organisation can determine the most appropriate level and scope at which integrated assurance should be implemented.

Table 15.1   Example Problem #1

Problem #1
Duplication of assurance reporting across all lines of defence. This can occur between line management and other key assurance functions such as risk, compliance, internal audit, information security, other quality assurance areas as well as external audit.

Causes and contributory factors
The main causal factors include:
- Silo approach to managing risks and/or organising assurance activities;
- Unclear specification or understanding of the respective responsibilities across the three lines of defence which can only be expected to increase without any positive intervention;
- Increased assurance activities in response to changes in regulatory and governance requirements; the expected trajectory of the approach of regulation that is more value and principles based will only increase the proliferation of assurance activities and aggravate the problem.

Consequence & impact
As a consequence, the business is likely to be experiencing:
- Inefficient use of resources and unnecessary costs;
- Duplicated reporting at both the board and executive management levels, resulting in potential conflicting picture of risks and controls as well as obscured vision of the real risks that matter; it also makes it difficult for appropriate challenge and discussion in the board room;
- Emergence of *turf wars* and lack of cooperation between the lines of defence, which can also further affect the efficient and effective operation at the local and organisation group level.

Table 15.2   Example Problem #2

Problem #2
There are gaps in the organisation's management of risks and system of internal controls. In defining the problem, it is useful to quote examples of known areas of risks where little or no assurance is being provided in the organisation, or where assurance is merely the verification of compliance rather than the integrity and effectiveness of the risk mitigation arrangements. Refer to Chapter 6 on Rethinking Assurance.

Causes and contributory factors
The main causal factors are similar to those for Problem #1.

Consequence and impact
As a consequence, the business could be experiencing:
- Unwanted surprises in the executive and board room where the board's risk appetite may have been exceeded or there is more frequent occurrences of near misses;
- Management distraction from more strategic matters in the business;
- Uninvited attention (or its potential risk of attention) from regulators.

Table 15.3   Example Problem #3

Problem #3
The executive and/or the board (including its subcommittees such as the risk and audit committees) do not feel sufficiently confident that the organisation's risk management and system of internal controls are as robust as they should be particularly in the current economic and regulatory environment. Furthermore, in anticipation of changes in the organisation's strategy, the executive and the board are concerned that the current approach to risk assurance may not be fit for purpose. A fresh look at the organisation's assurance framework is required.

Causes and contributory factors
The main causal factors include:
- Cumulative changes in the organisation's business model or strategy in recent years, which may not have been matched by adjustments in the relevant risk assurance and oversight activities.
- Delivery of the organisation's new strategy or business plans requires a more robust and holistic approach to the assurance of the organisation's risk taking and tolerance capability.
- Underlying weaknesses in organisation's risk management in the way new and emerging risks are identified, assessed and reported.
- Limited skills in the risk management and internal audit functions.
- Rising standards of governance and increasing breadth of board oversight means that a more efficient approach to assurance is necessary to help boards and senior management to focus on the more strategic matters while also demonstrating a high standard of governance.

Consequence and impact
As a consequence, the executive and/or the board could be experiencing:
- An increasing overload of assurance reporting that appears to confuse rather than inspire confidence in the organisation's ability to take risks sensibly within the board's risk appetite or the organisation's capacity for accepting risks.
- Unnecessary attention and distraction on operational matters of process in controls and risk management rather than the decisions and the oversight of decisions relating to strategic matters of the business.
General feeling of discomfort and concerns over the board's ability to demonstrate sound governance to its stakeholders that include its investors, customers, business partners and regulators. The discomfort may be arising from gut feel, actual events or remarks from the regulator regarding the robustness and completeness of the board's risk oversight and quality of assurance.

Key Question #2 – How Mature is Risk Management?

On the basis that assurance and the effective management of risk are intrinsically linked, it is unsurprising that the maturity of the organisation's risk management framework plays an important part in influencing the way integrated assurance is implemented. Risk management underpins the integrated assurance process in three main ways:

1.   Identification of the principal risks at the start of the integrated assurance mapping process.

2.   Assessment and evaluation of the effectiveness of controls and risk mitigation plans by all assurance providers.

3.   Application of the organisation's risk appetite by all assurance providers in their assessments and decision making.

In an organisation where risk management is well established, that is, where there is a defined system of policies and procedures for managing risks in line with the organisation's risk appetite, aligning the approach for integrated assurance will be more straightforward than in an organisation which has yet to define its risk management methodology. In other words, a less risk mature organisation will require some additional steps to be included in its implementation plan, such as:

- Developing and agreeing a common approach for evaluating the effectiveness of controls and risk mitigation by assurance providers; refer to Chapter 14, in particular, Figures 14.1 and 14.2 for example risk rating criteria.

- Agreeing a set of principal risks with senior stakeholders at the start of the integrated assurance mapping process.

These additional steps are constructive in developing risk management, and the case for implementing integrated assurance is increased rather than reduced in an organisation where risk management is less developed. An organisation that is unclear, or has inconsistent views, of its risks faces a greater challenge in aligning its assurance and oversight requirements. Organisations with less mature risk management practices would benefit from implementing integrated assurance up to Level 2. For these organisations, integrated assurance can be a catalyst and a positive influence for developing a holistic approach to risk management and oversight from the outset.

In summary, the maturity of the organisation's risk management will influence the overall size of the project, including number of additional steps that may or may not be required to get the integrated assurance project started. This in turn impacts on the type of resources required and the pace at which the project can be implemented.

Key Question #3 – What is the Mindset of the Organisation?

The approach and ease at which integrated assurance is implemented will also be influenced by the mindset of the organisation at the outset, in particular, the perception of the key stakeholders in the assurance food chain. The mindset of the organisation in this context refers to the level of buy-in and overall appreciation of the concept integrated assurance. Clearly, the greater the level of buy-in and shared vision, the lower the need for an aggressive communication or educational plan to secure a champion for integrated assurance at the top of the organisation.

Given the regulatory drivers for integrated assurance as discussed in Part 1 of the book, the initial proposal for such a framework is likely to be suggested by a director responsible for governance and risk management, such as the chair of the audit and/or risk committee, director of risk or internal audit. Conceptually, we categorise organisations who wish to implement an integrated assurance framework into three main types:

1.   *The Converted*, which refers to those who know why they want to implement an integrated assurance framework and have already started.

2.   *The Inspired*, which refers to those who know why they should implement integrated assurance but face some practical challenges and as a result, may not have started or have made limited progress.

3.   *The Encouraged*, those who have been encouraged by their boards to implement such a framework, or who might have heard from their peers about the concept but have yet to fully understand and be convinced of its benefits.

Those organisations falling into *The Converted* and *The Inspired* categories may need less help than others in defining the conceptual benefits for implementing integrated assurance. For those organisations that need more inspiration or help, the Key Points at the end of each chapter in Parts I and II provide the basis for developing their proposals. To help with the process, we anticipate some key questions which may be asked at the outset for strength testing the proposal:

1.   What problem is the framework trying to address?

2.   Is this the only solution to the problem?

3.   Who is going to benefit from its implementation?

4.   How are the expected benefits – tangible or intangible to be measured?

5.   How do the benefits contribute to the strategic aims of the organisation?

6.   What is needed to deliver the framework successfully and at what cost?

The answers may be obvious to those in the *Converted* and *Inspired* camps but within any organisation there are many hardnosed directors and managers who like to ensure that any investment in non-frontline activities are not only meaningful but have tangible benefits for the organisation. Many hardnosed directors and managers would also recognise that building confidence in the boardroom, which is the ultimate aim of an integrated assurance framework, cannot be priced.

Identifying and securing the buy-in of the key stakeholders in the organisation's integrated assurance framework is critical to successful implementation of the framework. Early identification of the key stakeholders is also necessary for shaping the communication strategy and formal set up of the project which includes mobilising the resources required. The key stakeholders of such a project fall under four main groups in the assurance food chain either as assurance providers or users of assurance:

1.   Boards and their sub-committees, particularly those with delegated responsibility for overseeing risk management and internal control.

2.   Executive management, as owners of the integrated assurance framework.

3.   The Executive Sponsor or champion of the integrated assurance framework.

4.   Key internal assurance providers across the three lines of defense.

The last three groups broadly represent the key players in the assurance food chain which are accountable for supporting the governance requirements of the boards and their sub-committees. In summary, knowing the mindset of the stakeholders and the starting position of the organisation helps to inform the approach required for instigating the project, in particular, the areas that relate to:

- Strategy for gaining buy-in and the challenge or ease at which allies and a visible champion at the top are available.

- Problem definition and the depth of work required to document and articulate the rationale for integrated assurance.

- Communication strategy and the need for preliminary discussions with key stakeholders in the assurance food chain.

The objective of the communication strategy and plan is to secure 'hearts and minds' and to gain approval for the project to be implemented. The communication strategy broadly consists of a plan for reaching each type or set of stakeholders, recognising that each set of stakeholders may require a different communication style, approach, as well as different timing. In this regard, where possible, it is useful to adopt an interactive approach particularly for stakeholders at the management level to refine the implementation approach and identify challenges to implementation that may not have been previously identified. Typical content of the communication plan for each set of stakeholders includes aspects of the following areas in greater or lesser degree of detail:

- Rationale for implementing integrated assurance in the organisation including an appreciation of the problem the framework is aimed to address, and the benefits it is expected to deliver.

- Scope of the programme, for example, group wide, an entity or business activities (see Key Question #4 below).

- Approach for rolling out the programme, for example, pilot scheme and phasing.

- Stakeholders in the assurance food chain and their respective roles in the project.

- Time scales.

- Project governance and oversight.

- Challenges, inter-dependencies and risks to the plan.

The case studies in Part IV of the book provide some practical examples of the way different champions at the top, and the vision they have, can influence the approach to implementing integrated assurance. For example, case studies 1, 2, 7 and 9 were inspired or encouraged by non-executive members of the board including the chair of the respective organisations' audit committees; the chief executive was behind two other case studies while the chief risk officers and chief internal auditors were the visionaries in the remaining case studies.

Key Question #4 – What Resources and Expertise are Required?

We begin our deliberations for Question 4 by distinguishing between the type of resources that are required for managing the project and those required for developing, implementing and maintaining the integrated assurance framework. We also discussed in Questions 1–2 the considerations for particular resources and skills that may be required to address the underlying issues, such as risk management expertise, which integrated assurance is expected to resolve.

The need for specialist project management support depends on the size of the organisation and scope of the implementation, and available resources of the business area leading the implementation. It also depends on the level at which integrated assurance is implemented to deliver the expected objectives, as discussed earlier. The considerations for resources are therefore set out for broad application.

In addition to project implementation skills, the expertise required for developing and maintaining an integrated assurance framework are typified broadly by those working in risk management and assurance functions, in particular:

- Understanding of the concepts of risk management at the strategic as well as operational level, for ensuring sharp focus on the principal risks for which assurance is required.

- Understanding of the concepts of internal control and their link to the effective management of risk and risk appetite.

- Appreciation of systems of governance and the obligations of the board in the assurance food chain.

- Ability to work across functional boundaries.

At a practical level, expertise is also required for the development of methodologies and underlying processes for supporting the assurance mapping process. Other resources required to support the implementation are those in the assurance food chain. Their input is the provision of information required during the integrated assurance mapping process although the effort required should not be substantial. It is worth noting that the clearer the definition of roles and responsibilities across the three lines of defence, the smaller the impact on the resources required in the implementation.

The governance of the implementation project should be broadly guided by the organisation's governance structures, identified sponsors and stakeholders of the integrated assurance framework. The progress of the project can be monitored by a unique governance body or as part of an existing governance body such as the executive board. The executive owner of the framework plays a key role in advising on the governance requirements of the project.

The project team would typically consist of the executive owner and operational owner of the integrated assurance framework and individuals who would be carrying out the detailed assurance mapping process, coordinating and facilitating the approval of the methodologies and outputs of the project. The operational owner of the Framework may also take on the role of project manager or assign the project manager role to a dedicated resource.

Based mainly on skills and knowledge, the operational owner of the framework is typically sourced from, or with, a background in risk management or internal audit. This is borne out by the case studies in Part IV of the book. The facilitation skills that are usually found in the risk and internal audit functions further lend themselves well to supporting the implementation of such a framework. The Chartered Institute of Internal Auditors have indicated in its professional briefing for coordinating assurance[1] that the internal audit function may facilitate but not own the integrated assurance map as this may compromise the independence of internal audit. This, however, depends on whether or not the assurance map is mainly used to support the internal audit planning process.

It is also worth acknowledging that the resources for implementing the framework may be different to that required for sustaining and maintaining the framework after *Day One* of implementation. The executive and operational owners of the framework are probably the two common denominators at the start of the project and after implementation. As the framework matures, responsibilities may also develop, for example, as seen in one organisation where a dedicated 'Corporate Risk Assurance' team was set up for maintaining and evolving the framework on an on-going basis.

Where appropriate, an organisation should consider using third parties to bolster limited internal resources or skill sets to help jump-start the project and lay the foundations of the framework implemented. External help may be used, for example, in defining and developing the methodologies for the assurance mapping process or aligning the risk management and assurance procedures. However, care should be taken to avoid over reliance on external resources as this could dilute the benefits inherent in the implementation process.

Key Question #5 – What is the Scope of the Implementation?

The considerations in Questions 1–4 come together to help to determine the options that are most practical and feasible for an organisation. There are a number of options for scoping implementation of integrated assurance and the choice is influenced broadly by four main considerations:

1. the nature and size of the problem;

2. mindset, size and complexity of the structures of the organisation;

3. speed at which the framework is required, which could be influenced by the nature of the problem or immediacy of the benefits expected; and

4. resources available.

In practical terms, the scope of implementation refers to how deep and wide the assurance mapping process and integrated discussions across lines of defence will be taken into the organisation. This means that integrated assurance can be implemented at a group or entity level, or risk or process level, each level of which is explained below. These options are illustrated diagrammatically in Figure 15.1.

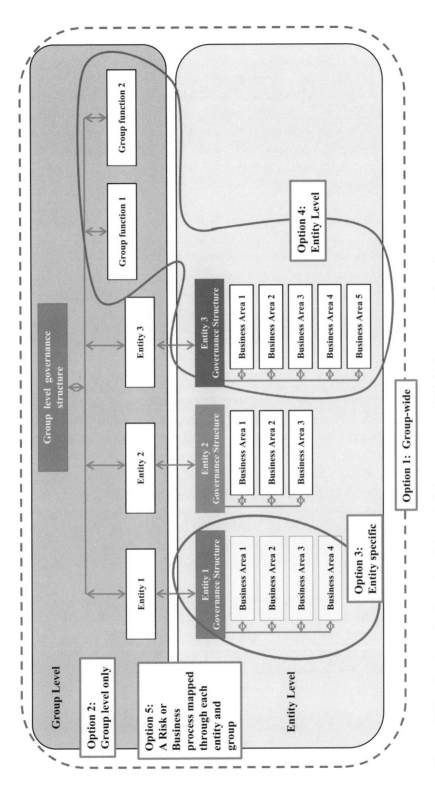

Figure 15.1   Options for Scoping Integrated Assurance and Risk Assurance Mapping

GROUP LEVEL

At the group level, the scoping of integrated assurance and its mapping process can be interpreted in two ways. Firstly, it could be implemented across the whole group (shown as Option 1 in Figure 15.1). Secondly, integrated assurance could be implemented only at the highest tier of the organisation – at group level functions to provide an aggregate and holistic view of risk assurance (shown as Option 2 in Figure 15.1). The mapping of assurance in either scope follows the same principles as described in Chapter 11.

Implementation at the group level is an effective way for gaining an overview of the programme of risk assurance activities (application at Levels 1 and 2) as well as the picture of residual risks based on the conclusions of the assurance activities (application at Level 3). It could be applied with limited resources to provide an initial reading of risk assurance planning and/or residual risks across the organisation before conducting any 'deeper dives' into particular areas of risks or business activities (see Case Study 7).

ENTITY LEVEL

An entity in this context refers to a business unit or subsidiary of an organisation. Integrated assurance and risk assurance mapping can be implemented within an entity for the purpose of providing an aggregate risk and assurance picture to the boards at the entity level quite successfully before attempting to roll it out to other entities across the organisation. This incremental approach is useful as a form of pilot exercise where the process can be used to *test and learn* prior to full implementation. Some organisations call it a *do and learn* pilot. Pilot implementations are useful, particularly for larger organisations where the enormity of the task is itself a challenge in its own right (see Case Study 3). Implementation at entity level is shown as Options 3 and 4 in Figure 15.1.

Having a visible advocate or executive champion at the entity level will be particularly useful as a springboard to full implementation across the group. In this regard, it is important to select an appropriate entity to pilot which can be held as the *leading light* for implementing integrated assurance across the organisation. The following are some key characteristics for selecting an appropriate entity to pilot the implementation:

- Presence of a visible and respected advocate or champion at the executive level within the entity. These individuals would serve to inspire others in the organisation in implementing integrated assurance.

- Known issues relating to the entity's risk assurance such as duplication of effort or gaps in the assurance supply chain, which would benefit from an end-to-end assurance mapping exercise.

- Concerns at group level over the adequacy of oversight of the entity or of the effectiveness or quality of the assurance received.

RISK OR PROCESS LEVEL

Applying integrated assurance in respect of a risk, process or particular business activity is the lowest denomination level at which the risk assurance mapping can be conducted. This is essentially the starting point for understanding and practising the mapping process. This involves taking a particular risk or business process through each step of the mapping process. The single risk or business process can also be considered for a business entity before widening the mapping to the other entities throughout the group. This is shown as Option 5 in Figure 15.1.

Some organisations may choose to only map a particular area of risk or business activity as a pilot while buy-in for a full integrated assurance framework is obtained or if constrained by resources. Table 15.4 provides examples of areas for assurance at the risk or business process level. They are usually selected because of regulatory attention or are commonly understood areas of control which lend themselves well for piloting and practising the mapping process.

In summary, as shown in Figure 15.1, there are five options for scoping the mapping of integrated assurance across an organisation, which allows for a phased and incremental approach to implementing integrated assurance:

Option 1:   Group-wide, involving all entities and business functions at group and entity levels.

Option 2:   Group level only, based on the assurance that is in place from a group perspective.

Option 3:   Entity or subsidiary level specific, providing an integrated assurance view that is limited from the entity's perspective.

Option 4: A variant of Option 3, whereby the assurance provided by group level functions is brought into scope.

Option 5: Particular focus on a risk, or business process, that is tracked through each entity and group level function.

Like any project, how quickly the integrated assurance framework is implemented will depend on the urgency of the identified needs, the priorities set by the key stakeholders, scope of the implementation and level of availability of resources. It is also worth considering the organisation's change agenda and business cycles, which may affect the availability of resources required in the implementation.

Table 15.4   Examples of Specific Areas of Risks or Processes for Risk Assurance Mapping

Example Area for Risk Assurance	Typical reason for attention and/or piloting risk assurance mapping	
	Specific interest of risk oversight	Common Area of Control
Acquisitions, mergers and due diligence	•	
Budgetary control and management		•
Code of conduct compliance	•	•
Environmental risks	•	•
Health and safety		•
Information security management		•
Outsourced arrangements and management	•	
Overseas oversight	•	
People recruitment and vetting process		•
Product and service development	•	
A specific risk class, which are popular in financial services organisations that include: • market risk • credit risk • insurance risk • liquidity risk • operational risk	•	
Strategy and business planning	•	

There are clearly a number of ways in which assurance mapping can be scoped and made manageable when implementing an integrated assurance framework. In other words, the project is framed according to the nature of the problem, size of the organisation and speed at which implementation is required. Attempting to implement the framework across very large organisations in one step is daunting. A phased or pilot approach is practical and enables implementation to be managed in bite-size chunks particularly in large organisations and/or where resources are limited.

However the scope is cut, it is worth reiterating that as a process, assurance mapping is not an end in itself but a route for gaining better insights to the organisation's risk governance and finding more value in the assurance food chain. By way of summary, Figure 15.2 sets out the options for scoping and applying integrated assurance and its mapping process at one of the three main levels.

Specifying the Benefits

The case for implementing integrated assurance should be cemented by the expected benefits. Depending on the exact nature of the problem, the five main types of benefits that could be gained from a successful implementation of integrated assurance include:

Level		Purpose of mapping	Main application	Typical Frequency	Scoping Options		
					Risk or Process Level	Entity Level	Group-wide
1	Risk Assurance Planning	Coverage: To identify gaps and overlaps in the contribution of risk assurance across all lines of defence	To inform risk assurance planning, in particular, internal audit planning	Audit planning cycle	▪	▪	▪
2	Enhancing Risk Assurance	Quality: To determine the quality of assurance contributed from each line of defence in order to assess areas for improving and optimising risk oversight	To improve and gain optimal value from risk assurance activities that include promoting greater accountability	Periodically as required	▪	▪	▪
3	Integrated Risk Oversight & Assurance	Confidence: To determine the overall level of confidence the organisation has of its system of risk management by aggregating the conclusions of risk assurance activity across all lines of defence	To harness shared and collective intelligence in order to gain a holistic risk and assurance picture, for challenging and improving the effectiveness of risk management	Half yearly, or at least annually	▪	▪	▪

Figure 15.2   Integrated Assurance – A Summary of Options for Scoping and Application

I. STRATEGIC BENEFITS

These benefits may arise from more confident decision making that is afforded by a holistic risk and assurance picture. By ensuring that assurance is fully integrated and aligned with the management of principal risks of the organisation, the board and its management are better positioned to make optimal decisions on risks they could take, accept or avoid. Confidence in the quality of assurance they are getting allows them to focus on more strategic matters.

2. FINANCIAL BENEFITS

Financial benefits may arise from the reduction in unnecessary duplication of effort in providing assurance at both the operational level and in the board room. The effect may be counterbalanced by the need to address gaps in the assurance activities although the net effect is likely to be a positive contribution because integrated assurance:

- promotes clarity of the assurance activities that is meaningful in relation to the principal risks of the business; and,

- enables management and the board to oversee the key decisions that matter to the sound running of the business and successful delivery of the business plans.

Tangible financial benefits could be estimated in terms of the release of duplicated resources and reduced assurance activity where there is no added value to the effective oversight of risks. Other benefits which are more difficult to measure include opportunity costs arising from reduced board and management distraction on operational issues and improved focus on managing those risks that could obstruct the successful delivery of the business plans. The reality is that it is probably impractical to attempt to measure the indirect tangible financial benefits that include subjective factors such as increased confidence and effective decision making.

3. OPERATIONAL EFFICIENCY

These benefits may arise through clearer understanding, better coordination and improvements in control processes across functional boundaries. Functions that should benefit particularly from better coordination across the lines of defence include risk, finance, compliance and internal audit. Tangible benefits arise where ineffective processes are identified, and associated recurrent costs are removed, although these may only be measured fully after implementation of the project.

4. PEOPLE RELATED BENEFITS

These benefits can arise through better understanding of people's respective responsibilities and improved performance at the individual and team level. Building effective relationships are intangible benefits that are not readily measurable but can affect improvements in efficiencies and confident delivery of the organisation's strategy and business plans. A culture of collaboration and joined-up thinking is also a benefit that could arise that is assessable over time.

5. REGULATORY RELATED BENEFITS

These benefits may arise in the form of management's ability to demonstrate with greater confidence the organisation's corporate governance and risk management policies. The costs of regulatory action, particularly in financial services, have been rising and are not expected to decline. The cost of investing in the framework is small compared to the cost of organisational distraction and management time required to rework and to address areas of governance and risk management that do not meet the current standards of regulation.

While there are several benefits we can point to when implementing integrated assurance, undoubtedly, there are implementation costs – particularly opportunity costs in respect of the time involved in getting the project started. By and large, implementing integrated assurance for the first time is likely to incur significant costs. In attempting to track efficiency savings, we should ensure that the effort does not outweigh the benefits of doing so. Where overlaps and duplication of effort are already being experienced, it is questionable as to its value in spending disproportionate amount of time to measure savings that could be achieved in implementing integrated assurance. A pragmatic approach is encouraged. Integrated assurance, if implemented practically, should be capable of delivering tangible benefits as a result of more efficient and risk informed decision making in the business.

Defining the Success Criteria

To complete the storyboard for the business case for implementing integrated assurance, it is helpful to consider ahead what success looks like. The success criteria can be defined at a high level with reference to the definition of the problem(s) and potential benefits, and which encompasses the key objectives of the project. Example statements for describing success include:

1.   Increased confidence and efficiency in the boardroom and overall improvement in management's risk and internal control at board level, which is attributable to a better focus on risk assurance rather than compliant operation of controls.

2.   Duplication in assurance activities across the three lines of defence are identified and removed appropriately.

3.   Greater collaboration and collective intelligence across functional boundaries is ensuring more timely identification of evolving and emerging risks, against which effective assurance can be determined.

4.   Gaps in respect of assurances required of principal risks are identified and responsibilities are allocated appropriately across the three lines of defence.

5.   The establishment of an assurance map and a mapping process gives appropriate focus on the *big ticket* risks and integrity of key controls.

6.   Rationalisation of assurance reporting at executive and board level, resulting in a more coordinated board agenda across its sub-committees.

The challenge here is clearly one of quantification and measurement. Like the earlier discussion on the benefits of implementing integrated assurance, the success factors are not always readily measurable. Unless disproportionate cost and time is incurred, measurement of success is likely to be subjective but success will be evident in the way the problems are addressed and impact the assurance stakeholders, and in particular, those in the boardroom. The degree of subjectivity can however be reduced by canvassing the views of board members and key assurance stakeholders.

To Conclude this Chapter ...

As a first step to implementing integrated assurance, it is essential to know the reasons why. Clear understanding of the problems the organisation is facing in relation to its risk oversight, or benefits it could enjoy with integrated assurance, enables an appropriate implementation approach to be determined. It is important that the problem is defined at a practical level, taking into account the constraints capacity as well as the capabilities of the organisation, or we risk trying to implement a project that is too big to manage – setting the project for failure.

The practical considerations include the communication strategy to gain buy-in, the level at which integrated assurance will be applied, the scope and pace of implementation and the resources required. Understanding the mindset of the organisation and its assurance stakeholders is essential for shaping the communication strategy, which will vary between the converted, the inspired and the encouraged. To implement integrated assurance successfully, it is worth stressing the importance of maintaining focus on the reasons for getting started – at the start, middle and at the end – of the implementation plan. Chapter 16 which discusses the main implementation challenges and the case studies set out in Part IV of the book provide further insights to developing an approach for addressing the particular needs of one's organisation.

Key Points from this Chapter

1. Knowing the reasons for improving risk governance and risk assurance is essential to gaining buy-in for implementing integrated assurance.

2. Time spent on understanding the mindset of the key assurance stakeholders helps to refine the communication strategy to gain 'hearts and minds' and securing successful delivery of integrated assurance.

3. The risk maturity of the organisation and other constraints or strengths such as capacity and capability will influence the ultimate size and speed of the problem and implementation project.

4. In defining the problem and implementation plan, it is important that the practical constraints and strengths of the organisation

are taken into account to ensure that integrated assurance is implemented pragmatically and successfully.

5.   Tangible benefits may include greater operational efficiency although intangible benefits, such as increased confidence in the boardroom and reduced distraction from more strategic matters that are less readily measurable, are often the more important benefits.

6.   Appointing individuals with appropriate skills, and good understanding of systems of risk management and internal control, with the ability to work across functional boundaries is another success factor for implementing integrated assurance.

7.   Implementing integrated assurance should be guided by established project management standards in the organisation.

Endnotes

[1]   Chartered Institute of Internal Auditors (IIA-UK and Ireland), *Professional Guidance for Internal Auditors: Coordination of assurance services* (London, IIA-UK and Ireland, 2010), 6.

Chapter 16
Key Implementation Challenges

In this chapter we discuss the common challenges to implementing integrated assurance. By discussing these challenges, I hope we can be more alert to the potential hurdles and better prepare the path to a successful implementation of integrated assurance within our own organisations.

Introduction

The implementation challenges have been drawn from practical experiences, including my own, and from discussions in open forums as well as private discussions with organisations and board members, for example, when developing the case studies in Part IV. My analysis of implementation challenges also includes the work of a focused study on integrated assurance involving some 24 member companies of the Insurance Internal Audit Group[1] (IIAG). Collectively, the challenges experienced can be described under six main headings, which are not mutually exclusive:

Challenge #1	Absence of a universally defined framework
Challenge #2	Maturity of risk management
Challenge #3	Ownership
Challenge #4	Availability of resources and appropriate skills
Challenge #5	Champion at the top
Challenge #6	Coordination and collaboration

Each area of challenge is considered below.

Challenge #1 – Absence of a Universally Defined Framework

Knowing what to implement can be vexing when there are different views and understandings within an organisation of what integrated assurance means and what it is expected to deliver. The term means different things to different organisations as well as to different individuals within the same organisation. This is unsurprising given the many 'faces' of integrated assurance as discussed in Chapter 9 and the different ways in which the term is perceived and experienced.

Defining the purpose, and therefore the scope of implementation, is not only the most pivotal step in the implementation project but also the most challenging. This is exacerbated with the absence of a universal definition of integrated assurance. The different perceptions and expectations need to be brought in line before the vision and likely benefits to the organisation can be put forward. 'If we do not know what it is we should build as a standard, it is rather difficult to define a plan of attack', said one chairman of an audit committee. The sentiment is echoed by a number of respondents in the IIAG focused study. In a similar vein, a finance director indicated to me that he believed he had instigated integrated assurance which involves coordinating the external and internal audit plans. He added enquiringly 'although it depends on what is meant by that [term, integrated assurance]'. This finance director's remark is not uncommon. The IIAG focused study identified an unclear definition of a framework as the most common hurdle to implementing integrated assurance.

An unclear definition of integrated assurance has the potential to impact the implementation in three main ways:

1.   inability to communicate the benefits or the rationale for integrated assurance which is necessary for gaining buy-in and support;

2.   inability to define a plan of action;

3.   a mismatch in understanding between what integrated assurance can deliver and what it is perceived to be.

Implementation of an integrated assurance framework has thus far been determined intuitively by organisations based largely on their specified needs. This approach, however, means that implementation could be limited to the perceived need or problem as well as the vision of the instigator and champion of the framework. The position of the champion in the organisation, as we will consider in Challenge #5 below, will also be influential in defining the approach and pace of the project. For example, the need expressed by the board's audit committee is likely to attract more buying power than one that had been identified at a lower level in the organisation.

Rather than trusting to luck of having a high profile champion, some organisations felt that the presence of a universally agreed definition of integrated assurance would help provide a vision, and baseline standards, for implementing integrated assurance. A universally agreed definition also gives confidence to those who are inspired by the concept but unclear what is involved. Due to lack of confidence, even the inspired can be inhibited and constrained in implementing a framework that is enterprise wide.

Perhaps the model and definitions set out in this book can start to give organisations greater clarity in vision as well as confidence to determine to the options they have for defining their needs. The case studies in Part IV illustrate how a number of organisations have intuitively developed the vision as set out in this book, and with the right conditions and support, were able to realise the benefits they had envisaged.

Challenge #2 – Maturity of Risk Management

The comment that 'implementing integrated assurance is difficult – we don't have the basics of risk management in place' which I have heard from more than one organisation may sound surprising yet it reflects a key challenge for many. On the basis that effective management of risks lies at the heart of integrated assurance, the maturity of an organisation's risk management policies, standards and processes can impact significantly on the way integrated assurance is implemented in the organisation. The impact can occur in three main ways:

1. IDENTIFYING PRINCIPAL RISKS FOR THE INTEGRATED ASSURANCE MAPPING PROCESS

Knowing which risks and core business activities are most important for inclusion in the assurance map and subsequent evaluation is the foundation step for implementing integrated assurance. Where an organisation has yet to define an approach for identifying and assessing risks or threats to its business consistently across the organisation, it can impair the view of what assurance is required and where assurance activity should be directed.

2. CRITERIA FOR ASSESSING AND EVALUATING CONTROLS AND RISK MITIGATION PLANS

Assessing the significance of risks and effectiveness of controls and risk mitigation plans is integral to any risk management process. It follows that the criteria for these assessments should be applied consistently when evaluating the quality of assurance by which the effectiveness of risk management is determined. The absence of defined risk assessment criteria will increase the challenge for providing a consistent view of assurance over the organisation's management of risks. The challenge is, however, not a show stopper. It can be managed with an explicitly defined assessment criterion, as is relevant by each level of implementation of the assurance map, although it will involve judgement to moderate any variations in practice between the lines of defence. The criteria can be redefined and aligned with the organisation's eventual risk management assessment approach.

3. APPLICATION OF THE ORGANISATION'S RISK APPETITE

Intrinsic to any decision making process within an organisation is the organisation's risk tolerance and risk taking policy. Clarity in an organisation's risk appetite enables risk based decision making, which is integral to the organisation's risk management process and therefore also to the implementation of an integrated assurance framework. In particular, risk appetite and tolerances are necessary to determine the level of acceptable residual risk and how much assurance is required. The absence of a clear risk appetite policy is not, however, a show stopper in the implementation of integrated assurance as, in practice, tolerance of risk taking in organisations is defined by a number of means, including authority manuals and escalation processes. By defining the approach for assessing assurance clearly, we can mitigate the effects of an underdeveloped risk management process.

In brief, underdeveloped risk management practice should not inhibit the implementation of integrated assurance. On the contrary, the integrated assurance mapping process could be a catalyst for defining and improving the risk management framework in the organisation. Implementing integrated assurance could provide the focus needed by the organisation for developing and enhancing its risk management. The implementation approach in such an environment will however need to allow for the extra work involved and to be alert to the availability in the level of skills, resources as well as support from the top. All of these could affect the scope and pace at which integrated assurance can be implemented. At this point, it is worth noting the advice from an insightful member of the audit committee of an organisation in the United Nations, who said that the development of risk management should not be rushed as the process offers beneficial development and learning for any organisation. Taking time over the implementation can have a high payoff in developing the risk culture.

Challenge #3 – Ownership

'Who should own this?' is a question that is discussed in almost every conversation and discussion I have had on the subject of implementing integrated assurance. Ownership in this context refers to the operational level which includes maintaining the framework and its use. By and large, ownership is more readily determined when the level of application or scope is limited than when integrated assurance is applied enterprise wide. For example, at Level 1 application of integrated assurance, which is used mainly to support and demonstrate the rationale of the internal audit plan, the natural owner would be the internal audit function. Similarly, in an implementation that is limited to a particular risk or business activity, such as outsourcing risks, major change project risks, information security risks or market risks, the owner of the risk could be regarded as the natural owner of the integrated assurance process.

The challenge therefore arises, particularly when the scope of the integrated assurance covers a broad spectrum of the organisation's risks and business processes. Organisations indicate that as there is a natural tendency to working within defined functional roles and silos, finding someone to own a framework that is enterprise wide can indeed be challenging. I would attribute the challenge to four interrelated reasons, which are:

1. lack of an executive level champion for the framework;

2. insufficient clarity of the vision and the purpose of integrated assurance, which affects the clear articulation of the benefits to the board and the rest of the organisation;

3. lack of a mandate and authority for implementing integrated assurance;

4. lack of appropriate skills, experience and resources for delivering such a holistic framework.

The lack of a universally agreed definition or common understanding of integrated assurance as discussed earlier is probably a major contributor to the first three reasons. In respect of appropriate skills and experience for owning the framework, there are three main contenders – the risk management function, the internal audit function and the function responsible for coordinating the organisation's compliance with regulations such as Sarbanes-Oxley s.404 attestation or Turnbull Guidance on internal control.

Many I have spoken to, including a number of board members, intuitively associate the concept of integrated assurance with enterprise risk management. In effect, risk management underpins the philosophy of integrated assurance so there is an argument for the risk function to own this framework. The pushback from some risk functions to owning such a framework is that 'assurance' is regarded to be the preserve of the internal audit function, which unfortunately reflects a common perception and limited interpretation of the term. Many risk functions already report on the residual level of risks facing their organisations which, by definition, would have taken into consideration the effectiveness of risk mitigation strategies and management controls. The discipline of integrated assurance merely enhances the evaluation and reporting of risk assurance to the board by identifying the level of confidence the board can have in the risk mitigation activities across the organisation. I am pleased to observe that there are some risk functions who have taken ownership of the integrated assurance framework.

The second area in the organisation which could own the integrated assurance framework is the function that is responsible for facilitating the organisation's board report on management's system of control, for example, as defined by the UK Corporate Governance or Sarbanes-Oxley requirements. The integrated assurance map lends itself to supporting the methodical analysis of the organisation's system of controls against the principal risks and core business activities required by these reports. Some organisations have created a dedicated function such as a 'Business Assurance' team in the second line of defence to coordinate, evaluate and report on assurance across the organisation on an integrated basis.

The internal audit function is the third option, although the Chartered Institute of Internal Auditors has indicated that while the internal audit functions are able to help facilitate the mapping process without compromising their independence, they should not own the organisation's integrated assurance framework. I would assert that the exception is if integrated assurance is being deployed by internal audit at Level 1 to assist its planning process. Nonetheless, organisations should take advantage of the professional input of internal audit given the natural alignment of their skill sets with those required for implementing an integrated assurance framework across functional boundaries.

Finally, it is also worth pointing out that credibility of the ownership of the integrated assurance framework at the operational level is important. Those whose support or involvement is required in the process need to feel confident that their efforts will not be wasted through lack of leadership, expertise or project management. This observation is cemented by a comment from one non-executive director who stated that any assurance process – whether at an individual or integrated level – begins and ends with the confidence the board has in the skills and expertise of those involved. There are many aspects of the integrated assurance framework that require skilled judgment such as the scoping of the assurance map and assessment of the coverage, quality and conclusions of the assurance; it is essential that the implementation process to be led and owned by a credible owner.

Challenge #4 – Availability of Appropriate Resources and Skills

There are three aspects to this challenge. Firstly, there is the challenge of the generally limited resources, particularly in demanding and changing business environments. Adopting a phased implementation approach, as discussed in the last chapter on getting started, is a pragmatic way to dealing with limited resources. Secondly, the challenge alludes to the type of skills and expertise required to facilitate the implementation of integrated assurance. This is covered in Chapter 15 on getting started, which discusses the type of skills required to facilitate the implementation as well as scoping of the project within resourcing constraints.

Thirdly, the challenge refers to the comment at the end of the last section which refers to the importance of the credibility of the owner and lead coordinator of the integrated assurance framework. This includes the fundamental matter of confidence in the quality of the assurance providers and reliability of subject experts in the assurance food chain. Where a board or audit committee has yet to gain confidence in the assurance being provided by a particular source in the assurance food chain, integrating the assurance would merely compound the issue. In these situations, the primary concern relating to the board's confidence in the assurance providers should be addressed before attempting to integrate the assurance picture. One organisation dealt with this by excluding any assurance provider that had not been 'certified' by its internal audit function for the integrated assurance process.

It is important that the board has reasonable confidence in most, if not all, of the assurance providers. After all, integrated assurance is designed to provide credible views from different perspectives in order to optimise shared risk intelligence across the organisation.

Challenge #5 – Champion at the Top

A champion at the top is necessary to provide visible support and leadership for the implementation project. This is particularly important for initiatives such as integrated assurance that are enterprise wide. It is somewhat reassuring to know that the lack of a champion at the upper echelons of the organisation is not the most significant challenge for implementing integrated assurance although it is ranked amongst the top 5 of challenges in the IIAG study in 2012. The focused study attributed the difficulty of finding a champion to the absence of a common understanding of integrated assurance for communicating its rationale and benefits.

I would agree with this conclusion, as in my discussions no director denied the benefits a holistic view of risk assurance could bring to the board room. Greater clarity was required to help organisations understand the options and benefits for implementation such the framework. To secure a champion at the top, we need to first be able to articulate the benefits that integrated assurance could provide including the potential for addressing problems such as overlaps or gaps in assurance. In Chapter 15, we discussed the importance of understanding the underlying issues pertaining to risk governance in order that the benefits of implementing integrated assurance can be determined and articulated. This is necessary to help gain buy-in and secure an appropriate champion at the top.

There is, however, another form of challenge which no amount of explanation of the benefits can overcome to secure buy in from the top. Here, I refer to the tension that occurs between some boards operating at the subsidiary and group levels, where there is little or no appetite by the boards at group level to provide the subsidiary boards with a broader risk picture across the group. This limits the ability of subsidiary boards to gain oversight or assurance over potential group risks and contagion risks. The merit for implementing integrated assurance at the subsidiary level in these scenarios remains as it allows the gaps in the risk picture and assurance to be made explicit.

Challenge #6 – Coordination and Collaboration

Coordination is essential to integrated assurance as it involves drawing together the efforts of risk management across the organisation. At least a third of the organisations in the IIAG study identified this as a challenge in the implementation process. Effective integrated assurance is dependent on good coordination, collaboration and communication across functional boundaries in the organisation. The size of the organisation can pose a significant challenge to coordination and communication, as pointed out by a member of the audit committee of an organisation that operates over 130 offices covering nearly 170 countries. Like its implementation of its enterprise wide risk management system, attempting to integrate assurance in such an organisation is highly complex. In such large organisations, implementing integrated assurance should follow the footprint of enterprise risk management (where one is in place) with assurance mapping being embedded locally as the building blocks for a fuller integrated view at the top.

While the complexity of the task increases with size in respect of scope, time and resources required, the challenges relating to coordination and communication is not confined to large organisations. Small organisation can equally experience challenges in coordination and collaboration although the underlying reasons may be different to those of large organisations. Putting aside the consideration of size, factors that are most likely to influence effective coordination of assurance within an organisation include:

OWNERSHIP, MANDATE AND AUTHORITY

Unclear ownership and authority for driving the implementation of the integrated assurance framework (the project) that is accompanied by an inappropriate mandate makes it more difficult to organise, coordinate and communicate the objectives of the project.

CONSISTENT AND VISIBLE SUPPORT FROM THE TOP

As mentioned above, visible championship at the top of the organisation can have a significant influence on setting priorities and mobilising resources.

Assurance is more likely to be developed and provided when the highest level of the assurance food chain is clearly interested in seeking it.

CLARITY OF RESPONSIBILITIES AND ACCOUNTABILITIES

The process of collaboration can be obstructed as a consequence of unclear responsibilities and accountabilities for particular areas of risks or business process. In this situation, the mapping of assurance can be completed with the identified gaps until the responsibilities are clarified. Unclear and overly rigid description of responsibilities can both have similar effects on ownership of risks and therefore the provision of assurance. Integrated assurance applied at Level 2 is designed to help highlight these issues for appropriate action.

CULTURE OF COLLABORATION ACROSS FUNCTIONAL BOUNDARIES

The inability to work collaboratively across the organisation in the form of silo working or so called *turf wars* can obstruct the implementation process even where the project has visible support from the top. This is particularly the case where silo working is institutionalised in the culture of the organisation, for example, as a result of rigid terms of reference and low encouragement or opportunity to work across functional boundaries of the organisation.

Organisational behaviours of this nature do not necessarily prevent the implementation of integrated assurance but can make the process more protracted and demanding of time and scarce resources. Some organisations which recognise the significant benefits of collaboration across functional boundaries – working outside the proverbial silos – actively incentivise team working through performance management. Many organisations recognise that the hurdles to coordination and collaboration provide the very arguments for implementing integrated assurance and joined-up management and oversight of risks.

To Conclude this Chapter ...

In summary, the main challenges for implementing integrated assurance reflect the immaturity of the concept of integrated assurance rather than the lack of desire, intention or inspiration. The rationale for implementing integrated assurance is hard to disapprove of once it is understood. It is the way in which the discipline of integrated assurance is framed for implementation at a practical level that is a source of confusion and concern. For this, it is imperative that the implementation plan first seeks to understand the issues relating to risk governance and assurance within the organisation before determining an approach that is demonstrably thoughtful and measured to enable the organisation to optimise the benefits through a test or 'do and learn' phase.

In setting out the considerations for getting started in Chapter 15, we have been mindful of the practical challenges discussed in this chapter. Those challenges that are deep rooted in the culture and mind set of the organisation are likely to be trickier to resolve than those of an operational nature but they are surmountable, with a vision and determination to make it happen.

To illustrate this point, I refer to the perception of the Chief Executive Officer of Police Mutual Group, UK's largest affinity insurance company, Stephen Mann, whose vision of a prosperous modern mutual organisation encouraged innovation in the way governance and business transformation is achieved. Integrated risk assurance, according to Mann, enabled the organisation to identify and then wrap its arms around the risks requiring oversight. He explains that:

> most insurance companies can be horribly siloed; structured on functional lines and introspective in the extreme. In reality they are much more complex with a range of interdependencies where traditional control functions and processes are not easily aligned to end to end or holistic risks which can often lead them to being blindsided to inherent risks. Having the confidence to seek to develop an integrated risk assurance framework in turn instils confidence that the board has a process for gathering a holistic view of the effectiveness of its controls and oversight. In turn, it provides further reassurance to a board that it is focusing on key risks and the effectiveness of the controls in mitigating them and has a process and framework that is both forward looking and structured.

Key Points from this Chapter

1.   There are six main challenges to implementing integrated assurance:

- – Absence of a universally defined framework
- – Maturity of risk management
- – Ownership
- – Availability of appropriate resources and skills

       – Champion at the top
       – Coordination or collaboration

2.   The challenges facing organisations are in many ways the very arguments for implementing integrated assurance and promoting more joined-up management and oversight of risks.

3.   Many of the challenges stem from the absence of a universally defined concept or framework for effective application of integrated assurance.

4.   The challenges are practical in nature and reflect the immaturity of the concept of integrated assurance rather than the lack of desire, vision or inspiration.

5.   Integrated assurance implementation plans benefit from being demonstrably thoughtful and measured in recognising the practical challenges peculiar to the organisation and which enable the organisation to optimise the benefits through a test or 'do and learn' phase.

Endnotes

[1]   Insurance Internal Audit Group (IIAG), Good Practice Development Group study on integrated Assurance in Summer 2012, the results of which discussed at the IIAG Conference in September 2012. Publication is limited to participants of the study. www.iiiag.org.uk.

PART IV
CASE STUDIES

Case Studies

Introduction

We dedicate this part of the book to a number of case studies selected to illustrate the different ways in which organisations have deployed the discipline of integrated assurance in order to support their governance needs. The nine case studies demonstrate the different drivers and implementation approaches for achieving better risk governance through integrated assurance. While the case studies share a common goal of effective risk governance, the variations in the way integrated assurance has been applied in each case reflect the flexibility of the discipline to meet the specific business needs of each organisation. A summary of these cases studies is provided in Table CS 0.1.

The case studies are shaped from my personal practical experience and dialogue with organisations, which were recommended for their progressive practice in integrated assurance. For each case study, we consider the level at which integrated assurance is being applied, the rational for using integrated assurance to address the perceived need and the challenges as well as positive lessons. The discussion in each case study is set out under the following main headings:

- The need and rationale for integrated assurance;

- Implementation approach; and,

- Key outcomes and lessons.

Table CS 0.1 Summary of Case Studies

Case Study	Implementation Level	Scope	Application Objective
1	Level 1	Group wide	Supporting audit committee approval of audit plans.
2	Level 1	Group wide	Supporting audit committee review of the need for an internal audit function.
3	Level 2	Business entity within a Group	Optimising risk assurance in a fast growing entity.
4	Level 2	Group wide	Enhancing risk governance to match growth ambitions.
5	Level 2/ Level 3	Group wide	Optimising risk assurance in line with strategic change.
6	Level 2/ Level 3	Group wide	Sharpening and simplifying risk governance and assurance.
7	Level 3	Business entity within a Group	Deep dive risk oversight for Group Board ahead of strategic change for the entity.
8	Level 3	Specific risk across the Group	Spotlighting a risk for oversight and assurance.
9	Level 3	Group wide	Promoting collective risk intelligence.

The key used for indicating the size of the organisation in each case study is based broadly on the annual revenue or number of full time equivalent (FTE) employees where annual revenue is not an appropriate measure. The key is shown in Table CS 0.2. Also, as a reminder, the three different levels for applying integrated assurance are:

- Level 1 – Risk assurance planning

- Level 2 – Enhancing risk assurance

- Level 3 – Integrated risk oversight and assurance

Table CS 0.2 Key to the Size of the Organisation

Size	Company annual revenue	Or	Number of Employees (FTE)
Large	In excess of £10bn		More than 5000
Medium	Between £1bn and £10bn		Between 1,000 and 5,000
Small	Less than £1bn		Under 1000

In examining each case study, we observe that the sector in which the organisation operates is less significant in influencing the way integrated assurance is being deployed than the strategic change experienced by the organisation. Regardless of industry or sector, each case study shares the same objective of both promoting and enhancing good governance, risk assurance and demonstrable accountability across the organisation. The size of the enterprise appears to be an important factor in influencing the overall approach, speed and scope of implementation within the organisation. These factors were discussed in Chapter 15 on getting started.

The overriding influence for applying the discipline of integrated assurance in all cases is the guiding hand of a chief executive, an audit committee chairman, an inspired audit executive or chief risk officer. In summary, I hope the case studies help to illustrate how specific risk assurance concerns can be addressed with the discipline of integrated assurance and will inspire the use of integrated assurance to promote optimal risk assurance across the organisation.

Audit Committee Approval of Audit Plans

In this example, integrated assurance is applied at Level 1 across the organisation for the purpose of supporting the Audit Committee's approval of the internal audit plans. The objective in this regard is clear.

Base Information for Case Study 1

INDUSTRY AND SIZE OF THE ORGANISATION

Sector: Financial Services

Size: Small organisation

LEVEL AND SCOPE OF IMPLEMENTATION

Level: Level 1

Scope: Group wide

Identifying the Need

Prior to approving a set of internal audit plans a couple of years ago, the Chairman of the Audit Committee requested additional information that related to other assurance reports which the Audit Committee or the Board was receiving or expected to receive in the same period. Increasing standards of governance in the industry have undoubtedly raised the awareness of the Audit Committee to the need for more explicit assessment of the completeness of risk assurance provided at board level.

Rationale for Integrated Assurance

The central feature of integrated assurance, that involves the mapping of risk assurance across the organisation, lent itself well to rationalising the internal audit plans. The concept of integrated assurance was, at the same time, being established in the organisation by a member of the Executive who is also the Chief Risk Officer for the purpose of gaining a holistic risk oversight, that is, application at Level 3. The need of the Audit Committee was well timed as it provided additional impetus for implementing the framework for the long term. The integrated assurance framework at Level 3 was not yet fully in place at the time the Audit Committee made its request but was sufficiently defined for the purpose of supporting the internal audit planning process at Level 1.

Implementation Approach

The integrated assurance framework is owned by the Chief Risk Officer and the Risk function leads the risk assurance mapping. The Risk function and Internal Audit work to a common timetable in order to synchronise the risk assurance mapping with the stakeholder meetings conducted by Internal Audit for the purpose of determining the initial audit plan. The risk assurance map charts the assurance being provided to the Board or the Audit Committee from the three lines of defence against the risks on the Board's strategic risk register and core business processes.

The mapping identified all formal reporting – from management in front line operations, as well as the monitoring by the Compliance function, to other second line of defence functions, such as customer complaints and external validation plans from independent parties. The agendas of the Board and subcommittees were also consulted to identify any known assurance reports that had recently been tabled or were scheduled for discussion.

The completed assurance map was compared with the proposed internal audit plan which had been derived from Internal Audit's own assessment of the risks and discussions with key stakeholders in the organisation that included the Executive, senior managers and members of the Audit Committee. Discussions between the Chief Risk Officer and the Chief Internal Auditor were held to ensure that any gaps and overlaps in the risk assurance map were resolved appropriately.

Management assurance, that is, formal assurance from the first or second lines of defence functions was considered where it may not have been necessary for independent assurance to be provided by Internal Audit, for example, for areas with low likelihood of the risk materialising but which are nonetheless important for risk oversight. The use of management assurance in this manner reinforced accountability at the local level and directed the use of Internal Audit resources to where it was needed most.

Since its request, the Audit Committee is furnished with four key documents when approving the Internal Audit Plan each year:

- proposed Internal Audit Plan;

- proposed Compliance Plan;

- proposed Management Assurance Plan; and,

- results of the Integrated Assurance Map, showing the key risks and core business processes considered and the sources of assurances from each line of defence.

The combined information of the four documents allows the Audit Committee to determine if its risk oversight requirements are adequately covered across the risk universe of the organisation.

Key Outcomes and Lessons

As a result of the integrated assurance planning process, the approval of the Internal Audit Plan is streamlined involving just one step at the Audit Committee. By comparison to previous years, the risk oversight and assurance agenda is considerably more transparent and visible. The feedback from the Audit Committee Chairman is that there is 'greater comfort' – not necessarily because there are no material risks but because the organisation is cognisant of them, allowing the Board as well as the Audit Committee to direct with greater confidence.

Assurance against particular risks will continue to be requested as the need arises which adds to the management assurance agenda or internal audit plan as appropriate. The key lessons which can be drawn from this case study include:

- The importance of having risk governance champions in the form of the Audit Committee Chairman and Chief Risk Officer; from the Audit Committee Chairman's perspective, it was the need for completeness in the risk assurance picture before approval of the internal audit plans that provided the driver for integrated assurance. From the Chief Risk Officer's perspective, it was the need for a systematic approach to minimising surprises and blind trust in managing principal risks across the group that provided the vision for implementing integrated assurance.

- Ownership of the integrated assurance framework by the Chief Risk Officer which enables efficient alignment of the assessments of risk assurance with the organisation's risk management approach.

- The importance of the Risk and Internal Audit functions, and indeed other key assurance providers, to work in a collegiate manner. Collaboration appears to be most effective when there is mutual understanding and respect for the responsibility each has in contributing to the total risk oversight required by the organisation.

Case Study 2

Reviewing the Need for an Internal Audit Function

In this case study, integrated assurance is applied at Level 2 across the organisation to assist the Audit Committee to determine if an internal audit function is required and also to enhance the organisation's risk management approach.

Base Information for Case Study 2

INDUSTRY AND SIZE OF THE ORGANISATION

Sector: Support Services

Size: Small organisation

LEVEL AND SCOPE OF IMPLEMENTATION

Level: Level 2

Scope: Group wide

Identifying the Need

The organisation has experienced rapid growth since it was established just under 10 years ago. It is a public listed company conforming to the UK Corporate Governance Code which requires the Audit Committee to review each year the need for an internal audit function. With a simple business operating model which supplies administration support and services to other organisations predominantly in financial services, an internal audit function has not been regarded as necessary so far. The organisation has, however, an established monitoring programme operated by front line management. This is complemented by the work of the Compliance and Risk function, which includes a formal risk management process introduced some two years ago.

A new Audit Committee Chair was appointed recently who requested a structured review to determine the nature and sources of assurance that is available across the organisation, in order to objectively assess the need for an internal audit function. In addition, the new Audit Committee Chair also wanted assurance that the risks facing the organisation have been recognised to allow appropriate oversight, taking into account the strategic changes in the organisation as well as changes in the external environment.

Rationale for Integrated Assurance

The primary attraction for using integrated assurance lies in the methodical identification of principal risks and core business processes, which provides a sound foundation for assurance mapping. The Audit Committee Chair thought that the integrated assurance approach facilitates a fresh look at the risks and core business processes with reference to the organisation's strategy and business model, so as to better inform the assurance programme being implemented by management and the Compliance and Risk function. Recognising the limited skills typically available in a small organisation, the Audit Committee Chair thought that the integrated assurance implementation process would also help to identify solutions for addressing any skills gaps.

As a result, the Audit Committee will be better placed to determine whether or not an internal audit function is required in proportion to the risk profile of the organisation. In other words, integrated assurance would enable the organisation to recognise the monitoring programme it has established in the front line functions as an operational feature of the business, and that the monitoring strategy is fully aligned with risks that are critical to the success of the organisation. The approach was discussed with the Chief Executive and Head of Risk and Compliance.

Implementation Approach

The Head of Risk and Compliance is leading the implementation of integrated assurance with the vision being championed by the Audit Committee Chair and supported by the Chief Executive. The implementation is in progress and the plan of action includes:

1.   As a first step, the Risk function is facilitating discussions with the key parts of the business for reconsidering the risks on the risk register in light of the business operating model and also its strategy in the forthcoming year. The refreshed risks, which now include strategic as well as financial, operational and regulatory risks, are agreed with the Audit Committee for the risk assurance mapping exercise.

2.   Core processes of the business operating model that have not been identified as potential risks will be determined for the risk assurance map.

3.   The established monitoring programme will be mapped against the risks and core processes on the map. A number of the monitoring processes and controls are embedded in the management of front line operations, a feature that reflects the nature of the service model of the organisation.

4.   The Risk function will make an assessment of the degree of independent assurance that is provided by front line operations, the Risk and Compliance function as well as any external parties in the third line of defence. The assessment, which is shown in the risk assurance map, is determined by a simple rating as follows:

    –   3–Impartial: Assurance is independent from the ownership or accountability for the risk or process, for example oversight and monitoring carried out by the Risk and Compliance function, and the external auditors.
    –   2–Neutral: Assurance is partially or indirectly linked to the ownership or accountability for the risk or process. Examples include the quality control monitoring conducted by individuals who are not directly involved in the line operations.
    –   1–Partial: Assurance is provided by a source that is an integral part of the process or risk control under consideration. Examples include the monitoring and self-certifications by individuals who are located within the processes and directly accountable for the risk.

5.   The completed risk assurance map, with the assessments, will be initially discussed with the Management team for the purpose of identifying any potential actions and recommendations for consideration by the Audit Committee.

6.   The key matters for consideration by the Audit Committee include the adequacy of risk assurance and sufficiency of objective assurance that is being provided by the group as a whole. The key factors that will influence the decisions for more or less assurance and, if an internal audit function is required, include the risk appetite and tolerance of the Audit Committee, the strategy of the business and the changing risk profile of the organisation.

As mentioned earlier, the implementation of the integrated risk assurance mapping is in progress. Should the Audit Committee, as a result of the risk assurance mapping, require additional comfort, it has three main options which include enhancing the organisation's existing risk management and assurance arrangements, commissioning external reviews of certain key risks and establishing an internal audit function.

Given the current business operating model and size of the organisation, early indications are that the Audit Committee can gain the risk oversight it needs by focusing on improving and strengthening the existing risk management and assurance arrangements. This focus should help position the organisation for more substantial and accelerated growth as part of their strategic plan. An internal audit function may then become more pertinent for providing the additional pair of eyes required by the Audit Committee over the changing risk environment of the organisation.

Optimising Risk Assurance in a Fast Growing Entity

In this example, integrated assurance was implemented at Level 2 for a business entity within a large multi-national financial services group. The implementation began as a pilot project in a form of a 'test and learn' exercise within a single entity prior to rolling out to other parts of the Group.

Base Information for Case Study 3

INDUSTRY AND SIZE OF THE ENTERPRISE

Sector: Financial Services

Size: Large organisation

LEVEL AND SCOPE OF IMPLEMENTATION

Level: Level 2

Scope: Option 3 – Business unit or entity

Identifying the Need

The cash generation of this organisation was growing both consistently and rapidly due to relentless cost focus and increasing income, the effects of which increased the complexity of giving assurance over 300 auditable activities across six business entities located across the UK, Europe and the USA. Unsurprisingly, the risk profile of the organisation was complex and also changing with the dynamic regulatory environment which attracted greater focus of the governing bodies of the Group. The strategic vision and regulatory environment affecting the Group triggered a number of transformation initiatives across the organisation.

Like the rest of the organisation, Group Internal Audit recognised the need to transform its approach to better serve the organisation's assurance requirements in a holistic manner. An approach that was both efficient and effective was necessary to provide the required level of independent and credible assurance expected by the Group Audit Committee of independent nonexecutive directors (NEDs). The relentless cost focus made this a need to 'do more with less'.

Influenced by a sympathetic vision of holistic assurance for the organisation, the Group Executive Director of the Group's most profitable business division (£500m Operating Profit per annum) was also seeking to raise the standards of management assurance at the local level as well as to minimise unnecessary duplication of effort. Group Internal Audit and the Group Executive Director of this business division developed strong relations as transformation partners.

Rationale for Integrated Assurance

Integrated assurance was identified by Group Internal Audit as an appropriate discipline and methodology which would help deliver the transformation required for developing the Group's future assurance strategy. It was envisaged that the integrated assurance mapping process would initially provide insights to the assurance capabilities across all three lines of defence within the Group so that assurance arrangements and strategies could be optimised across the Group. This was critical because the Risk, Compliance and Internal Audit governance structure reported to monthly Risk and Compliance Committees, and any discrepancies in opinions could lead to confusion when trying to draw together a coherent and holistic view of the Group's control environment. On a number of occasions the Compliance and Group Internal Audit teams had separately planned similar pieces of work, and executed them independently in close succession, which had been generally detrimental to first line management's views of the reputation and credibility of governance functions.

Recognising the scale of the Group, a pilot implementation within a single business entity was determined to be a practical way to help Group Internal Audit 'test and learn' from the exercise prior to rolling out to the rest of the organisation. The rationale for implementation up to Level 2 in the pilot took into account the interests of, and more critically, support of senior management:

- One of four Group Board Executive Directors

- The Group Board Director for the Distribution function

- The Commercial Director for the Distribution function.

Full implementation of integrated assurance at Level 3 would have been impractical to achieve at this early stage. It is envisaged that when integrated assurance is implemented eventually at Level 3, it could enhance the basis for Group Internal Audit in its preparation of the thematic and Business Entity focused control environment reporting to the Group Audit Committee.

Implementation Approach

The mapping process for the control environment was iterative. Initially the existing activities and controls were mapped from the Group Internal Audit (GIA) 'Universe' database and prior audit reports. Secondly, the Commercial Director for the Distribution function was instrumental in arranging a series of workshops where GIA facilitated discussion and recording of first line and second line of defence controls. Varying degrees of comfort to GIA (although not reliance) were then assigned to each control, at four levels – none, low, medium and high level of comfort.

This approach enabled GIA to re-prioritise the local audit plans to reflect the audit of areas with the highest expected net risk, rather than only the original gross risk rating. In addition, the series of workshops allowed appropriate 'tweaking' and refinement of individual audit scope.

The next phase was to coordinate planning with the Risk and Compliance functions, leading to more coherent reporting on the control environment.

Key Outcomes and Lessons

A clear lesson from the pilot is that although GIA owned the integrated assurance framework and led the process, the implementation of integrated assurance required a high level of commitment by all stakeholders throughout. Ensuring that this level of commitment was obtained at the outset helped to make sure the pilot phase was successful. The pilot also highlighted the significance of a strong understanding of the business and business risk drivers as pre-requisites for maintaining appropriate focus throughout the course of the implementation process. The key benefits were:

- GIA avoided clashes or duplication with other governance functions.

- GIA could be more effective in other ad hoc work, and particularly assurance on distribution regulatory programmes.

- Governance functions could collaborate in providing assurance on identified distribution areas.

Incidental broader benefits were also realised as part of further roll-out:

- The initial review identified that the same level of assurance could be provided to the Group Executive Director of the Group's most profitable business division using fewer audits. A series of 56 audits consisting *circa* 350 man-weeks of effort was recalibrated to only 38 audits consisting *circa* 228 man-weeks of effort (a saving of 122 man-weeks).

- The Annual Audit Planning routine was refined to include a full listing of all planned audit activities in risk priority. This was overlaid with the Group risk appetite and available resourcing for the year, to provide comfort that the relevant activities were being covered.

The positive outcomes of the pilot were generally broader than initially estimated and GIA plans to pace the roll out to other parts of the Group on an incremental basis, recognising that the maintenance of net risk based priorities will be an ongoing challenge, particularly during periods of significant change.

Case Study 4

Enhancing Risk Governance to Match Growth Ambitions

In this example, integrated assurance is implemented at Level 2 across the group of a financial services firm whose business is the provision of retirement annuities to individuals. The organisation is relatively young, but has experienced significant growth and recently became a listed public limited company.

Base Information for Case Study 4

INDUSTRY AND SIZE OF THE ENTERPRISE

Sector: Financial Services

Size: Medium organisation

LEVEL AND SCOPE OF IMPLEMENTATION

Level: Level 2

Scope: Option 1 – Group wide

Identifying the Need

As a rapidly growing company, selling complex financial products to retail consumers in a highly regulated industry, it was extremely important to the Board that an effective risk culture was embedded throughout the company's operations. The company's private equity investors and senior management were keen to ensure that the company grew safely, treated its customers fairly and proactively developed effective governance and risk management frameworks. Effective governance was needed to support Board accountability for risk and controls and to prepare the company for meeting the requirements of the European Solvency II Directive and, in due course, a stock exchange listing.

The company had recently appointed a new Chief Financial Officer and a Director of Risk and Compliance (Risk Director) and there had been significant investment in developing the Board Governance and Enterprise Risk Management (ERM) frameworks, which were built on a 'three lines of defence' model. Following the recommendations of the Walker Review, a Board Risk Committee was also created, which had the same Chair and membership as the Audit Committee.

For the Board, it was imperative that the risk management and assurance agendas were complementary, coherent and consistent, to ensure a common understanding and oversight of risk exposures and mitigating actions and controls. There was therefore an expectation that the new Internal Audit Director would work closely with the Risk Director to implement an assurance strategy that was fully aligned with the three lines of defence model.

For the Executive Committee, the priority was for the organisation to grow safely. Over a two year period the company underwent significant business change and increased its headcount from 200 to over 500 full time staff; at this rate of growth, which inevitably involved management stretch, it was essential that the risk and control disciplines were operating consistently. It was not only expected but imperative that Risk and Internal Audit work closely together to support a consistent and coherent risk and control culture throughout the organisation.

Rationale for Integrated Assurance

To develop an Internal Audit strategy that would add demonstrable value to the Board and the Executive, it was self-evident that the communication of internal audit assurance plans and results would need to be aligned with the company's ERM framework. Both the Risk and Internal Audit directors and the Chair of the Audit Committee had worked in organisations with three lines of defence assurance models and some element of 'combined assurance' reporting, so it was recognised by each of the key assurance stakeholders that an integrated approach should be followed.

As part of the ERM framework, the Risk Director had produced a report to the Audit Committee on the company's internal control framework, which defined key controls for each of the company's key risks and the first, second and third line assurance mechanisms in place for each risk. This report enabled the Board to assess how effectively risks were being managed and to better direct and prioritise its future assurance requirements. The Risk report mapped recent internal audits against relevant risks, however audit coverage was patchy and there was no linking of key risks with Internal Audit's plan, methods or reporting. The new Internal Audit Director therefore felt that there was considerable scope to align the function's assurance activities far more clearly with the company's ERM framework, to support a consistent, consolidated understanding of risks, controls and assurance at Board level.

Implementation Approach

The first step was for the Internal Audit Director to present the revised assurance strategy to the Audit Committee. This strategy set out the blueprint for aligning Internal Audit with the ERM framework with the following objectives:

- Aligned assurance – to align independent assurance with governance and risk frameworks.

- Business briefings – to gain closer engagement with business stakeholders and consider emerging risks.

- Core controls – to identify a comprehensive programme of control checks based on risk registers.

- Deeper dives – to provide where appropriate additional assurance on high risk areas and emerging risks.

- Expertise – to develop existing skills and leverage other internal and external expertise.

Each objective was designed to bring Internal Audit activities more closely into line with the ERM framework and to support a consolidated assurance perspective at board level without impacting the Internal Audit team's independence from first and second line of defence activities.

ALIGNED ASSURANCE

Internal Audit plans continued to be based on an independent risk assessment of the company's strategy and business model, but now the annual audit plan was also clearly mapped against the company's key risk register with the Internal Audit response set out against each risk. This approach ensured that the company's risk profile, as reported to the Risk Committee, was fully considered in the annual audit plan. It also enabled the Risk Director to present a consolidated assurance map that showed the Board a more complete and consistent coverage of key risks and controls by the third line of defence.

Internal Audit adopted the same risk ratings for audit observations as the ERM framework and evaluated exposures on the same risk assessment criteria and basis of materiality used by Risk. Also, the overall grading of Internal Audit reports was assessed by reviewing the aggregate impact of the individual observations. These assessments enabled Internal Audit to provide an annual assurance opinion which was aligned with the ERM framework and clearly set out its coverage of the company's key risk profile and its assessment of controls for each risk.

BUSINESS BRIEFINGS

Regular relationship management meetings were held with key contacts and stakeholders across the business as well as with the Risk and Compliance functions. These meetings enabled the Internal Audit team to be aware of emerging issues and of activities being carried out by other assurance functions so that perceptions of duplication or gaps in assurance activity could be escalated and resolved promptly.

CORE CONTROLS

To ensure comprehensive audit coverage, and support the corporate risk culture, Internal Audit instigated a programme of core control reviews, which covered every business function on a two year cycle. As well as validating the effective operation of key compliance and governance controls, these health checks validated the operation of controls set out in the corporate and departmental risk registers. Core controls reviews were supplemented by similar reviews of controls in significant outsourced operations. These reviews enabled Internal Audit to support its annual assurance opinion with a 'heat map' of the business control environment, which mapped audit ratings against each risk in the company's risk profile.

DEEPER DIVES

Internal Audit planning also identified areas of critical risk that require focused assurance activity. These 'deeper dive' audits, which included reviews of the Risk and other governance frameworks, generally made use of subject matter expertise provided by Internal Audit's co-sourcing partner or by second line assurance teams. The results of these audits supported Internal Audit's annual opinion on more technical areas of the company's risk profile.

EXPERTISE

Clearer alignment with the company's risk profile ensured Internal Audit engagement with all critical risks including complex, technical risks such as reinsurance, pricing, actuarial valuation and underwriting. There was therefore a need to develop the technical skills of the audit team and to procure subject matter expertise to provide appropriate insight to the evaluation of controls. A focus on resource development and co-sourcing strategies was therefore critical to support the delivery of aligned assurance activity and reporting.

Key Outcomes and Lessons

The key outcome of implementing an integrated approach to the company's assurance activities is that the Audit Committee now has a clear statement of consolidated assurance on key risks and controls and supports the Board in its discharge of its responsibilities and demonstrates its accountability to investors, customers and regulators. Furthermore, the Board and the Executive Committee are now able to clearly see how Internal Audit activity supports their overall assurance responsibilities. From Internal Audit's perspective, the more integrated approach gives a clear framework and body of evidence to support its annual opinion on controls, which both corroborates, and is corroborated by, the ERM framework. Overall, there is a greater level of confidence in risk assurance across the assurance food chain.

The aligned approach has built a common agenda and understanding between the Risk and Internal Audit functions and a highly productive working relationship with the Chairman of the Audit Committee. In a recent stakeholder survey of its effectiveness, the Internal Audit function was rated by the company's nonexecutive directors, Executive Committee and senior management as 'fully effective' on 18 out of 20 criteria and 'mostly effective' in the other criteria. The function also received a number of favourable comments on its planning, reporting and assurance approach.

Above all, the Risk and Internal Audit functions have continued to operate and to report independently of each other, without any blurring of roles and responsibilities. The company is now investing in the development of other second line of defence activities, particularly with respect to actuarial risk management and information risk and the Internal Audit team has a clear operating model to follow in aligning its activity with these functions.

The success of the implementation of an integrated assurance approach has been driven largely from the top at board level through the inspiration of the Chairman of the Audit Committee and experience of the Risk and Internal Audit directors. Underpinning this motivation is the need to growth safely through the recognised value in joined up risk management and assurance activity across the organisation.

Case Study 5

Optimising Risk Assurance in Line with Strategic Change

In this multinational telecommunications services organisation, integrated assurance is implemented at Level 2, progressing to Level 3 that covers the identified group wide risks. The implementation is led by the organisation's Risk and Internal Audit leadership teams, in particular, the Head of Enterprise Risk Management working in conjunction with a senior manager from Group Internal Audit. The progress achieved so far reflects a process of conceptualisation and development over a period of two to three years. While the overall objective was to provide enhanced assurance to the group's audit committee of the effectiveness of the management of the group's most significant risks, the framework also enabled the organisation to recognise the validity of other sources of assurances and encourage even more ownership and continual improvement in the organisation's system of internal control and risk management.

Base Information for Case Study 5

INDUSTRY AND SIZE OF THE ENTERPRISE

Sector: Telecommunications

Size: Large organisation

LEVEL AND SCOPE OF IMPLEMENTATION

Level: Level 2, progressing to Level 3

Scope: Group risks

Identifying the Need

There were probably a number of factors that came together and influenced this telecommunications company to seek the benefits offered by an integrated assurance framework. Firstly, there was a desire to be able to present a holistic 'one truth' view to senior management and the Audit Committee, and to address the fragmented approach to assurance that had developed over time. Secondly, Group Internal Audit recognised the limited resources it has as the organisation continued to evolve and grow, and which led it to actively consider the other credible sources of assurance across the group. Thirdly, the strengthening of the group's enterprise risk management also led to greater exploration of more effective ways in which assurance of the organisation's aggregate risk management could be provided. Finally, there was an understanding that integrated assurance was an approach explored by leading edge organisations as a way of strengthening and maturing the overall governance arrangements.

The integration of the Internal Audit and Enterprise Risk Management functions under the leadership of the Director of Risk and Internal Audit has been a key driver in the development of assurance maps and the exploration of an integrated assurance framework. The presentation of a joint approach has also helped provide clarity on direction with other assurance providers, and ensures that the focus remains on enterprise threatening risks and close alignment to the Internal Audit programme.

Rationale for Integrated Assurance

The core role of integrated assurance to present a clearer 'one view truth' to senior management and the Audit Committee is a primary reason for implementing an integrated assurance framework. In addition to providing the top of the organisation with visibility of the work of assurance providers other than that of Group Internal Audit, the integrated assurance framework would help the organisation optimise the scope of internal audit activity and resources at Group Internal Audit's disposal by leveraging the work of others.

In particular, it was anticipated that the assurance mapping process would provide a structured approach for identifying assurance providers across the three lines of defence. The vision for implementation included promoting greater recognition, accountability as well as the visibility of assurance received by the Audit Committee from the first and second lines of defence. In the course of mapping the assurance, it was also envisaged that improvements to the quality of assurance would be identified particularly where assurance was required to qualify or meet a certain credible standard for it to be used by management or the Audit Committee.

Implementation Approach

The integrated assurance framework is led and owned by the integrated Group Internal Audit and Risk function. The assurance mapping process involves the support of senior managers from Internal Audit and Risk Management in deriving and determining the assurance maps. The implementation project is championed by the Head of Enterprise Risk Management with the support of the Director of Risk and Internal Audit, who recognised the potential benefits which could be delivered by the integrated assurance framework although some preliminary work is required to secure full support of the group's Audit Committee.

Taking into account the size of the group which operates in over 170 countries, the implementation team adopted an approach that focused initially on the identified 'group risks'. Limiting the scope to the group risks enabled the team to develop a pilot with which it could ensure a pragmatic approach is determined sensibly and incrementally to gain buy in at the board level prior to full roll out. Implementation involved six key steps:

1. Confirming the most significant or group level risks for assurance mapping across the three lines of defence. The risks were translated into 'risk themes' to ensure that the risks are considered more broadly in respect of the underlying key systems of internal control and risk mitigation. This approach also allowed a degree of 'future-proofing' of the assurance map, minimising the need to update the nature of the assurance as the detailed aspects of the risks change. A version of the assurance activity map is shown in Table CS 5.1 below.

2. Identifying the owners of the risks and respective providers of assurance across all parts of the business.

3. Assessing the validity and credibility of the assurance available in respect of each risk. The team defined a set of parameters against which the quality of assurance was assessed. The parameters involve considering the degree of independence, robustness of the

process, skills and nature of the assurance reporting, the extent and scope of work undertaken. The initial or first tranche assessment identified some immediate credible assurance providers. There is the potential to develop a further number of other sources of assurance, once preliminary work on the first tranche has been completed and the process is more mature.

4. Engagement with senior and operational management in the identified assurance providers. A senior sponsor is appointed for each assurance provider whose role is to champion the integrated assurance approach, represent their area of activity at senior management forums and to formally review and approve the submission for their area. Operational leads are responsible for compiling the assurance report submission and acting as liaison with Group Internal Audit and Risk.

5. Establishing a quarterly verification review process conducted by the Head of Enterprise Risk Management, the Director of Internal Audit and the senior sponsors of the other assurance providers. This is to ensure that consistency is maintained and to identify any potential questions that may be asked by the Audit Committee so that any further supporting detail required can be prepared in advance of the Audit Committee meeting.

6. Defining and preparing the quarterly integrated assurance report. The report that is being piloted aims to provide the Audit Committee with an understanding of the scope of activity covered by the identified assurance providers, how they are aligned to group risks and a brief overview of the function, summary of work undertaken by the assurance provider in the quarter together with a commentary on key findings including highlights and lowlights arising.

Table CS 5.1 Sample Assurance Activity Map

Area of Risk (Examples)	Group Risk Reference	Validated Assurance Providers (AP)									
		AP1		AP2		AP3		AP4		AP5	
Strategy and M&A	GR1	A	P	A						A	P
Economic & market conditions	GR2	A	P	A	A	P					
Research & development	GR3	A	P	A	A	P					
Technology	GR4	A									
People resourcing strategy	GR5	A	P	A							
Remuneration & governance	GR6			A							
Business continuity/ disruption	GR7	P									
Regulatory change	GR8	A	P	A				A	P		
Customer experience	GR10		P	A							
Corporate responsibility	GR11	A		A							
Competition	GR12		P	A	A	P					
..etc	GR13										
..etc	GR14										

Key:

A	Assurance Provider Activity (Year To Date)
P	Planned (next period/year)

Key Outcomes and Lessons

Implementation of the integrated assurance framework is in its first year and the benefits have yet to be fully realised by the organisation. At this early stage of implementation, we believe the organisation has gained greater visibility as well as a better understanding of the nature and value of the work of each assurance provider. There is also greater clarity and common understanding of the concept of 'materiality' or level of acceptable risks and tolerances in the business.

The process has achieved consensus to work towards standardised reporting and identified opportunity to improve working between Group Internal Audit and one of the assurance providers. By embracing the opportunity to work collaboratively with other assurance providers Group Internal Audit has been able to enhance the service it provides to its internal clients by sharing work plans, intelligence and findings.

The formal recognition of valid sources of risk assurance across the organisation is helping to promote and embed sound risk management in the business, reduce the over reliance on a single provider of assurance from Group Internal Audit and enable more effective use of resources within Group Internal Audit. The sum benefit of the integrated reporting which is being implemented is the visibility and rounder view of the organisation's overall assurance to senior management and the Audit Committee.

These benefits are, however, not always readily measurable or could materialise in the short term. This poses challenges for gaining wide support for integrated assurance. In this regard, the implementation team recognised the importance of the quality of communication with the assurance providers in the business and devoted time to develop the quarterly report that would improve the risk oversight of the Audit Committee. The other key challenges or lessons which the implementation team would highlight are:

- The importance of senior management and Audit Committee support and engagement at an early stage – this not only ensures buy in at the highest level but that resources are available to develop collaborative working arrangements and that recipients of the assurance statements can help shape the reporting.

- Establishing a common risk and assurance language as well as understanding of the concepts of materiality – this helps all assurance providers focus on key issues and ensures information reported to senior management is balanced and risk based.

It is also worth mentioning that having credible champions for integrated assurance in the form of the Head of Enterprise Risk Management and the Director of Internal Audit has been critical for the success of the implementation thus far. Full implementation is potentially long for such a large organisation and necessitates vision and commitment from the champions to provide the support required by the implementation team for the rest of the journey.

Case Study 6

Sharpening and Simplifying Risk Governance and Assurance

In this example, integrated assurance is implemented across the organisation at Level 2 with elements of Level 3 being applied. This organisation plays a significant role in this multibillion dollar industry and provides mandatory services to other organisations at the national and international level. Integrated assurance has evolved as an approach over the last six years, with experience and reflecting change within the organisation as well as the industry. There are further plans to improve the current approach with the continued aim of increasing risk based assurance and oversight at the board level.

Base Information for Case Study 6

INDUSTRY AND SIZE OF THE ENTERPRISE

Sector: Aviation

Size: Medium organisation

LEVEL AND SCOPE OF IMPLEMENTATION

Level: Level 2, progressing to Level 3

Scope: Group wide

Identifying the Need

The need for risk based assurance was first identified by an external quality assessment of the organisation's internal audit arrangements six years ago. In brief, assurance being provided to the Executive Committee (ExCo) and Audit

Committee was not being aligned to the organisation's risks or assurance oversight requirements. The Audit Committee tasked Internal Audit with developing an approach for aligning the organisation's assurance activities with its risk profile and appetite. The approach was expected to provide comfort to the ExCo and Audit Committee by:

- Ensuring that all assurance activity, both generated internally and from third parties, is coordinated and leveraged off by all assurance providers within the organisation (including Internal Audit).

- Delivering a complete picture of the relevant control framework to ExCo and the Audit Committee.

- Driving discussion and identifying areas for further analysis.

- Complementing the organisation's existing business risk process.

- Informing the risk-based internal audit programme.

- Ensuring that overall assurance is maximised at minimum cost.

A view of the plans for the future is provided at the end of this case study.

Rationale for Integrated Assurance

The integrated assurance map was recognised as an appropriate tool by which the organisation could get a better understanding of its assurance activities against the key processes, risks and projects it is managing. The current framework described in this case study reflects the evolved process, which as a result of more simplified but thoughtful reporting provides better focus and clarity of risk assurance to the ExCo and Audit Committee. The early versions of the integrated assurance reporting evolved over time to consist of two 'A3' size pages, with 86 rows and 44 columns of data (approximately 3,800 fields). At this point the Audit Committee requested a more refined approach be developed as the level of detail included was both no longer fit for purpose and 'migraine-inducingly complex'.

Implementation Approach

By this stage of its implementation it could be said that the organisation had bought into the concept of integrated assurance, although a fresh approach was required. With this mandate from the Audit Committee, the new Head of Internal Audit revisited the key principles of integrated assurance and introduced a number of changes. It was agreed with the Audit Committee that the risk assurance mapping and reporting in the new approach should focus on the organisation's *core* business processes, top *Board Level* business risks, and *Tier 1* projects. These were defined as follows:

- *Core* business processes are those that impact across multiple organisational groups and/or locations such as Procurement, Contract Management and Crisis Management.

- *Board Level* business Risks are those business risks rated via the Business Risk Management process, with either – a combined *likelihood* and *severity* rating of eight or above, or any risk assigned the maximum impact rating of four that are *black swan events*.

- *Tier 1* projects are those projects deemed most significant in aggregate based on the organisation's tiered approach to defining the status of projects. The approach considers elements such as total project costs, risks, organisational impact, scale of stakeholder involvement and scope complexity.

For each area of focus, a separate assurance matrix was constructed. The mapping of the relevant core business processes, risks and projects was carried out against the specific assurance activities that were in place across the three lines of defense such as management self assessments, business case signoffs and internal audit reviews. An example of the assurance matrix with reference to key business processes is provided in Figure CS 6.1 below. The figure also shows the assurance rating used to assess the quality of the assurance in place and residual risks.

The assurance matrices are updated on a quarterly basis by Internal Audit. The updates involve identifying any gaps in assurance and providing a subjective residual assurance rating for each item on the assurance matrix. Any item with a red rating, that is, requiring *active management*, is highlighted and discussed at ExCo and Audit Committee meetings. Often this discussion centers on recent or upcoming internal audit work relating to the process, risk

Assurance Source

Key Business Process	Internal Audit	External Audit	Project Milestone Review	Departmental QA Audits	HMRC	External Consultant	Procurement Department	Regulator Audits	Investment/ Business Case	Finance Review	End Year Assurance	Benchmark/ Self-Assessment	Assurance Gap Noted / (Comment)	Residual Assurance Rating
1.4 Governance Structures	●	●									○	○	(Board self- assessments were last conducted in July 2012. External review of Board in Q4 2011)	NC
1.5 Financial Management	●	●			◓				◓	◓	○		(IA review of Payroll in November 2012 – rated as Substantial Assurance) IA review of Charge Collections in February 2013 – rated as Partial Assurance. IA review of the Application of Charges in February 2013 identified key areas requiring enhancement.	PM

Legend – Assurance Source Rating

● Substantial Independent Assurance – Detailed evidence/testing eg full internal audit

◓ Medium Assurance – e.g. high level review only

○ Unsubstantiated Assurance – e.g. management representation

Legend – Residual Assurance Rating

AM Active Management
No/unsubstantiated assurance available. Must complete treatment strategies. Requires regular Board/Audit Committee review.

CR Continuous Review
Limited/unsubstantiated assurance available. Must complete treatment strategies. Requires regular ExCo review.

PM Periodic Review
Limited detailed evidence/testing, and/or some assurance gaps identified.
Note: there may be opportunities for improvement, however a moderate level of risk may be accepted in some circumstances (e.g. cost versus benefit, availability of additional assurance sources).

NC No Major Concern
Multiple sources / strong assurance. Consider excess or redundant controls. .

Figure CS 6.1 Example of Assurance Matrix

or project in question and how any gaps in assurance could be addressed by the audit work. Implementation of the assurance framework was led by Internal Audit which was facilitated by clear support and mandate from ExCo and the Audit Committee, such that assurance providers within the organisation worked cooperatively across functional boundaries.

Recognising the benefits of an integrated approach to assurance, the Chief Executive recently challenged Internal Audit and the Corporate Planning team to develop the framework further; the aim being to mature the risk and assurance activity across the organisation for delivering the strategic objectives and managing the business on a daily basis. This has resulted in bringing many aspects of the risk and assurance activities closer together to create a more streamlined and risk focused approach to business planning, assurance, business resilience, health and safety and internal audit.

In practical terms, those responsible for each of those functions now meet regularly as the 'Risk and Assurance Team' (RAT) to identify emerging issues and areas requiring additional assurance work as well as opportunities for combining the scope of assurance work, its delivery and reporting. An example of such an opportunity involved the inclusion of multiple elements of risks within the scope of Internal Audit's business unit reviews; the 'touch it once' approach meant that the five or 10 day audit included a more in-depth coverage of health and safety, business continuity, business planning and performance management.

The results of such reviews would be provided as part of the final Internal Audit report or discussed at the RAT meetings. In addition to improving the efficacy of risk based assurance across the key risk and assurance functions, this process has also allowed Internal Audit to validate the coverage and timeliness of assurance activities that are necessary for supporting the decision making of the ExCo and to assure the Audit Committee accordingly on an ongoing basis.

Key Outcomes and Lessons

The feedback from both the ExCo and Audit Committee has been very positive. The refined reporting format is a key tool for facilitating focused discussion on risk and assurance and provides a visual aid for assessing the strength and sources of assurance over key processes, risks and projects. In addition, the new streamlined assurance approach is allowing *light-touch* monitoring on topics where assurance may only be traditionally sought and provided on a bi-annual or annual basis to be undertaken on an ongoing basis. For example, by including the performance management assurance discussions in the revised, more integrated Internal Audit approach enhancements to the process are being addressed between each of the bi-annual performance management cycles. As a result, there is more optimal use of increasingly stretched internal resources, collaboration and working across traditional functional boundaries.

The developments, and the process of implementing a more integrated approach, over the past six years have resulted in a number of lessons learned. These include the need to:

- Have open discussions with key stakeholders in order to gain clarity over their risk and reporting appetites, and to revisit these issues frequently to ensure assurance practices remain current and relevant.

- Utilise local knowledge from in-house audit and assurance team members where possible for more effective review of similar business practices in other parts of the organisation; for example, a member from one department in one location was able to provide real insights on assurance over case management practices to colleagues from a different department in a different geographical location.

- Formalise the integrated assurance programme with clear road maps to guide and steer its implementation, as this helped secure success of the new approach and assurance arrangements.

- Link the integrated assurance programme to the organisation's performance management process; the organisation did this by revising job descriptions and including related business plan objectives in the personal objectives of the Internal Audit and Corporate Planning teams.

With an eye on future assurance developments, the organisation is looking to track the benefits of the new assurance arrangements. An annual report to the Audit Committee is being considered to illustrate the following types of benefits:

- Demonstrable contribution of the RAT.

- Examples of the nature of cross-skills developed and transferred between teams in the business units and in-house audit team members.

- Savings on external consultancy fees from more optimal use of in house resources.

As more experience is gained by the organisation in aligning its risk and assurance activities, another enhancement which the organisation is considering is the practice of plotting net position assurance maps to demonstrate to the ExCo and Audit Committee that the balance of risk and assurance is appropriate. An early illustration of the net position risk assurance map is shown in Figure CS 6.2 below.

This would involve considering the relevant risk assessments and current assurance sources when mapping the assurance activity in the Assurance matrix. The current assessment of assurance gaps would be adjusted to include the balance of assurance activity against the risk, that is, whether there is too much or insufficient assurance based on the level of risk exposure and appetite

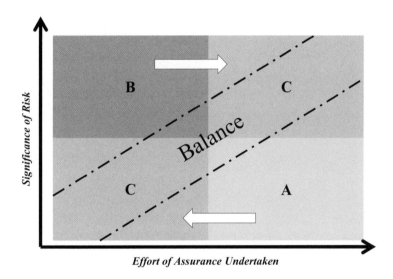

Key
A = Assurance effort exceeds level of risk
B = Insufficient assurance effort relative to risk
C = Balance between risk and assurance effort

Figure CS 6.2 Net Position Risk Assurance Map

within the organisation. The respective assurance activities would be plotted in the net position risk assurance map. Adjustments to assurance activities could then be made, for example by diverting Internal Audit attention and resources from processes where there is an 'excess' of overall assurance effort.

Case Study 7

A Deep Dive Risk Oversight
for a Subsidiary

In this example, integrated assurance mapping was deployed at Level 3 with particular focus on a subsidiary within the group. An integrated assurance framework is already in use at the group level and the discipline was used to provide a *deep dive* into the risks and residual risk profile of one of its subsidiary. The report that resulted from the *deep dive* complemented the integrated assurance reporting at group level.

Base Information for Case Study 7

INDUSTRY AND SIZE OF THE ORGANISATION

Sector: Financial Services

Size: Small organisation

LEVEL AND SCOPE OF IMPLEMENTATION

Level: Level 3

Scope: Subsidiary, incorporating assurance provided by group level functions

Identifying the Need

Discussions by the independent non-executive directors (NEDs) at the Group Board have over a period of time raised queries about the specific risks of a subsidiary which was acquired by the Group some seven years ago. The queries were operational in nature as the strategic plans of the subsidiary are developed and approved by the Group Board as part of the overall strategy of the Group. The queries were attributed to the rapid growth of the subsidiary and its potential for significant expansion.

It was as if the Group Board, having focused its attention on the strategy of the subsidiary thus far, sought to refresh its understanding of the operational risks of the subsidiary. The subsidiary has a local board, which is responsible for executing the strategy and business plan as approved at the Group level; the Group Audit Committee has oversight of the Group's risk management and system of internal control which includes that of the subsidiary.

The Group Executive Management sought to understand the queries raised by the independent nonexecutive directors of the Group Board. The Group Audit Committee and the Group Board are furnished with reports and briefings on the subsidiary that include periodic risk reports and independent audits since the entity was acquired. Nonetheless, the NEDs 'rumblings' would invariably surface in the boardroom at times when strategic developments relating to the subsidiary were being discussed. It was identified that while the NEDs had been furnished with numerous and relevant reports throughout the age of the entity, the principal issues were two-fold:

- Firstly, the information provided to the NEDs at the Group Audit Committee or Group Board was either too specific or too high level. Examples include development of a new product, selection of new business partners and 'overly' aggregated risk reports at the group level. Like many boards, discussions on financial and operational performance of the entity also tended to occur frequently while reports on the entity's risk and assurance perspective occurred periodically.

- Secondly, with the effect of the passage of time, the NEDs were potentially missing the full and evolving picture of the entity since its acquisition particularly from an operational perspective. The jigsaw pieces had started to move apart and needed to be brought back together again. The risk perspectives of the NEDs and of the Group Executive Management were potentially moving apart which was causing the disparity in views.

The growing information gap that was highlighted by the queries from the NEDs had effectively arisen from incremental changes in the business operating environment and strategic growth relating particularly to the new entity. To help minimise distractions in the boardroom and discussions on growth and development plans for the entity, the Group Audit Committee and Group Board required affirmation of the risk and control picture of the entity.

Rationale for Integrated Assurance

It was assessed that an integrated assurance report with particular focus on the entity was helpful in bridging the information gap at this juncture of the Group Audit Committee and Group Board's oversight. It was also assessed that the various management reports that are prepared for the Group Board and Group Audit Committee remain relevant and designed for their respective purposes. The integrated assurance report would not replace the existing management reports but would bolster the views of the NEDs from a different and holistic perspective.

Implementation Approach

The integrated assurance exercise was led and owned by the Group Risk function. It was assigned to a member of the Risk function whose portfolio included the subsidiary in question. The scope and approach was agreed with the Audit Committee and relevant Group Executive responsible for the subsidiary prior to commencing the exercise. This approach leveraged the Group's existing risk management and internal control frameworks that were already in place. With the agreed scope in hand, there were three key steps to implementing the integrated assurance report.

STEP 1

Step 1 involved confirming the key risks and core operational processes for the integrated assurance map. The subsidiary's risk register was reviewed and updated in the process, taking into consideration the concerns of the NEDs and their perceived risks of the entity and external operating environment, such as fraud claims, risks and reliance on third parties. Two risk workshops or round table discussions involving key senior managers of the entity were held in the process of refreshing the subsidiary's risk register. Working with the subsidiary's local operational team, the subsidiary's core processes were also confirmed against a map of the entity's current internal operating model and external environment. This map of the subsidiary's internal operating model and external environment was regarded to be important for providing an objective frame of reference to validate the scope of the integrated assurance map.

STEP 2

Step 2 involved completing the integrated assurance mapping for the subsidiary across all three lines of defence, taking into account any risk assurance activity provided by Group level functions such as Risk, Compliance and Internal Audit. This step was conducted up to Level 3 as defined in this book. The ratings and assessments required for the assurance map were readily aligned with the Group's risk management policies for consistency, aided by the exercise being led by a member of the Risk team. As expected, this step which involved mapping the assurance, and collating and recording the details was the most time consuming. The level of details recorded was to some extent influenced by the anticipated format of the integrated assurance report. On completion of Step 2, the following outputs were produced:

- An integrated assurance map with assessments of the risk assurance activities at Level 3.

- Details of the nature of risk assurance activities (Level 2) that support the assessments at Level 3.

- An updated risk register for the subsidiary.

STEP 3

Step 3 involved preparing the integrated assurance report to the Group Audit Committee. Based on the identified needs of the NEDs of the Group Audit Committee, the report consisted of two main documents:

- An update of the subsidiary's business operating model and a summary of the subsidiary's internal and external risk environment in which it operated – this was particularly useful to assure the Group Audit Committee and the Group Board that the entity's management and the Group Executive were cognisant of the risk profile of the entity which formed the basis of the entity's risk mitigation and assurance strategies.

- A completed integrated assurance map at Level 3 that is consistent with the entity's risk profile and current operating environment.

Extracts of the integrated assurance report were also used at a general discussion with the Group Board while considering the strategic development of the entity.

Key Outcomes and Lessons

The integrated assurance mapping exercise and report helped to provide the assurance that the risk assurance strategy and activities of the Group are appropriately aligned with the profile of the subsidiary. The report helped to draw together the various strands of the risk mitigation strategies deployed allowing the NEDs of the Group Audit Committee and Group Board to gain a full and current picture of the subsidiary's risk profile and operating environment since its acquisition some seven years ago. As a result, the risk perspectives of the NEDs and the Group Executive Management were more closely aligned than before.

The other benefits of the exercise included an increased awareness by the Group of relevant assurance activities carried out at the entity level and the improvements in the documentation of certain assurance activities to help minimise the potential duplication of effort at the Group level, particularly in the second and third lines of defence.

While valued by the NEDs and Group Executive Management alike, the integrated assurance exercise was undoubtedly time consuming particularly with limited resources in a small Group Risk function. The exercise should not, however, be required to be repeated each year unless the risk profile, operating environment or business model of the subsidiary changes significantly. The exercise highlighted the importance of helping the Group Board pull together a full risk picture of the subsidiary (and indeed other entities) within the Group periodically to ensure that the individual subject specific discussions or group level reports are given appropriate context. In other words, periodic *deep dives* of each entity within the Group are not only a good idea but necessary for supporting the risk oversight of the Board across the Group.

The organisation believes that the overall improvements in board reporting of risks and risk assurance justify the cost and effort invested in the initial exercise.

Case Study 8

Spotlighting a Risk for Oversight and Assurance

In this example, integrated assurance is implemented at Level 3, at the group level, within a large international financial services group that is based in the UK. The implementation is focused on the need of the Group Executive to gain assurance over the organisation's collective compliance requirements and obligations from a group level perspective. The scope was later extended to other key areas of risks, as defined by the industry regulator, including market risk, credit risk, liquidity risk, insurance risk and operational risk.

Base Information for Case Study 8

INDUSTRY AND SIZE OF THE ORGANISATION

Sector: Financial Services

Size: Large organisation

LEVEL AND SCOPE OF IMPLEMENTATION

Level: Level 3

Scope: Group level

Identifying the Need

The development of integrated assurance reporting with a specific focus on compliance in this organisation was largely influenced by the proliferation of regulatory requirements combined with the need to demonstrate personal accountability under the UK financial services *Approved Persons* regime.

Following the retirement of the Executive responsible for compliance and redistribution of accountabilities between the Executives, the Group Executive began to seek clarity of its obligations and more importantly how they were being discharged. The Group Executive also anticipated that regulatory developments and governance standards would continue to rise, which has proven to be true.

The Group had been operating a risk management and internal control framework that was generally biased towards the reporting of financial risks with operational risk reporting occurring at a higher level. While this reporting was appropriate for board level oversight of risks, the Group Executive felt it beneficial to gain particular assurance and confidence in the way the Group was managing its compliance obligations and risks. The Group Executive wanted clarity over the delegation of authority, responsibility and accountability for delivering the organisation's compliance obligations.

Rationale for Integrated Assurance

The concept of mapping provided by an integrated assurance framework was recognised as a logical approach for meeting the assurance needs of the Group Executive. The mapping of the legal and regulatory risk landscape, as it was referred to by the organisation, against the respective risk owners was accepted as a logical first step to understanding the organisation's obligations. The mapping of compliance risk assurance was thought to complement the Group's existing risk management framework by providing a magnifying glass on the regulatory and legal risks.

Implementation Approach

The implementation was led by the Senior Officer responsible for the Group's Risk and Compliance functions. Following the principles of the integrated assurance mapping process, the principal legislation, regulation and statutory requirements applicable to the Group were first identified. The regulatory and legislative landscape of the Group which operated in the UK, US, Ireland and five other countries in continental Europe was potentially large.

A pragmatic and risk based approach was adopted whereby the principal regulatory regimes were given more granular attention; for example, the particular requirements of the UK regulation that related to prudential regulation and fair treatments of customers were distinguished separately for the purpose of mapping the expected assurance. The final assurance map consisted of some 30 key regulatory and legislative obligations, which included a small number of trade and industry standards that the Group had committed to maintain.

The Executive Owner, as well as the key assurance providers and nature of the assurance being provided across the three lines of defence, were mapped against each of the regulatory and legislative obligations. The assurance map and the mapping process were completed with the help of the key risk assurance providers, mainly in the first and second lines of defence. The process was assisted by the organisation's existing risk management framework where the key assurance providers were part of an established network of 'business risk champions'.

A self certification or declaration of the compliance process was agreed with the key assurance providers and implemented. The declarations were collated by Group Risk and Compliance. The self certification returns were checked for consistency with the risk reporting that includes the analysis of loss events and incidents. To minimise overlaps with the quarterly risk reporting in place, the returns in respect of compliance with the regulatory and legislation requirements took place every six months.

Key Outcomes and Lessons

The assurance mapping of the regulatory and legislative landscape of the organisation provided the Group Executive with the insights it required of the compliance obligations of the Group, respective ownership and potential strengths or weaknesses in the assurance across the organisation. As a secondary outcome, the assurance map helped to highlight the potential areas of conflicts of interest that could arise between the legal entities at the group and local levels. In sum, the Group Executive gained most comfort, firstly, with the clarity of the Group's compliance obligations and ownership of the respective requirements, and secondly, with the collective view of the status of compliance across the organisation.

The four main lessons worth noting from implementing integrated assurance in this case study are:

- Given the detailed work entailed by the mapping process, a clear understanding of the assurance needs of the Group Executive was helpful to ensure that the resulting assurance map remained focused and manageable.

- Collaboration from other key assurance providers was essential to completing and expediting the process of the mapping and implementation of the self-certifications required. This was clearly assisted by an established network of 'business risk champions' which included a number of the key assurance providers.

- Duplication of effort can arise rapidly if the integrated assurance report in respect of the compliance obligations is not aligned with the Group's risk reporting.

- Integrated risk assurance reports, with a particular focus, complement the high level risk reporting that is typical in many large organisations; these 'spotlight' reports promoted discussion at the Group Executive and Group Risk and Compliance Committees.

The experience of this process led the Group Risk and Compliance to recognise the benefit of spotlighting a particular risk periodically and which complements the aggregated risk assurance reporting that covers the full spectrum of risks on the Group's radar. While there are benefits in risk reports providing an aggregate picture, they can dilute the underlying messages. The likelihood of overlooking specific risks increases in larger groups.

The integrated assurance framework, which the organisation has proceeded to define and implement to complement its existing risk management, consisted of two elements:

1.   A high level integrated assurance map of the principal risks of the Group, which covered all the key risk classes (market, credit, liquidity, insurance, operational and strategic risks) and their respective subcategories, whereby compliance is a subcategory of the operational risk class. This high level integrated assurance map was prepared on an annual basis and was provided to the Group Risk and Compliance Committee as part of the suite of risk reporting collated by the Group Risk and Compliance team. Figure CS 8.1 show a simplified version of the template used for mapping assurance across the risk classes.

	Key Risks and Business Activities requiring core assurance	1st Line Operational Line Management	2nd Line Monitor & Oversight	3rd Line Independent Assurance			
Risk Class	Key Risk/Business Activities	Split by source	Split by source	External Audit	Internal Audit	Other external	Overall Assurance
Market Risk	Asset-Liability Matching	Finance Monthly Reporting	Actuarial Qtrly Capital Report External Annual Review				
	Investment Mandates compliance	Finance Monthly Reporting	Investment Committee				
Insurance Risk	Asset Liability Management	Finance Monthly Reporting	ALM Committee Actuarial Qtrly Capital Report Watsons Annual Review				
	Mortality, Morbidity assumptions		Actuarial Qtrly Capital Report				
	Underwriting	Finance Monthly Reporting	Actuarial Qtrly Capital Repor				
Credit Risk	Reinsurance Admin (Premiums and Claims)	Finance Monthly Reporting	Actuarial Qtrly Capital Report				
Liquidity Risk	Cash flow	Finance Monthly Reporting	Actuarial Qtrly Capital Report				
	Budgeting and Treasury	Planning Monthly Reporting	Board MI/Dashboard				
Group Risk	Contagion risks	Line Management Reporting	Actuarial (capital) Risk KPI				
Strategic Risk	Strategic planning & execution Affinity engagement	Line Management Reporting	Executive Reporting Project Board				
Operational Risk	Project Realisation Monitoring	Line Management reporting	Executive Board MI				
	Client Administration – New Business?	Line Management reporting	Board MI Risk KPI				
	Fraud/money laundering detection	Line Management Reporting (incidents)	Board MI MLRO reporting Risk KPI				
	Financial Process – Payments Financial Process - Premiums/Receipts	Line Management Reporting (incidents)	Risk KPI				
	Property/Facility – Business Continuity	Property/Facility line reporting	Property/Facility MI Risk KPI				
	Product – Development controls	Line Management Reporting to Exec	Board MI Compliance				
	Legal – Contractual controls Regulatory – Compliance breaches	Line Management Reporting (Self Certs)	Legal KPI Compliance Reporting Risk KPI				
	Sales/distribution – Customer data	Line Management Reporting to Exec	Compliance Risk KPI				
	Tax risk exposure	Finance	Risk KPI				
	Technology- Development controls IT security breaches	IT KPIs	Risk KPI				
	People – Fit & Proper/Vetting checks Mandatory training	Line Management Reporting	HR reporting/MI Risk KPI				

RAG Status of Assurance
Red
Amber
Green

Figure CS 8.1   Simplified Assurance Map by Risk Class

2.   Specific integrated assurance mapping was carried out in respect
        of a particular risk class to provide particular focus to the Group
        Risk and Compliance Committee of the aggregated view of the
        assurance activities in respect of the particular risk. These specific
        risk assurance maps would be provided on a cyclical basis every
        six months.

The organisation regards implementation of the framework to be work in
progress, as the process is refined with each cycle of experience.

Case Study 9

Promoting Collective Risk Intelligence

In this example, integrated assurance is implemented across the organisation at Level 3, with particular focus on the key control functions working collaboratively. This global financial services organisation, with locations in some 18 countries, was established over 150 years ago. The board's commitment to maintaining high standards of corporate governance is necessary as the organisation continues to strengthen its international presence. It is unsurprising that the current approach to integrated assurance within this organisation is a product of continual development and improvement over the past 10 to 15 years.

This case study illustrates a relatively mature state of application of integrated assurance where the risk assurance mapping process is embedded and where the focus is on discussion and risk based decision making between the assurance functions as well as at the Board's Group Audit Committee and Group Risk Committee.

Base Information for Case Study 9

INDUSTRY AND SIZE OF THE ENTERPRISE

Sector: Financial Services

Size: Large organisation

LEVEL AND SCOPE OF IMPLEMENTATION

Level: Level 3

Scope: Group wide

Identifying the Need

There were probably a number of drivers that led to the development of an integrated approach to managing assurance across the organisation. These drivers include regulators' focus on risk management, increased transparent internal and external stakeholder reporting as well as optimal use of resources, all of which contributed to raising market confidence and share price of the organisation. The key assurance functions such as compliance and internal audit were not represented at the *top table* for various reasons that include skills and a focus that tended to be at an 'inspection' rather than at the strategic level. Undoubtedly, it was the need of the Board, and in particular of the Group Audit Committee, for effective assurance over the risks and exposures of the organisation that influenced the direction and outcomes so far.

Rationale for Integrated Assurance

The case for an integrated approach to assurance where the respective roles of the key assurance functions – namely compliance, internal audit and risk management – were joined up and coordinated can be attributed to a change in the organisation structure. The appointment of the Chief Risk Officer (CRO) at the group level with responsibility for the three functions, each of which was managed separately by its own manager, laid the foundations to an integrated approach to risk management and assurance in the organisation. While some regulatory regimes may have concerns that such a structure would impair the independence of internal audit, this view is not shared by the organisation's regulators on the basis that there are sufficient safeguards in the approach and that the benefits outweigh the risks.

With such an umbrella role and vantage point, it could be argued that the development of integrated assurance by the Group CRO was both an intuitive as well as a natural step forward for the organisation. The other developments which the Group CRO took into consideration was the direction of local governance codes which were promoting a more 'combined' approach to assurance whereby the external and internal auditors would work in a coordinated way to provide more holistic assurance required by audit committees.

Implementation Approach

Implementation did not occur overnight (to use a cliché though it is highly relevant for this point) but through a methodical plan that spanned a number of years laying the foundations of the approach that is in place today. For a start, the Group CRO commenced his journey by identifying the transformation required in the three assurance functions for which he was responsible. This involved expanding and changing the leadership, skill sets, experience, methodology as well as focus in respect of risks.

It was recognised that for the assurance functions to influence change amongst senior management and engage them effectively across all lines of defence in the organisation, the assurance functions were required to have sufficient credibility and to demonstrate a consistent approach for promoting robust risk management and assurance. This involved determining common terminology, modernising technology and developing models as well as appropriately skilled validation teams in the relevant assurance functions. Transformation within the compliance and internal audit functions took up to four years with certain areas taking no more than two years as their development was accelerated in response to increasing regulatory attention. By comparison, the risk function was already broadly aligned with the expectations of the organisation as well as its regulators.

The foundations laid down have enabled a clearer understanding of how assurance activities occur across the three lines of defence and should be managed. A communication strategy to engage management and gain confidence for their buy-in for a new approach was a gradual process. The assurance mapping process is now fully integrated in the assurance planning cycles internally and externally with the company's financial auditors.

The Group CRO recognises that the real benefits of the integrated assurance framework reside in the discussions rather than the physical state of the assurance maps. To this end, the Group CRO has established a Risk Strategy Committee whose aim is to provide a forum through which a forward looking view of risks, issues and assurance are considered on a regular basis. The Risk Strategy Committee consists of senior personnel from across the organisation that includes chief risk officers, chief internal auditors and compliance officers who meet every four months. The agenda of the Risk Strategy Committee includes:

- Identifying key risks and big issues with a strategic and forward looking view, which include horizon scanning across economies in which the organisation operates, such as risks relating to treating customers fairly.

- Agreeing respective responsibilities with the aim of coordinating effort and minimising duplication internally and with the external auditors in relation to remediation or future assurance activities.

- Determining areas where independent internal audit and compliance monitoring would be appropriate in respect of the risks on the assurance map or landscape.

- Adapting scorecards, risk limits and other measures in light of current experience and projected risks tolerances.

- Assisting with the planning processes, such that the risk and assurance plans are the results of different perspectives but appropriately integrated in their approach to minimise gaps and overlaps.

- Identifying appropriate assurance reporting and escalation of risks and issues to the relevant committees.

In brief, with the 'best interest of the organisation at its heart', the members of the Risk Strategy Committee recognise that by working collaboratively, they can promote more risk-aware management across the business that is both efficient and effective for the organisation on a sustainable basis.

Key Outcomes and Lessons

A key outcome of implementing an integrated approach to risk assurance in the organisation is the overall increased level of confidence in the boardroom and by regulators. As the approach continues to mature there is more focus by the Group Audit Committee and Risk Committee on discussing the risks and related assurance rather than only concentrating on the physical reports. 'Less is certainly more', asserts the Group CRO in respect of board level reporting; and work is underway to refine the risk and assurance reports to support discussions that are holistic and strategic.

For example, trend analysis of the last two years (backward looking) is complemented by forward looking views for each key risk and development of audit plans that are directly linked to the risk profile of the organisation. These developments are under consideration by the Risk Strategy Committee. On the basis that implementing an integrated approach to risk assurance in the organisation involved strengthening a number of key foundations in the organisation's risk, compliance and internal audit arrangements, the organisation has also benefited from a higher level of performance of the assurance functions which work collaboratively in the interest of the organisation.

The assurance functions are joined up, seamlessly, to promote efficient management of risks across the three lines of defence. This has also resulted in savings in external audit fees. Implicitly, the culture of the assurance functions has changed which resonates with the expectations of the board.

The Group CRO identifies that a key ingredient to establishing the path to an integrated approach to managing the organisation's risk and assurance is the support of the chair of the Group Audit Committee, managing directors of the business units and senior management. The encouragement and support, particularly of the chairman of the Group Audit Committee, most probably set the tone for the board and direction of travel which was picked up by the Group CRO as he rolled out his transformation plans for achieving integrated assurance. The other key lessons and practical tips which the Group CRO would share for implementing and embedding an integrated approach to assurance are:

- Ensure that the assurance functions are led by appropriately skilled leaders who have mutual respect for each other as well as having the respect of the business unit heads.

- Agree common terminology and align the methodology for identifying and assessing risks, and for determining assurance against the risks.

- Pay attention to the style of delivery when communicating and engaging appropriately with management to gain their buy in and support.

- Focus on promoting discussion of risks and assurance of risks when developing integrated risk and assurance reports – avoid over engineering and focusing on the quantification of risks, which can limit the nature of discussions and therefore of any real insight that could be gained from the risk management and assurance activities across the organisation.

- Ensure that appropriate assurance is provided over the key models used by the organisation for decision making, and that discussions of the bases used are encouraged;

- Consider a forum such as a Risk Strategy Committee for risk and assurance champions to come together across functional boundaries to identify and determine preemptive actions regarding potential risks and issues in a joined up way.

The Group CRO acknowledges that as an approach, integrated risk management and assurance cannot remain static if it is expected to support the governance of risks across the organisation, especially one that is operating in a heavily regulated environment and is continuing to strengthen its global presence. As mentioned above, one of the key areas of development which the Group CRO is working on is improving and refining the risk and assurance reports to facilitate deeper discussions at board level.

Bibliography

Audit Commission for Local Authorities and the National Health Service, *National Report: Taking it on trust – A review of how boards of NHS trusts and foundation trusts get their assurance*. London, Audit Commission, April 2009.

Bailey, Andrew, 'The UK Banking Resolution Regime', a speech delivered to the Institute of Chartered Accountants England and Wales Financial Services Faculty breakfast, London 26 November 200, retrieved 27 May 2011 http://www.bankofengland.co.uk/publications/Documents/speeches/2009/speech414.pdf.

Basel Committee, 'Basel III: A global regulatory framework for more resilient banks and banking systems', December 2010, rev. June 2011. Accessed 27 December 2013. http://www.bis.org/publ/bcbs189.htm.

Brundred, Steve CEO, Audit Commission, Press Release on 29 April 2009 'NHS boards should challenge more to assure themselves', retrieved 24 May 2011. http://archive.audit-commission.gov.uk/auditcommission/pressoffice/pressreleases/Pages/29042009takingitontrust.aspx.html.

Cambridge Dictionaries Online, s.v. 'assurance'. Accessed 03 August 2013. http://dictionary.cambridge.org/dictionary/british/assurance_2.

Cass Business School/AIRMIC, *Roads to ruin – A study of major risk events: their origins, impact and implications, Executive Briefing, 2011*. Accessed 4 October 2011 http://www.airmic.com/roads-ruin-study-major-risk-events-their-origins-impacts-and-implications.

Chartered Institute of Internal Auditors (IIA-UK and Ireland), *Professional Guidance for Internal Auditors: Coordination of assurance services*. London, IIA-UK and Ireland, 2010.

Chartered Institute of Internal Auditors (IIA-UK and Ireland) and Institute of Directors (IoD), *What every Director should know about Internal Audit –*

Essential Information for Boards and Audit Committees. London, *IIA- UK and Ireland*, April 2013.

Committee of Sponsoring Organizations of the Treadway Commission (COSO), New Jersey, American Institute of CPAs. *The Enterprise Risk Management – Integrated Framework*, 2004.

——*Internal Control – Integrated Framework*, 2013.

—— *Demystifying sustainability risk – Integrating the triple bottom line into an enterprise risk management program*, May 2013.

Doherty, Sharon, 'Terminal 5 comes alive', *Director*, March 2008, accessed 16 July 2013, http://www.director.co.uk/MAGAZINE/2008/3%20March/terminal5_61_8.html

Dr Foster Intelligence, a joint venture with the Department of Health, 'The Intelligent Board, 2006'. Retrieved 25 December 2012, http://drfosterintelligence.co.uk/thought-leadership/intelligent-board/.

European Confederation of Institutes of Internal Auditing (ECIIA) / European Confederation of Directors' Association (ecoDa), *Making the Most of the Internal Audit Function: Recommendations for Directors and Board Committees*. Brussels, ECIIA/ecoDa, January 2013.

European Confederation of Institutes of Internal Auditing, 'Spotlight on global assurance'. Brussels, *European Internal Audit Briefing*, July 2009 Issue 15.2.

European Commission, Press Release IP/10/918 Brussels 12 July 2010, 'Commission proposes package to boost consumer protection and confidence in financial services'. Retrieved 27 May 2011. http://europa.eu/rapid/press-release_IP-10-918_en.htm.

European Commission, 'Directive 2009/138/EC of the European Parliament and of the Council of 25 November 2009 on the taking-up and pursuit of the business of Insurance and Reinsurance (Solvency II)'. Accessed 11 April 2011. http://eur-lex.europa.eu/LexUriServ/LexUriServ.do?uri=OJ:L:2009:335:0001:0155:EN:PDF,

Eversheds LLP, *The Eversheds Board Report: Measuring the impact of board composition on company performance*. London, *Eversheds LLP*, May 2011.

Federal Deposit Insurance Corporation (FDIC), Bank List Updated 12 July 2013. Accessed 20 July 2013 http://www.fdic.gov/bank/individual/failed/banklist.html.

——'2010 Annual Report Highlights', accessed 20 July 2013 http://www.fdic.gov/about/strategic/report/2010highlight/chpt1-02.html.

Federal Reserve Board, Press Release September 16 2008 'Announcing the authorisation of the loan from the Federal Reserve Bank of New York to AIG under Section 13(3) of the Federal Reserve Act'. Retrieved 30 May 2011. http://www.federalreserve.gov/newsevents/press/other/20080916a.htm.

Federation of European Risk Management Associations (FERMA) / European Confederation of Institutes of Internal Auditing (ECIIA), *Guidance on the 8th EU Company Law Directive, Article 41 – Guidance for boards and audit committees*. Brussels, FERMA/ECIIA, September 2010.

Fermi National Accelerator Laboratory (Fermilab), *Integrated Quality Assurance*. Number 1001, Revision 001. Batavia, IL, Office of Quality and Best Practices Fermi National Accelerator Laboratory, 2010.

Financial Crisis Inquiry Commission (May 2009–February 2011), *The Financial Crisis Inquiry Report – Final Report of the National Commission on the Causes of the Financial and Economic Crisis in the United States*. Official Government Edition. Submitted by Pursuant to Public Law 111-21. Washington DC, U.S. Government Printing Office, 2011.

Financial Reporting Council (FRC), *Internal Control: Revised Guidance for Directors on the Combined Code 2005* ('Turnbull'). London. 2005.

—— *Boards and Risk: A summary of discussions with companies, investors and advisers*. September 2011.

—— *Effective Company Stewardship – Enhancing Corporate Reporting and Audit*. January 2011.

——*Guidance on Audit Committees*. September 2012.

——*The UK Corporate Governance Code*. September 2012.

——Risk Management, Internal Control and the Going Concern Basis of Accounting: Consultation on Draft Guidance to the Directors of companies applying the UK Corporate Governance Code and Associated Changes to the Code. November 2013.

—— Going Concern and Liquidity Risk: Guidance for Directors of UK Companies. 2009. This paper is under review alongside the Turnbull Guidance to create more integrated guidance under the UK Corporate Governance Code in 2014.

Financial Stability Board, 'Enhancing the Risk Disclosures of Banks Report of the Enhanced Disclosure Task Force', 29 October 2012. Accessed 1 November 2012, http://www.financialstabilityboard.org/publications/r_121029.htm.

Financial Stability Board, 'Thematic Review on Risk Governance – Peer Review Report', February 2013. Retrieved 15 February 2013 http://www.financialstabilityboard.org/publications/r_130212.htm, Section 2.2 on Risk Management Tools.

Frydman, Roman, and Goldberg, Michael, Imperfect Knowledge Economics: Exchange Rates and Risk. New Jersey, Princeton University Press, 2007.

Frydman, Professor Roman, 'Mechanics of risk'. Business & Finance, 15 February–28 February 2008, 38–39.

Geithner, Timothy F., 'A message from the Secretary of the Treasury, Department of the Treasury, Washington D.C.'. Accessed on 22 July 2013. http://www.gao.gov/special.pubs/longterm/debt/debtbasics.html#largefeddebt.

Hamilton, Stewart and Micklethwait, Alicia, Greed and Corporate Failure – The lessons from recent disasters. Hampshire, England and New York, Palgrave MacMillan, 2006.

H.M. Government, UK Companies Act 2006. London, HM Stationery Office, 2006.

H.M. Treasury, The Spending Review 2010: Presented to Parliament by the Chancellor of the Exchequer by Command of Her Majesty, London. October 2010.

—— A Review of the Corporate Governance in UK Banks and other Financial Industry Entities – Final Recommendations. ('The Walker Review'). Published 26 November 2009. Website last updated 7 April 2010. http://webarchive.

nationalarchives.gov.uk/+/http:/www.hm-treasury.gov.uk/walker_review_
information.htm.

——Major Project Authority – Integrated Assurance, 2012.

House of Commons, Culture, Media and Sport Committee, 'News International
and Phone-hacking, Eleventh Report of Session 2010–2012 Volume 1 (C)'.
London, The Stationery Office, 2012), Sections 201, 226–229.

Insurance Internal Audit Group (IIAG), Good Practice Development Group
study on integrated Assurance in Summer 2012, the results of which
discussed at the IIAG Conference in September 2012. Publication is limited
to participants of the study. www.iiag.org.uk.

Institute of Internal Auditors (IIA), International Professional Practices Framework
(IPPF), Orlando, FL. 2009. The IPPF consists of authoritative guidance
developed by the IIA international technical committees that include
mandatory and highly recommended practices that refer to the IIA's Code
of Ethics and the International Standards for the Professional Practice of
Internal Auditing ('The Standards'). --- Global Practice Guide: Coordinating
Risk Management and Assurance. March 2012.

International Federation of Accountants (IFAC), The Global Financial Crisis.
Accessed 29 May 2011 http://www.ifac.org/financial-crisis/international-
resources.php

Irving, Janis, J., Groupthink, 2nd Edition. Boston, MA, Wadsworth, 1982.

King Committee on Corporate Governance and Institute of Directors in
Southern Africa (IoDSA), King Code and Report on Governance for South Africa
('King III' Code). Johannesburg, IoDSA, 2009.

Lieberman, Senator Joe, Chairman of the Senate Government Affairs Committee,
'Statement at the hearing on 7 May 2002: The Role of the Board of Directors
in Enron's Collapse'. Accessed 20 July 2013. http://hsgac-amend.senate.gov/
old_site/050702lieberman.htm.

Massachusetts Institute of Technology, 'Collective Brainpower. Using new
technologies to amplify human intelligence'. Boston, MA, MIT Spectrum,
Summer 2010. Retrieved 25 May 2011, http://scripts.mit.edu/~cci/HCI/index.

php?title=Main_Page. See also definition in the Handbook of Collective Intelligence, MIT Centre for Collective Intelligence.

NASA John F. Kennedy Space Center, 'IDAS Challenge, Vision, Mission and Goal', May 2007. Retrieved 10August 2013 http://kscsma.ksc.nasa.gov/Reliability/Documents/IDAS/7_IDAS_Challenge_Vision_Mission_and_Goal.pdf.

National Audit Office, *Financial Management and Governance Practice – The Statement on Internal Control: A Guide for Audit Committee*. London. January 2010.

——*Assurance for High Risk Projects*. June 2010.

National Association of Corporate Directors (NACD), *White Papers Series I: Risk Oversight, Strategy, Transparency, Executive Compensation*. (Washington, DC, NACD, 2009).

National Association of Insurance Companies (NAIC), News Release September 2008, 'AIG: Conversation should stay focused on the facts'. Retrieved 22 October 2011. http://www.naic.org/Releases/2008_docs/AIG_facts.htm

Novo Nordisk, *Annual Report 2011*. Retrieved April 2013. http://annualreport2011.novonordisk.com/web-media/pdfs/Novo-Nordisk-AR-2011-en.pd, 11.

Prudential Regulation Authority and Financial Conduct Authority, *Handbook*. Accessed 28 December 2013. http://fshandbook.info/FS/html/PRA/PRIN and http://www.fshandbook.info/FS/html/FCA/D3.

Reynolds Porter Chamberlain LLP, 'FSA hands out record breaking fines against individuals in 2011', 19 December 2011. Retrieved 03 August 2013. http://www.rpc.co.uk/index.php?option=com_flexicontent&view=items&cid=130:insuranceandreinsurance&id=15822:fsa-hands-out-record-breaking-fines-against-individuals-in-2011&Itemid=27

Sants, Hector, Chief Executive FSA, 'Delivering effective corporate governance: the financial regulators role'. A speech delivered on 24 April 2012 at Merchant Taylor's Hall. Accessed 26 April 2012. http://www.fsa.gov.uk/library/communication/speeches/2012/0424-hs.shtml.

Schedler, Andreas, Larry Diamond, and Marc F. Plattner (eds). *The Self-Restraining State: Power and Accountability in New Democracies*. Boulder, Colorado and London, Lynne Rienner Publishers, 1999.

Sjostrom, William K., Jr., 'The AIG Bailout'. Lexington, Virginia, *Washington and Law University School of Law Review*, Summer 2009.

Soros, George, 'One Way to stop Bear Raids'. *The Wall Street Journal*, 23 March 2009. Retrieved 22 October. 2011 http://online.wsj.com/article/SB123785310594719693.html.

Taleb, Nassim Nicholas, *The Black Swan – The Impact of the Highly Improbable*. Rev. Ed. London, Penguin Books Ltd, July 2011.

Thornton, Grant, 'A new risk equation? Safeguarding the business model'. London, Grant Thornton UK LLP, 2010.

Turner, Adair, 'Successful regulatory reform'. A speech delivered on 28 September 2010 at the Eurofi Conference, Brussels, retrieved 29 October 2011, http://www.fsa.gov.uk/pages/Library/Communication/Speeches/2010/0928_att.shtml.

UK Department of Health, *Building the Assurance Framework: A Practical Guide for NHS Boards*. 2003.

——*Integrated Governance Handbook – A handbook for executives and non-executives in healthcare organisations*. London. 2006.

UK Parliament, *Financial Services Act 2012*. London, The Stationery Office, 2012.

U.S. Government, Sarbanes-Oxley Act 2002, 'Public Law No. 107–204', formally known as the 'Public Company Accounting Reform and Investor Protection Act and Corporate and Auditing Accountability and Responsibility Act'. Washington DC, *U.S. Government Printing Office*, 2002.

U.S. Senate, Permanent Sub Committee on Investigations of the Committee of Governmental Affairs, 'The Role of the Board of Directors in Enron's Collapse', 107th Congress 2d Session. Washington, DC, *U.S. Government Printing Office*, Senate Prints 107–70, July 8, 2002. 11–16, 55.

Webster's Online Dictionary, s.v. 'assurance'. Accessed 03 August 2013. http://
    www.websters-online-dictionary.org/definition/assurance

William, George, 'Board governance depends on where you sit'. February 2013.
    Retrieved 16 March 2013. http://www.mckinsey.com/insights/leading_in_
    the_21st_century/board_governance_depends_on_where_you_sit

Index

If you have found this book useful you may be interested in other titles from Gower

Bribery and Corruption:
How to Be an Impeccable and Profitable Corporate Citizen
Michael J. Comer and Timothy E. Stephens
Hardback: 978-1-4094-5357-4
e-book: 978-1-4094-5358-1 (PDF)
e-book: 978-1-4724-0452-7 (ePUB)

Detecting and Reducing Supply Chain Fraud
Norman A. Katz
Hardback: 978-1-4094-0732-49
e-book: 978-1-4094-0733-1 (PDF)
e-book: 978-1-4094-6117-3 (ePUB)

Fraud:
The Counter Fraud Practitioner's Handbook
Edited by
Alan Doig
Hardback: 978-0-566-08832-2
e-book: 978-0-7546-9209-6 (PDF)
e-book: 978-1-4094-6112-8 (ePUB)

Visit **www.gowerpublishing.com** and

- search the entire catalogue of Gower books in print
- order titles online at 10% discount
- take advantage of special offers
- sign up for our monthly e-mail update service
- download free sample chapters from all recent titles
- download or order our catalogue